Playing Host to Deity

Playing Host to Deity

Festival Religion in the South Indian Tradition

PAUL YOUNGER

OXFORD
UNIVERSITY PRESS

2002

OXFORD
UNIVERSITY PRESS

Oxford New York
Athens Auckland Bangkok Bogotá Buenos Aires Cape Town
Chennai Dar es Salaam Delhi Florence Hong Kong Istanbul Karachi
Kolkata Kuala Lumpur Madrid Melbourne Mexico City Mumbai Nairobi
Paris São Paulo Shanghai Singapore Taipei Tokyo Toronto Warsaw

and associated companies in
Berlin Ibadan

Published by Oxford University Press, Inc.
198 Madison Avenue, New York, New York 10016

Oxford is a registered trademark of Oxford University Press

Library of Congress Cataloging-in-Publication Data
Younger, Paul.
Playing host to deity : fesitval religion in the South Indian tradition /
Paul Younger.
p. cm.
Includes bibliographical references and index.
ISBN 0-19-514044-3
1. Fasts and feasts—Hinduism—India, South. I. Title.
~~BL 1239.76.S68 Y68 2001~~
294.5'36'09548—dc21 00-033621

1 3 5 7 9 8 6 4 2

Printed in the United States of America
on acid-free paper

Contents

Note on Transliteration

Because this study is concerned with a primarily Tamiḻ-speaking tradition that originated in South India, the transliteration of Indian words is in accord with the system of the *Tamiḻ Lexicoṉ* (1936).

Playing Host to Deity

Introduction

The annual festivals that are a central feature of the South Indian religious tradition are among the largest religious gatherings anywhere in the world. These festivals are held in hundreds of locations, and the important ones attract well over a hundred thousand worshipers. Most of the festivals last about 10 days, some for shorter or longer periods. Most are associated with Hindu temples, but some are linked with Buddhist, Christian, or Islamic centers, and many involve people or symbols from more than one religious tradition. An outside observer might find the many activities of a South Indian festival somewhat chaotic, yet the participants see the activities as the ritual focus of a distinct religious experience and frequently testify that they and their ancestors have found their most profound sense of religious meaning in the activity of a festival.

Despite the festivals' obvious importance in the religious life of many people, they have not received much scholarly attention. There are two interrelated reasons for this neglect. First reason is that Brāhman scholars, and priests within Brāhmanical temples, generally did not understand or value festival religion. Festival religion had its roots within the non-Brāhmanical communities that were traditionally not allowed to worship within the Brāhmanical temples; in many ways it represents an alternative religious form to that offered within the Brāhmanical temples. Although Brāhmanical temples later developed their own modified festival traditions, the difference in worship style between festival worship and the daily rituals inside the temples is great, and Brāhmans continue to be uncomfortable about festival religion. Second, the festivals have been neglected by scholars because in the nineteenth century when western scholars began the study of Hindu religion, they looked primarily at texts. Judging by the role texts played in the major western religious traditions, these scholars assumed that they would eventually understand what went on in Hindu temples,[1] and in festivals and pilgrimages as well. Only slowly have scholars reassessed these mistaken assumptions and recognized that the literature produced by the Brāhman community was linked to their special concerns, and that many of the most popular religious traditions were not tied to those same concerns. In the case of festival religion, these two prejudices worked neatly together in that Brāhmans were eager to provide western scholars with texts about their own special interests, and even more ready to minimize the importance of festival religion. As anthropological references[2] to festivals became more rich and interesting a few decades back, students of religion began to reflect on this popular form of religious life.[3]

The first couple of times I was escorted to a festival by an enthusiastic acquaintance, I was puzzled about how I would gain an understanding of this complex and unfamiliar style of religious life. As I watched people go into ecstasy at the sight of the image in procession, or watched people dance themselves into a trance, I had a strong sense that profound religious experience was taking place. Again, as I listened to stories of how people organized themselves in distant villages for the trip to the festival, and to the reasons why they felt that their family or their caste had to attend the festival, I realized that the social meanings of the festivals were much more complex than I was accustomed to observing in other religious settings. Then, when I began reading thousand-year-old inscriptions, and found that people then were donating money for the celebration of the same festival I was witnessing today, I realized that the religious meanings had been effectively handed down from generation to generation, even though that meaning remained in oral or nonliterate form throughout many centuries.

South Indian festivals are public celebrations. The festival crowds always include people unfamiliar with the ritual routine, who must decide, as I did during my early visits, if the forms of emotional ecstasy they see, the statements of social meaning they hear, or the set of symbols being handed on from generation to generation provide structures of meaning they find attractive. In some important sense, the many individual and social units that participate in the festival constitute the festival community, and they believe that the deity has agreed to join "their festival." In modern circumstances the administrators of a temple, church, or mosque often get involved in arrangements for a festival, but the crowd, inclined to be critical of those administrators, will forcefully overrule any attempt to change festival tradition, such as in the time or location for the deities' arrival.

In saying that this religious form belongs to the community of persons and groups who choose to participate in it, I am distinguishing it from two other types of religious societies. On the one hand, these festivals are not the ritual expression of predefined social units such as tribes, castes, villages, or nations. Although the ritual of such "natural religious groups" (Wach 1951) is thought to be controlled by the designated leadership of those units of society, festivals normally take place outside the jurisdiction of such social units. Sometimes the leaders of those units of society join in festival celebrations, but they are usually begging for recognition rather than leading or directing the ritual. On the other hand, the religious communities involved in a festival are not defined by a group of priests or religious specialists, who invite members of the public to affiliate with their "distinctive religious society" and a particular deity, doctrine, or ritual pattern. In the context of a festival, it is more as if a community of worshipers invites certain deities to join in its festivity. When the deities arrive, priests or religious specialists associated with those deities often perform peripheral ritual functions, but they are clearly involved only in specific parts of a larger festival celebration. In many ways the festival is located outside the specific social units that govern everyday social behavior; it can, therefore, serve as a context for reversing the values associated with those social units and reexamining them from a perspective that transcends them. At the same time, the festival is an explicit statement of social solidarity and serves as an opportunity to examine a deeper sense of social identity. It is as if the deities are invited to be part of a reformulation of the highest psychological and social ideals of this collection of human society.

I have chosen to describe these festivals as belonging to the "South Indian tradition," and I realize that description needs some explanation. Readers will have already noted that some of the festivals to be described do not take place within the geographical limits of South India. The first clarification concerns Śrī Lanka. Until colonial times, communication in the region around South India took place primarily along the coasts, and Śrī Lanka traditionally shared a common cultural region with the rest of South India. As a result, the festivals of Śrī Lanka fit very neatly into what I call the "South Indian festival tradition." The second clarification concerns the "diaspora" communities that have emigrated from South India and Śrī Lanka. When South Indians began to settle in other parts of the world during the last century, they tenaciously carried their religious traditions with them. Now South Indian communities can be found in Guyana, Trinidad, South Africa, North America, and many other places, and one can observe the "South Indian tradition" of festival practice in different corners of the world.

A different problem with attaching the label "South Indian" to these festivals arises because the label indirectly implies that popular religious practices in "North India" are quite different. In North India the primary form of popular religion is "pilgrimage,"[4] but individual ritual features such as ecstatic behavior, healing, and large excited crowds are common in both North Indian "pilgrimages" and South Indian "festivals." Some of the oldest of the South Indian festivals are in fairly remote locations and might well be called "pilgrimages." The first of those to be described (chapter 1) is indeed often called a "pilgrimage." Although a systematic distinction between popular forms of religion in North India and South India will have to await further study, a preliminary distinction will focus this study.

What distinguishes the South Indian form of popular religion from similar North Indian forms is the more elaborate social arrangements that are part of the South Indian "festival." The "Dravidian" marriage arrangements[5] characteristic of South India permit marriages with first cousins on the mother's side. This arrangement helped keep land within the larger family network and led to the creation of tight endogamous caste groups. To operate in the economic, political, and cultural arenas, these relatively small caste groups needed forms of common social interaction with others, and festivals provided one of the most effective forums for social interaction. Of course, other structures of social interaction define everyday economic and political relations among the castes, and psychological and religious dimensions of festival activity transcend the social, but South Indian "festivals" have a specific social function in both reflecting and redefining social structures. This distinguishes them from the more diverse "pilgimage" traditions so prominent in North India.

Interpreting Festival Activity

Festivals are arenas of action; the activity should speak for itself without being burdened with too much interpretation.[6] On the other hand, the extended conversations possible in the relaxed atmosphere of the festival are all about interpretation. Precisely because there are no religious specialists giving "sermons" of predefined meaning, the participants constantly converse about the kind of meaning each is experiencing. Whereas those who chose to engage me in conversations of this sort presented me with somewhat more elaborate styles of interpretation than those I overheard as I walked about, nevertheless the activity of interpretation is central to the meaning of the festival for all participants. This form of religious life has an "openness" about it that invites both participants and observers to interpret activity.

I begin examining the problem of interpretation by describing styles of interpretation offered to me by participants in the festivals and asking how they relate to patterns of interpretation in the scholarly literature. After reflection on the interpretations I heard, I thought that participants tended to use three different lines of interpretation in describing what was happening: they wanted to tell me how the participants in the festival *think*, to tell me how the *social and cultural meanings* of the festival are worked out, and to tell me what the *religious experience* they enjoyed was like.

1. The most serious among those who volunteered to interpret the festival usually provided a meta-explanation as to how the primary group of participants in the festival "thought." Usually they would define the human unit they were talking about in terms of language. "Tamiḻs classify things into *aham* and *puram*" was a common starting point. Or "Sinhalas are really Veddas [tribal forest dwellers] with a touch of Sanskrit/Pāli culture." Or "You must remember that Malaiyāḷis love reversals, that Onam [the national celebration of Kerala] honors a demon."

Quite often these pretentious openings did not lead very far, because people find reflection on their own system of thought more difficult than they expect. In the case of the Tamiḻs, people tended to feel more confidence because the classification schemes of the ancient grammarian Tolkāppiyaṉ (circa second century BCE) are generally regarded as having influenced all subsequent Tamiḻ culture. Tolkāppiyaṉ's central contribution was to divide all poetry into aham and puram, or poetry expressing the emotions of the inner person and centering on eroticism and fertility, versus poetry expressing the perspective of the king or other public person and centering on heroic action. Explaining the many activities of the festival in terms of polar balancing between themes of fertility and heroism was often quite helpful; when an interpreter started by making this underlying "grammar" of the interpretation explicit, the conversation about the many specific features of the festival often went quite smoothly.

In the explanations of the Sinhala thought of Śrī Lanka, there was less consensus, but a balance was usually defined in terms of moving back and forth between the spontaneous forces of nature and the restraint and dignity of culture. The worshipers in Kataragama, for instance, frequently "explain" why they like to spend part of each day visiting the small shrine of the tribal goddess Valli, engaging in the wild emotion of the *kavati* dance, or splashing in the river, and then go off to the quiet of the Buddhist *stūpa* or burial mound for a time of meditation. The meditation takes them away from the world of "nature" and the round of fertility and allows them to enter what they consider the highest form of human "culture."

For the Malaiyāḷis of Kerala, the explanations of the underlying thought system are almost always offered mischievously, because they involve some suspending of ordinary values. For them, the underworld is fascinating, and learning to control the tigers, snakes, and *yakṣis* or tree spirits that endanger human life is the center of the spiritual quest. In this version of the polarity of nature and culture, the natural powers initially appear dominant, but humans can engage the spirit world underlying this natural order, and courageous action can often allow humans to manipulate that world to their advantage.

Many of the discussions of the local thought patterns drifted away from the events of the festivals I was trying to understand, and I was sometimes tempted to ignore those who spoke in this vein altogether. What should one make of these local structuralists' efforts at interpretation? Scholars such as Durkheim and Mauss (1903, trans. 1963) long ago initiated the study of "primitive classification," but they barely scratched the surface in figuring out what to do with such systems of thought. Claude Lévi-Strauss (1958, 1962, 1970), of course, studied structures of thought but followed a number of unproductive directions in the process. He insisted that the classification systems of even the earliest forms of human society involved structured patterns of thought and that the structures of language would provide clues as to how the other patterns of thought worked. But poststructural critiques of Lévi-Strauss have raised doubt about what he meant by "structure," and his detailed studies of the fragmentary stories and myths collected from simple societies scattered here and there did not produce a convincing picture of an early system of thought. Van Gennep (1960) and Turner (1969, 1974) turned our attention in more promising directions when they pointed students of religion to the more universal expression of thought in ritual behavior. The widespread forms of religious behavior, such as initiation and pilgrimage, attracted their attention for initial investigations, but the underlying pattern of the interaction of structure and antistructure they identified is also evident in other types of ritual settings.

The ritual setting of these festivals almost certainly reflects patterns of thought, some more than a thousand years old, but it did not seem to be easy for local participants to describe those patterns satisfactorily. They seemed to grope for some way in which to explain how the abstract structure, which they thought was there somewhere in their culture, was linked with their own participation in the festival. Those who recognized the problematic nature of linking an abstract pattern with their own concrete and historically defined behavior would suddenly shift to another line of interpretation more directly related to their historical situation, but many just ended the conversation in frustration, feeling that deep in their consciousness was an underlying meaning to the festival that they could not quite express.

2. The most extended and interesting conversations I had with festival participants were when someone would try to "explain" a festival to me by outlining the interaction of the different groups in their society, usually concluding by showing me how their own group's participation in the festival reaffirmed the particular values it brought to the society as a whole. The sense of group participation and the inclination for people to define their world in social terms were both quite striking features of these descriptions. Some of these discussions involved the tracing of complex historical patterns that I sometimes knew a bit about from other sources. Others were quite mythical and involved the speaker's community in great heroism. In either case, the focus was on identifying some pattern of social history and defining the world in terms of it.

Those who painted the picture on a grand scale always seemed to start with some version of the first contacts between hunting or fishing groups and the early agriculturalists. Most then went on to outline the complex divisions of labor within the agricultural operation. And, finally, when relevant to the story of their own group, they would provide a version of how the small groups of craftpersons, traders, weavers, and planters of palmyra and coconut groves operated in interdependence with the dominant agricultural sector of South Indian society. The discussions also usually included internal caste group analysis as well, with an explanation of male and female roles, family splits, and the general complication of maintaining an endogamous community with enough proper subdivisions for the provision of brides.

When all the nuances of the social interactions a speaker linked with the festival were laid out, he or she usually concluded by saying that the social function of the festival was the reestablishment or reformulation of all these many alliances. Having stated this conservative social agenda, however, they then felt obliged to add that radical social change could come out of the festival. As people loved to point out, there was an unstructured feeling about the festival activity, which made the people happy and the leaders of society nervous.

The primary question about social grouping that people in South India are concerned about, of course, involves the boundaries of the endogamous group, or the group within which one can arrange marriage. Although theoretically flexible, these boundaries do not change much over time. They must, however, be ritually reexamined regularly so that each group may imagine that its status is rising in the estimation of the society as a whole. Tangentially related to boundaries of the endogamous group are the economic alliances in which an endogamous group is involved (Beck 1972). Endogamous groups that hold their unit together carefully with well-arranged marriages can be valuable to a landlord group or a craft group with an interacting economic interest, but a group's dream of a better life depends on its ability to use the ritual context of the festival to demonstrate the solidarity of the group and the ways other groups might benefit from an economic alliance with them. Finally, for all the endogamous groups and economic groupings together there are questions about political alliances, and the ways the whole society participating in the festival might seek out its long-term interests.

Because people attend festivals in two or three locations, each group's loyalty to a particular economic or political alliance can be regularly reexamined, and new social dreams explored. Festival activity provides an acceptable apolitical forum for extensive reexamination of a group's alliances, and groups can ease themselves in or out of one alliance or another without appearing to bring about a major shift in the larger social fabric, and, perhaps most important, without getting involved in the violent tactics of rulers and would-be rulers.

The scholarly language needed for describing the role of religious forms in a society defined primarily in terms of endogamous groups has not been carefully worked out. Marxists have recognized the general possibility that ritual forms sometimes reflect social interaction, but their concern has been to confront official religion, which they hold both reflects and provides legitimation for established patterns of power. Mary Douglas (1973) used the felicitous phrase "implicit meaning" to point out that ritual interactions can be highly ambivalent, and often hide the social structures they reflect. Clifford Geertz (1973) and Victor Turner (1969, 1974) went a step further by making us aware of ritual's role in social change, as patterns of potential social conflict or social change can be tested in terms of symbolic conflicts in the dramas enacted in ritual events. South Indian festivals lend themselves especially well to being described as social dramas because they reflect a society that has freed itself from more primitive and monolithic social forms such as tribes (wherein political authority and religious authority are coterminus) but has not yet evolved into a society wherein subgroups, such as endogamous groups or "castes," have disappeared and individuals are free to associate with religious institutions that appeal to them for ideological reasons. These festivals are still "social" because there is great pressure on families and caste groups to participate as social units, and the meaning individuals find in the experience is often expressed in terms of the social aspirations their group brought to the festival.

3. Some of the more thoughtful of the worshipers used the two ways of "explaining" the festivals that I have already described. A somewhat larger number tried to use the third pattern of explanation and tell me, as they continued with their worship routines, why they were attracted to some specific feature of the deity being worshiped. Worshipers would quickly explain as they paused near me that the goddess was "powerful" or "angry," or that the god was feeling "playful" or "hungry" or "tired." Others would explain that the two wives of the god represented the two types of devotion worshipers could offer, that certain hymns were sung at the special request of the deity, or that the deity required certain offerings on that day. Some deities were said to bring healing, others possessed worshipers, and others could be "glimpsed" only in the most fleeting way.

In later reflection on these spontaneous and intentionally idiosyncratic expressions of faith, I found myself thinking of Wilfred Cantwell Smith's fascination with statements of belief. In *Meaning and End of Religion* (1963), he taught us that the historically defined "great religions," with their prescribed formulas of belief, were a product of the eighteenth century, and not typical of the way many people speak of their faith. He suggested that we allow our neighbors to state their "faith" and listen carefully. He expected we would then discover faith had more to do with "persons" than with philosophical abstractions. Festival expressions of faith are probably even more personal than anything Smith (who had studied primarily Islamic and Christian religion) had in mind.

The attribution of personal and even idiosyncratic qualities to the divine in festival vocabulary at first puzzled me, but I soon grew to expect it. Festival worshipers at times found the experience of deity awesome and overwhelming, but the context in which any such experience took place was considered home-like and familiar and could be described in everyday language. Whether full of fear or joy, the experience of the divine was an intimate and personal one happening on that day, in that place, to be described in terms of the appropriate local vocabulary of the worshiping community to whom the deity had come.

In later reflection on the three styles of interpretation I was given at the festivals, I realized they were complementary accounts provided by three different types of personalities. The first style was used by a small number who walked around the edge of the crowd and felt uncomfortable with the passion of the festival activity. They felt that it all made sense on an unconscious level, but the abstract truths they tried to find to express that level of truth tended to elude them. Those who used the second style of social analysis did not need to remove themselves completely from the immediate experience of the festival, because their group was there at the festival, but for them too reality was a rationally constructed story of the past that they had been taught. Those who blurted out a near-ecstatic statement about deity as they went about their worship were expressing their faith with a consciousness hardly distinguishable from the ritual action itself. These expressions of faith were not inconsistent with theological statements I could find in written texts, but they were different in kind in the sense that, with the abstract framework removed, they were expressing an immediate confidence that at any moment they would be in touch with a special form of ultimate reality.

I realize that having mentioned some of the participants' efforts at interpretation only begins to explain the many layers of interpretation the reader will discern in the ethnography in the chapters to follow. Clifford Geertz's (1973) concept of "thick description" provides a general explanation of how both participants and observers are involved in the interpretive process, but as James Clifford and George Marcus (1986) and others have shown, the "writing" of the story "thickens" the description in a number of new ways. The writer is no longer able to pass along a story tailored for a particular audience, but must guess what questions unknown readers might ask. I found that even in describing this book to colleagues they interrupted with unexpected questions, such as: "Is there a similar kind of religion in the West"? "How similar are these celebrations to the medieval 'carnivals' Bakhtin writes about?" "How can you be sure that these festivals were celebrated in a similar way a thousand years ago?" "How do you know that these aren't just social events without any religious significance?" I soon realized that an infinite number of questions could be generated in this way, and that the best I could do would be to acknowledge that similar questions occurred to me throughout the period of research and at least some would be partially answered as the narrative progressed. The first two questions, for instance, had also bothered me for quite some time.

Of course, watching people go into a trance in the context of a South Indian festival reminds one of Pentecostal Christian services. And the sequence of taking a vow and following it with ascetic practices and pilgrimage is as common in Marian pilgrimages in Europe as it is in South India. Specific religious phenomena are often comparable in two different settings, and I certainly let myself make comparisons from time to time in order to explain what is going on in a particular situation. The problem with comparing specific phenomena in very different settings is that one then has to hasten to explain that, of course, the comparison does not go any further and in a number of other ways the situation in South India is quite different from that found elsewhere. In general I found that the further I got into a particular festival celebration the less I wanted to entertain comparisons with particular phenomena elsewhere; they seemed to distract me from seeing the main lines of thought in the local situation.

The discussion of the nature of "carnival" that the Russian literary critic M. M. Bakhtin has stirred up seems to me to provide a more open-ended and creative comparison. Bakhtin has distilled from the medieval European experience of carnival a set of philosophical notions and wants to measure all other forms of culture in terms of them. Bakhtin's scholarly work involved showing that as early as the sixteenth century, the French novelist Rabelais recognized the cultural loss that would occur if the principles underlying the medieval carnival were to disappear, and he tried to illustrate those philosophical principles in the carnival characters portrayed in his novels (Bakhtin 1984).

At first glance, there are striking similarities between the medieval European carnivals as portrayed by Bakhtin and the festival tradition of South India. In both "festivals" and "carnival," a notable independence of the official political and clerical authorities emerges; a warm, playful, and physical form of expressing the religious vision appears; and a creative genius originates within a nonliterate mass of humanity and eventually profoundly influences the higher forms of culture within its society.

The philosophical interests that led Bakhtin to examine Rabelais, and the medieval folk culture that had inspired Rabelais, are complex and can be pointed out only in passing here.[7] Even in his first essay, *Toward a Philosophy of the Act* (written 1919, trans. 1993), written in his early twenties, Bakhtin was already puzzling over the question of how the gap in experience between an individual act and even the most immediate effort to explain it could be overcome. Whereas the act itself was part of the world of life, to which he felt we are answerable in some special way, the "explanation" is already part of a world of Being experienced in a different framework of moral answerability.

In the decades that followed, Bakhtin tried to bridge this gap by developing the idea of the "dialogic imagination" to describe the experience of discourse in which every particular word is understood to echo a host of other voices and is itself addressed to many others. In great novels, such as those of Dostoevsky, some of the echoing voices can be found within one character, and those being addressed can also represent a number of different moral universes. The dialogic truth Bakhtin sought to identify and use allowed him to directly address certain realities of the Soviet cultural scene he lived within, while simultaneously engaging other eras and other contexts of historical consciousness in dialogue.

In turning his primary scholarly attention to Rabelais, Bakhtin was looking for an example of the dialogic imagination operating in full freedom. In examining the cultural forms of seventeenth-, eighteenth-, and nineteenth-century Europe, he found increasingly constricted monologues of theology, science, rationalism, or romanticism, in which powerful cultural voices used political and cultural monopolies to restrict discussion to the abstract framework of truth they were setting forth. In this situation he thought that Rabelais was the last thinker to voice the philosophically different "carnival" discourse of the Middle Ages.

As Bakhtin understands it, "carnival" was a festival style of the Middle Ages in which for periods of time the lower classes of society celebrated with plays, processions, and feasts that mocked the clerical and political leaders and voiced their radical freedom. The laughter that characterized these celebrations was ambivalent because it put everyone at one level, and although it mocked the usually revered biblical figures, clergy, and politicians, it was equally adept at self-mockery. The "open" discourse of the carnival generated multivoiced laughter about important issues such as death and fertility, and on these issues all share alike. Those who pretend otherwise prove themselves fools.

In illustrating the free discourse characteristic of the medieval carnival, Rabelais, and Bakhtin after him, insist on especially bawdy examples and extreme forms of hyperbole. In Bakhtin's special vocabulary, this language is "grotesque realism," and the focus of the vocabulary comes from the "lower half" of the human body. Because both Rabelais and Bakhtin clearly intend to exaggerate this point, and Bakhtin wanted to contrast this "carnival" language with the restrictions on the use of such language in, for example, nineteenth-century literature, it is not easy to say how central this language style was to the actual discourse of the medieval carnival. Was the language of the carnival just the normal everyday language of a celebrating crowd—which would, of course, in any era and any part of the world include more references to the body and more hyperbole than nineteenth century literary convention would allow—or were the participants in the carnival crowds intentionally bawdy and hyperbolic?

I raise the question as to whether bawdy and hyperbolic language is an essential feature of "carnival," because it is not a major feature of South Indian festivals. The language of the South Indian festivals is free and includes the deities in a great deal of everyday fun and laughter. In Koṭuṅkaḷūr (chapter 3), for instance, the goddess is considered to be sexually aroused, and the crowd promises to satisfy her; in Kataragama (chapter 2) and Śrīraṅkam (chapter 4) the deity gets into romantic entanglements that produce much emotion; and in Tiruvāṉaikkā (chapter 5) both a priest and a deity don female dress and create a lot of good fun. In Koṭuṅkaḷūr one might think of the bawdiness of the language as intentionally exaggerated because the whole dramatic structure of the festival involves an overthrow of the priestly role and the temple is actually closed for the duration of the festival. In general, however, the "everyday" quality of the South Indian festival language seems to be intended simply to share with the deity the normal warmth and excitement of the people's life.

South Indian festivals are certainly like a "carnival" in the way they insist on being the voice of the people, which is expressed with all its multivocality and all its joyous affirmation of life. Because they express voices spread over a thousand years (see discussion to follow),[8] however, the exact nature of the "official" clerical and political voices they counter continually changes, and the tone of mockery is muted. Today's festival participants are fascinated by the variety of older voices embedded in the ritual, but like the carnival celebrants of Europe, they intensely focus on the physical energy the celebration calls forth and the healing and sense of well-being the visit of the deity promises.

The Festivals Scattered through Time: The Three "Parts"

Even though festival worship in South India is focused very clearly on present and future well-being, the participants truly believe that festival religion is a tradition with great antiquity. Although the nature of the discourse within the festival is ahistorical, the integrity of the festival is closely related to its ability to preserve and repackage ritual features from ancient times. Although the ritual materials incorporated in the festival do not include datable figures such as founders of dynasties, some clearly reflect earlier eras of a hunting or sea-faring society. In addition to the internal evidence that the festival reflects some ancient voices, sometimes datable inscriptions describe a donation for a festival, or a piece of datable literature mentions a festival.

After I had attended a few different festivals, I realized that they projected their sense of antiquity differently. Some festivals were really much like pilgrimages, in that they involved people going to a fairly remote sacred spot reputed to have been recognized from primordial time as having sacred power. The rituals of these festivals assumed that they were taking place in a preagricultural society, and they brought together a festival community from a widely scattered and socially diverse region. Even if a temple developed on this sacred spot, it is thought of as marginal to the festival activity. A second type of festival is much more closely associated with one of the great stone temples built in medieval times, even though the festival religion in the streets outside the temple continues to contrast sharply with the daily rituals within the temple. In these settings the formal rituals for opening and closing the festival and for some of the processions involve the temple priests, but when the festival is large, the celebratory tone of the festival remains with the crowd, even as it does in those with a more primordial sense of the sacred. Third, there are a fair number of festival events today that even the participants recognize as recent developments. Some of these "modern festivals" model themselves on the earlier pilgrimage type or the medieval temple type, but others are explicitly designed for a particular community's needs.

These three types of events all are part of the South Indian tradition of festival religion, but their different senses of antiquity may help us approach the difficult question of how to deal with a clearly old tradition that does not acknowledge the kings and clerics who provide the guideposts for the usual "official" histories. Each chapter in this study is a description of a particular festival that is still celebrated. Nevertheless, in some festivals participants insisted that the festival had been celebrated in exactly the same way since preagricultural times and that the hunting symbols providing the basic structure of the celebration were taken from the everyday occupation of the early celebrants. While I was skeptical at first, and made determined efforts to find external evidence to date the celebrations, in the end I found the internal evidence convincing, and suspect that the festivals structured around preagricultural ritual symbols might well be quite old. Whatever the date, three festival types project their antiquity differently. In organizing this study into "Parts," I use this threefold typology as a guide.

In part I I describe four festivals that I interpret as pilgrimage-like gatherings at ancient sacred spots. This section is entitled Ancient Patterns. Part II presents another group of festivals which center on elaborate ceremonial flag raisings and processions around great medieval stone temples. The studies in this section are described as Medieval Structures. Finally, a somewhat larger number of festivals are described in part III under the label Modern Forms, because each can be described as a self-conscious effort to develop a religious community in a particular historical circumstance.

Playing Host to Deity

When worshipers approached to interpret the festival activity for me, they were invariably excited and proud of what was going on. Initially I interpreted this attitude as a kind of lower-class hospitality directed at me as a visitor. After attending a number of festivals, I realized that the excitement and pride were ubiquitous and that the fever pitch for this style of hospitality occurred just before or just after the arrival of one of the deities. At these times excited cries ("She is coming!" "He is feeling playful!" "She is so-o beautiful!" "Can you see Him?") ring through the air.

There are two important aspects to this sense of hospitality. One is the way it presents the human community in the worship experience, and the other is the way it relates the worshiper with deity. Some religious traditions are described as "otherworldly" because the deity is believed to belong to a completely different realm from the world of everyday experience, and people learn to worship by establishing ties with that other world. In the South Indian festival, the preparation is all in the form of tidying the everyday world. Shelters near mountaintops or streams are spruced up, social relations are all renewed and carefully checked out, and vows are performed so that the body and mind are all ready. No one is exempt, so that leaders put on the dress and manners of the common folk, and those who need healing of body or mind are brought into the center of the celebration. The worship takes place within the community and it is an affirmation of the life of the people in all its variety that is being celebrated.

The deities have been invited to share in the celebration of the community, but there is no certainty that they will come. Stone temples in South India were built like fortresses with a number of concentric walls around the "seat" of the deity, or "seats" of the deities. Priests fed, bathed, and worshiped the deities within these temples daily, and landlords or kings who made major donations for building the temples could arrange for worship within one of the corridors. However, for the mass of the people, entry to the temple was restricted and the primary worship of the deity took place on festival occasions. For the deity to come out of the temple into the community was a major event and involved transferring the power of the deity into either an *utsava ayūdha* (festival instrument) or an *utsava mūrti* (festival image). Sometimes this transfer itself is a frightening experience,[9] but the utsava form of the deity is thought to have a totally different personality and can be known only in the context of its encounter with the festival crowds.

When the deity meets the festival crowd, its personality is defined. The formidable and frequently angry goddess of Koṭuṅkaḷūr is said to be "swept off her feet" by the offerings of meat and toddy and the chanting crowds awaiting her in the festival (chapter 3). The playful *aḷakīya maṇavāḷaṉ* or "bridegroom" form Viṣṇu assumes at festival time seems to get so involved in the premarriage party laid out for him that he almost forgets to go back for his arranged marriage (chapter 4). And Māriyammaṉ, who is considered vengeful and even the cause of smallpox before she comes to the festival, is considered relaxed and stunningly beautiful by all the festival celebrants who approach her with the stories of their lives (chapters 8 and 12).

In defining the religious experience of these festivals as "playing host to deity," I wanted to indicate the special dimension of the religious experience, without distracting from either the great variety within the festival tradition or the important "living" quality of a religious tradition held together almost completely by ritual action alone. The people involved in these festivals today are for the most part no longer nonliterate, but they still consider it important that the ritual remain the expression of the mass of the community as it celebrates its joy with the deities that have come to be part of the community. For those who have thought of worship as removing oneself from everyday society and approaching a special domain of the divine, this different sense of worship will not be easy to appreciate at first. But it is a rich religious tradition, one from which others can learn.

I

ANCIENT PATTERNS

These four studies explore the relationship of the ancestral society and the divine. The first two are undergoing dramatic revivals in recent years and are profoundly linked with the political visions of modern South India and Śrī Lanka, respectively. The other two appear to have had links with the ancient royal capitals of their respective regions, but the celebrations now seem to reach behind the royal power and address the divine presence found in this location before the royal power was established.

Consistent with their theme of reaching for the primordial past, each of these four festivals involves great physical exertion from the worshipers. In each the worshipers seemingly must break with the normal social order in order to renew themselves and appropriate the power that can be derived from a wilder and more natural domain. In the first example the feminine presence is left behind in the social order when the worshiper leaves to search, whereas in the other three, the discovery of the feminine provides the energy of the mythic encounter at the heart of the festival.

In the first two cases, temples now stand on the festival site, but in the first case the temple is open only during the festival time, and in the second the priesthood and the ritual are unique to this festival site. The third temple has a year-round ritual, but the temple is known primarily for its festival. The fourth festival has been woven into the larger ritual pattern of one of the most important temples of South India, and therefore the festival is no longer easily recognized as belonging to the ancient pilgrimage-like festival group.

1

Return to the Mountains

The Ayyappan̲ Festival in Sabarimalai, Kerala

The classical Tamil̲ grammar, written by Tolkāppiyan̲ before the beginning of the Christian era, identified five types of geographical regions that poets might use symbolically. Among the five, the "mountainous" or *kur̲iñci* region was first, described, among other things, as the region where a poet might place a young male deity. Probably at one time a large percentage of the population in South India and Śrī Lanka actually lived in the mountains, where the tropical forests contain a wide variety of animals and are still rich in natural fruit and root produce. In recent centuries these mountains have become world-renowned for their spices and tea.

Even in Tolkāppiyan̲'s time, however, the mountains seem to have been associated with nostalgia. We know that by the beginning of the Christian era, trade along the coasts of South India and Śrī Lanka was prospering. Although the products that made the trade possible came from the mountains, the urban trading centers along the coast provided the sophisticated political and literary forms for which the Classical Age in the region is known. Somewhat later, the focus of activity shifted once again, this time to the river valley areas under irrigation. In these river valleys Śrī Lanka and later South India were able to produce major agricultural surpluses, and in these densely populated areas they went on to develop highly structured societies and elaborate institutions. The mountainous region continued to play a minor role in the economy as a supplier of raw materials, but its most important role was as a symbolic reminder of the social origins and roots out of which the South Indian understanding of human experience developed. For all of South India and Śrī Lanka, the mountains continue to represent freedom and naturalness, or the liberating antistructure that stands against the highly structured society in the more heavily populated areas.

The most dramatic expression of the symbolic contrast between life in the mountains and the plains is the annual festival pilgrimage to the shrine of Ayyappan̲.[1] This festival now involves a pilgrimage in which more than 175,000 males reach the remote shrine in the mountains on each of the 51 days the shrine is open during December and part of January. For these 10 million worshipers, and for the many millions who help them prepare for the trip or just watch them along the route, the whole experience represents a total reversal of values, as they leave their busy (often urban) lives and return to roots that involve arduous physical exertion and the challenge of the wild natural order. The huge numbers that make the pilgrimage today are a relatively new phenomenon that I will try to explain later, but the festival certainly has been celebrated faithfully over the centuries, and its symbols vividly recreate the vision of the origins of the social order. Those who join in this celebration participate in the kind of life people knew during the earliest phase of human experience in South India. Their participation renews their sense of identity as South Indians and provides them with perspective on the narrower focus in which their daily life is ordinarily lived.[2]

The Core Story

The story that provides an explanation of the festival is set within a small mountain kingdom known as Pantalam. One day the ruler of Pantalam was hunting and found a baby boy alone in the forest. The ruler went to an ascetic living in the forest to ask who the baby was. The ascetic told him to take the baby home and raise it as his own son, and he would discover the explanation of his identity by his twelfth year. The king followed this advice, and the baby grew into a fine young prince named Manikantha.

When Manikantha reached the age of twelve, the king wanted to crown him as his *yuvarāja*, or heir apparent. The king and queen had a younger son of their own who was disabled and therefore unable to rule. An evil minister, because he hoped to be the de facto ruler himself one day, convinced the queen that her biological son was about to be set aside unjustly. On the evil minister's advice, the queen feigned illness, and the evil minister called a physician friend. The medication prescribed by the physician was tiger's milk. Manikantha insisted on going into the forest to bring the necessary milk. The ruler was distressed that Manikantha face the dangers of the forest alone, but he eventually provided him with a coconut to carry the milk.

When Manikantha returned from the forest riding on the back of a tigress, the ruler knew he was in the presence of a divine being. He promised to build Manikantha a shrine, and when Manikantha shot an arrow to indicate the spot where the shrine was to be, it landed thirty kilometers from Pantalam in the thick of the forest. Manikantha then indicated that the image should be a boy crouching with a band around his legs, as hunters in the area crouch when resting. Manikantha was then transformed into the divine being Ayyappaṉ, and the day of his transformation, Makara Saṅkrānti (about January 14), became the day on which the heavenly lights (*viḷakku*, Sanskrit: *jyotī*) spread across the northeastern sky, the day on which the festival now reaches its climax.

This core story is carefully structured. On one hand, the social order has serious flaws (a younger and incompetent son claiming the throne, a sick queen, and an evil minister). On the other hand, nature holds mysterious power (the tigress's milk and an ascetic who had been able to solve the mysteries of the forest). The resolution involves an interdependent balance of political and divine intervention. The Pantalam ruler, as the embodiment of the political order, is able to uphold *dharma*, or righteousness, to care for the baby, and to build the shrine for the deity. His role is still reenacted each year as a member of the Pantalam ruling family (which no longer has any political role) proceeds to the shrine with a box of jewels just as the lights in the sky flare for the climax of the festival. The young male deity, Ayyappaṉ, joins the spiritual power of the ascetic with the natural power of the tigress's milk and applies them to the needs of the kingdom.

The Pilgrimage

Participants in the festival, not really devotional worshipers in the ordinary sense, seek temporarily to become "Ayyappaṉs," males who can meet the challenge of the forest and return to society emboldened with new power. For either 41 or 51 days (there seems to be a difference on how long the vow should hold) a small group (I observed groups as small as three and as large as fifty) is bound together in the three activities of preparation, travel, and celebration. They call one another "Ayyappaṉ," or just "Swāmi" (Lord), and use no personal names. For the duration of the pilgrimage, this small group cuts itself off from the rest of society and tries to leave all distinctions of age, status, or any other form of social identity behind. Acting as one unified personality, they assume the personality of an exuberant male youth familiar with the forest.

For a rather high percentage of the participants, the "first-timers" (*kaṇṇis*), the entire exercise is an initiation, much like Manikantha's when he went into the forest for tiger's milk just before he was to be crowned as *yuvarāja*. Probably in years past this initiatory aspect of the pilgrimage was more central, and almost the whole of the ritual was an initiation of South Indian youth. Even now, most of the preparatory rituals are much like initiation rites.

The most important step in the preparation is saying the solemn vow in the hometown temple. For this ceremony a large number of family members usually accompany the participant to lend their support. The vow involves a promise to wear a black *lungi* (a dramatic contrast to the usual white one worn by South Indian men), to eat only the simple fruits and millets in the forest, to abstain from sexual activity, and to grow a beard. The vow is sealed by the wearing of a *rudrākṣa* necklace. The group takes this vow together and thereby place themselves under an experienced spiritual guide, or *periyaswāmi*, who will take charge until they return.

Under the strict guidance of the *periyaswāmi*, the trip begins with each *kaṇṇi* wrapping up a two-compartment packet (*irumuṭi*). The front compartment holds items for the final act of worship (a coconut filled with ghee, dried rice, betel leaves, arecanuts, and a coin), and the back compartment holds other coconuts for worship along the way and more rice and gram for the pilgrim's consumption. The packet is carried on the head throughout the trip. Once the packets are ready, the *periyaswāmi* leads the group off toward the mountains, visiting as many temples as he can find along the way. All along the way (under some *periyaswāmis* for 24 hours of every day), antiphonal chants ring out (called the *śaraṇam viḷi*) varying the name from "Ayyappaṉ śaraṇam" ("I take refuge in Ayyappaṉ") to "Swāmiye śaraṇam," to "Śaraṇam Ayyappaṉ," until the participants are dazed and participate in the nonstop activity of the group with blind impulsiveness.

When the group reaches the little town of Erumeli at the edge of the forest, the second-year *swāmis* paint the *kaṇṇis* in colored paints and require them to perform the wild *petta tuḷḷal* dance until they reach uncontrollable frenzy. After this, the initiates are again warned that the forest is full of tigers and wild elephants and reminded that the trip involves the climbing of steep slopes and the swimming of turbulent rivers, so that only those spiritually prepared are likely to live. Thus prepared, the group undertakes the last part of the pilgrimage, which involves walking through the dense forest for 4 days and 45 kilometers of arduous climbing.

Finally the pilgrims arrive at the long-sought wondrous shrine. There the noisy crowd becomes an object of reverence itself, and the cries of thousands constantly ascend. Gradually groups line up at the 18 steep stone steps before the temple, and in a last cry of exuberance throw ghee-filled coconuts against the stone. Then, with the assistance of anchored ropes and calm police constables standing on carefully braced platforms, the worshipers climb the sacred steps and enter the quieter confines of the temple. There they watch in wonder as the priests pour the ghee from their coconuts over the image of Ayyappan̲. In a surprisingly short time, they head for home.

One of the most notable features of this festival, which distinguishes it from all others I know in the area, is that women are not allowed to participate. Women were not allowed to participate in the past because the central ritual is really a male initiation rite that tests the young man's ability to stand up to the rigor of a dangerous forest. A minor ritual involving Ayyappan̲'s *śakti*, or female counterpart Malikappuram, links the idea of initiation and the exclusion of women. Malikappuram has a separate temple nearby, but the story is that Ayyappan̲ agreed to marry her in any year when no *kaṇṇis* arrive for initiation. Each year now on the evening before the final celebration, her image is brought near Ayyappan̲'s temple only to find the appropriate door locked once again because hundreds of thousands of *kaṇṇis* are still awaiting initiation. Now that many worshipers drive to within 8 kilometers of the temple by car or bus and many women wish to worship, the authorities have had difficulty explaining the exclusion of women. They have recently made a new distinction and now allow young girls and women who have passed menopause to participate, on the premise that only women of menstruating age carry pollution. The logic of this new position may be hard to maintain because women who are actually menstruating do not normally worship in any temple in India, and no other temple considers that menstruating age alone would make one polluting.

The spirit of the core story about Manikantha/Ayyappan̲ and the tone of the initiatory pilgrimage to the mountain shrine fit beautifully together. The symbols of an older understanding of the wild power of the natural order are abundant throughout the pilgrimage, and worshipers truly relive the story of the human engagement with that power in a drama that challenges their physical limits. The ascetic dimensions of their behavior enables them to overcome the dangers of the forest, and then they are renewed by the power that flows from the forest through the figure of Ayyappan̲, whom they embody as they reenter society.

Medieval Interpretations of the Story

A number of supplements to the core story have appeared over the centuries that reflect the sequence of political and religious changes the region has undergone during that time.[3] In many ways these supplements do not appear to have been the basis for major changes in the festival activity itself, because the original story of a courageous initiatory trip into the forest is still the central focus of the action. Nevertheless, the supplemental stories are interesting in their own right, and one or another of them often becomes quite central in the story of the festival as told by any single pilgrim.

One set of supplementary stories appears to reflect the period of prosperous international trade in the history of South India between the beginning of the Common Era and the third century. During this period, apparently the stories of the festival were modified to reflect not only the original setting of a hunting and gathering society living in the forest but also one in which trade was important and plundering outlaws were the primary enemy. Although the temple itself remained in the forest, the main trade route between the east and west coasts of South India passed through the kingdom of Pantalam nearby. The Pāṇṭya capital of Maturai, the eastern anchor of this mountain trade route, was the link between all of South India and Śrī Lanka. The Nair and Pulāyan castes of Kerala, who worshiped in this temple, provided most of the mercenaries who protected the mountain trade route and even regularly assisted the kings of Maturai and Śrī Lanka. Trade on the Kerala or western side of the mountains was in the hands of Syrian Christians during this period, and archaeological ruins 20 kilometers from the temple include many crosses from buildings that were probably part of a Syrian Christian trading post. Buddhist traders were influential on both the east and west coasts of South India, as well as in Śrī Lanka, during the fifth and sixth centuries. Although there is no archaeological evidence of Buddhism near the temple, many scholars think there was Buddhist influence on the ritual in that Ayyappaṉ is often called Dharma Śāstā, or just Śāstā, or "Teacher" as the Buddha was, and the chant of "*ṣaraṇam*," or "I take refuge," is like the best-known chant of the Buddhists. By the late seventh century Muslim traders began to take primary responsibility for the trade routes, and as we will see shortly, a number of Muslim tombs are in the immediate area and do play a role in the present pilgrimage ritual.

The primary change in the stories that reflects this concern with trade, outlaws, and social order is that Ayyappaṉ comes to be pictured as a military genius able to challenge the outlaw Udāyanaṉ, who had been plundering all the small kingdoms in the region. In one of the military stories, Ayyappaṉ is portrayed as the child of a young priest, whose ascetic father had been murdered by Udāyanaṉ, and a royal princess, who had been abducted by Udāyanaṉ. Raised with the mission of taking revenge for his ancestors, Ayyappaṉ proved to be a daring military commander when he assisted the ruler of Pantalam against the fearsome Udāyanaṉ. In one variation of this story, the Pantalam ruler actually sent Ayyappaṉ to Maturai to serve as a mercenary with the Pāṇṭya rulers to whom the Pantalam ruler was related. Finally, in one version of the story, Ayyappaṉ forms an alliance with the Muslim warrior Vāvar against Udāyanaṉ. This last version is the basis for a direct modification in the festival celebration itself. A mosque sits beside the tomb of Vāvar, right next to a little shrine of Ayyappaṉ in the town of Erumeli, where pilgrims assemble for their trek through the forest; everyone is expected to worship in both the mosque and the temple before commencing the journey through the forest.

The second set of supplements to the core story arose from the fact that by late medieval times (seventh century to the twelfth century) the vast majority of pilgrims were devotees of well-known Hindu deities at home, and they felt the need to provide a clearer account of the mythic heritage of Ayyappaṉ. When irrigation was developed in the Kāvēri river valley during the seventh and eighth centuries, many people moved into that area. The primary cultural vehicle binding the extensive valley together during this period was the construction of temples in each of the many *nātus* or petty kingdoms spread up and down the valley. During the seventh and eighth centuries, hymnsingers of Śivaṉ and of Viṣṇu traveled from temple to temple, and their devotional religion became orthodox Hinduism in South India in the centuries that followed. It became necessary to link these religious stories with that of Ayyappan̲.

One of the mythic supplements to the Ayyappan̲ story focuses on the female demon buffalo, Mahiṣi. The story is that two divine beings, Datta and Līlā, took human form and wandered on the earth for a time. Datta wanted to go back to the divine realm, but Līlā was enjoying his company and pleaded with him to remain. In anger, he cursed her so that she would become Mahiṣi, so she cursed him to become a Mahiṣa, or a male buffalo, and keep her company. (Other versions make the two buffaloes cousins.) He eventually did become Mahiṣāsura, or the famous demon buffalo, and oppressed humankind as the central "enemy" of many goddess stories popular in South India. Finally the goddess Candika was called upon, and she put him to death. Mourning his death, Mahiṣi then ruled in the forest as a frightening tree spirit, or *yakṣi*. When Ayyappan̲ entered the forest to look for tiger's milk, he was confronted by her; he killed her and threw her body down a steep bank into the A̲luta River (tributary of the Pampa) just below the present shrine.

Other orthodox Hindu stories recount that Mahiṣi had once been granted a boon and had requested that no one be able to kill her except a child born of the two male deities Śivan̲ and Viṣṇu. There was, however, an old Vedic story of how Viṣṇu was transformed into the beguiling female form of Mōhinī to entice the demons, or *asuras*, away from the nectar of immortality they had stolen. In the crisis produced by Mahiṣi's boon, Viṣṇu again took the form of Mōhinī, Śivan̲ was attracted to this female form, and the child thus produced was the mysterious baby found in the forest by the Pantalam king. In this story the name of the baby becomes HariHara after his two parents, Viṣṇu (Hari) and Śivan̲ (Hara).

Much like the political clarifications of the story supplements described earlier, these supplements to the mythic story also clarified and enriched the whole story complex without modifying the core story. The introduction of the sympathetically portrayed Mahiṣi figure in the role of spiritual "enemy" allowed the rich Kerala tradition of *yakṣi* myth to be brought into the worship. Yakṣis, as portrayed in both old temple paintings and modern films in Kerala, are the voluptuous young mothers who turn into fanged and frightening women who often try to seduce those they wish to conquer. The Mahiṣi of this story too has a legitimate right to be angry, but the sympathy one feels for her just makes her all the more difficult to overcome. In much the same way, the including of the youthful, vigorous, and righteous Viṣṇu/Hari and the ascetic and formidable Śivan̲/Hara in the same personality portrayed the mountain deity Ayyappan̲ as an engaging being who could overcome the sectarian religious divisions of the plains. Worshipers still wanted the unknown mystery and danger of encountering the forest deity, but by linking the identity of the deity with widely known mythic figures, they could also now think that their worship was relevent to all kinds of problems, including those they would encounter as they returned to their complex responsibilities in the plains.

Modern Meanings

No one seems to know when the modern craze for undertaking the journey to the shrine of Ayyappan̲ began, but only during the past 50 years has the festival grown from a modest-sized one to one of the largest anywhere in the world. Reasonably accurate figures are kept by the Devaswaram Board of the State government that now manages the temple, and they claim that as they now encourage people to complete their worship any time during the 51 days prior to Makara Saṇkrānti, that 10 million worshipers visit the temple during that period. For a two-month period every year, trains, buses, and highways all over South India are jammed with Ayyappaṉ worshipers shouting their antiphonal chants. During the last 50 years a new sense of what is meaningful about this pilgrimage of renewal has arisen.

However, the modern resurgence in the worship of Ayyappaṉ has not triggered new storytelling or a conscious new reinterpretation of the worship. In some ways it almost seems that the absence of religious specialists, or the priests and monastic leaders commonly found in South Indian temples, makes this worship experience different. When the Kerala government took over the management of the temple from the Pantalam ruler, they appointed civil servants to manage the finances of the temple and the great crowds, and they also appointed a new team of nonlocal priests to see that the care of the image was proper. Contact with religious specialists is minimal throughout the festival, and the patterns of meaning the festival holds are conveyed to each generation of worshipers almost completely by word of mouth among those on the pilgrimage route on any one day.[4]

As the crowds have grown, there have, of course, been important organizational changes, some serving to encourage the growth of the crowds even further. Paved roads now lead to the Pampa River crossing, just 8 kilometers from the temple, for those who choose a less arduous path to worship. The state government's assurance that offerings are handled correctly has helped increase the income of the temple. In 1950 a charitable organization called the Ayyappa Seva Sangham was established. It is now highly organized and provides medical facilities and other amenities for the festival itself and includes 600 branches spread around South India that serve as facilitators to help set up the pilgrim groups.

A wider public has come to be interested in this pilgrimage to the past because South India is witnessing a period of deep self-examination stimulated by the creative politics of the Dravidian movement. Most people trace the Dravidian movement to the protests (under the name of the Justice Party) the educated non-Brāhmans made at the beginning of the century against the near monopoly the Brāhmans had on the employment opportunities that British rule made available in the civil service and the universities. At this point for the first time one heard the argument that the Brāhmans were North Indians who had immigrated into the area in medieval times and that there was a distinct South Indian (or Dravidian) culture that should be rediscovered. By the twenties this anti-Brāhman anger had taken the next step, and E. V. Ramaswamy Naicker argued that South Indians should reject the religion of Brāhman priests and the temples they dominated. Unlike Naicker, most South Indians began to cling to religion more thoroughly than ever through this period of self-examination, but the temples (and particularly the festivals of those temples) that owed little to the Brāhman-defined traditions of North India began to attract the largest crowds.

The special role of the Ayyappaṉ pilgrimage in this new era of South Indian cultural renewal, was to represent the deepest roots of the culture. Scholars were involved in the recovery of the classical literary heritage in Tamiḻ, and were enthusiastically supported by the Dravidian governments. The temples of Murukaṉ and Māriyammaṉ were also involved, but in those cases the wild dances and self mutilation that the lower class worshipers have carried out over the centuries were not easy for others to adapt to. In Ayyappan̲ worship, the rituals are also arduous, but the activity begins in one's home village with close associates, and individuals assign meaning to the ritual for themselves. All South Indians could participate in their own way and feel that they were contributing to the overall sense of cultural renewal.

Many of the "new" participants in the Ayyappan̲ pilgrimage seem to come from the educated urban class. I watched the creation of a small group of some of the best-placed professionals in South Indian society. The organizer of the group was a high court judge from the Kavuntar caste of landlords in the central drylands of South India. He had been distinctly areligious until he was elevated to high court judge by the Dravidian government, but his zeal for Ayyappan̲ quickly became contagious. He soon recruited his physician, who was a western-educated dean of the medical school married to a Christian but still anxious to rediscover his roots. A third member of the group was the most senior South Indian in the whole New Delhi civil service, who began to save his leave each year so that he could relinquish his powerful hold on the finance ministry of India and fly off to trek to the mountain deity of South India. Along the pilgrim way, one recognizes widely known journalists, musicians, or athletes, and one can speak with a majority of the worshipers in English, the primary language of higher education in South India. The formation of the Ayyappa Seva Sangha has certainly encouraged the educted elite among the non-Brāhmans to join in this worship; its board consists entirely of "Pillais" and "Nairs," the two traditional landlord castes of the region, many of whom are now English-educated professionals.

While the wider public became interested in the Ayyappan̲ pilgrimage as a return to the roots of South Indian culture, in this festival they see and now tend to articulate, two more specific religious emphases. One is the ecumenical atmosphere of the festival. Many worshipers comment that Śivan̲ and Viṣṇu are both included in the myth, but they seem to exult even more enthusiastically about the wider inclusivity of the pilgrimage and mention the stop at the sanctuary of a Muslim saint, the visits of the famous Christian singer Jesudasan, and the Ayyappa Seva Sangha's plans to sponsor a world parliament of religions. South India has always had an intense religiosity, and its villages have always had religious institutions of many rival sects and rival religions. If the pilgrimage to Ayyappan̲ represents a return to the root of the culture, it must be inclusive as much as possible, even if its devotional tone remains intensely Hindu in many ways (and it continues to exclude most women).

The other religious emphasis that the modern worshipers mention often is the ascetic dimension of the worship of Ayyappan̲. With the development of urbanization and industrialization, many people are enjoying new wealth and new social freedom that they are not comfortable about. Asceticism has always had a respected place in the religious traditions of India, but it has generally been associated with the worship traditions of meditation rather than with traditions involving specific requests to the deities. In the tradition of Ayyappan̲, one can have it both ways. On one hand, the Ayyappan̲ tradition is Dravidian and has little to do with meditation, yet on the other hand, it is in certain ways characterized by asceticism and can legitimately claim some of the prestige associated with that style of religious practice. As the worshipers now remark, this annual "conquering of the senses" is good for the soul in this world of social freedom and temptation and links an individual to a respectable religious tradition without the more permanent implications of traditional ascetic vows.

Conclusion

The festival worship of Ayyappa<u>n</u> is different from the other religious festivals of South India in that it takes place in connection with a temple that does not now operate year-round. Because the worshipers make a special trip to get there, and the trip is an important part of the worship, one is tempted to think of it more as a pilgrimage than a festival. In some limited ways, it is comparable to pilgrimages, but its origin almost certainly reflected its local society, as do the other temple festivals. It continues to keep that basic character despite major changes in the size of the celebration.

The central theme of the celebration is an exploration of the interrelationships between "nature" and "society." Nature is portrayed as full of mystery and terror, but its power is essential to the healing and proper functioning of the social order. Humans normally live in the realm of society, but they are capable of dealing with the powers of nature through careful discipline and divine assistance.

The deity involved in this worship is actually never thoroughly described. He is experienced in "intimate comradeship." To break trust with him is indeed dangerous, because the venture into the realm of nature is dangerous for all concerned, but he is not a mysteriously unpredictable personality that humans find difficult to understand. He confronts what humans confront in the dangers of the natural order, and in that sense he empowers the worshiper.

The worshiper who comes to this festival sets aside his social identity for a time so that he can test the limits of his personal power. For the hunting society that first developed the ritual, this test would probably have been an important part of an initiation that provided each person with the courage needed for life and death encounters with dangerous animals. For the male members of the Nair and Pulāyan castes of Kerala, (who made up the bulk of the worshipers over the years), the test of personal and group courage made it possible to function as mercenaries, even though their role in the matrilineal and matriarchal family arrangements of Kerala was tenuous. For the modern professional class, which has turned to this festival with so much enthusiasm, the test involves knowing how far they can go beyond the bounds of the social identity into which they were born without losing touch with their roots and the power that contact provides.

The public that reads about the record-setting numbers who visit Ayyappa<u>n</u> each year reflect on the trends in social and political behavior and conclude that a general rootedness still exists in their society. Other festivals I will analyze affect the social life of their region in important ways, but the Ayyappa<u>n</u> festival plays a special role in this regard. Its influence, one assumes, was once limited to the region of the Kerala mountains and the hunters and warriors who lived there, but those localized symbols have now assumed a different meaning and have become some of the most widely accepted symbols around which the whole society of modern South India is attempting to redefine itself.

2

On the Edge of the Forest

A Festival of Romance in Kataragama, Śrī Lanka

One of the best known festivals in the South Indian tradition is held in Kataragama in southeast Śrī Lanka, climaxing on the full moon of the month of Esala (July–August) each year. This festival takes place on the edge of the great Yala Forest, which is now a government reserve for animals. The primary figures in the ritual—the priests of the main deities, the *ālatti ammas* or "mothers of light," and the tribal chieftain—are all reputed to be linked to the ancient Vedda population that inhabited Śrī Lanka long before it had contact with India.[1] So although this festival has important roles in the social and political life of contemporary Śrī Lanka, it can be seen as an ancient Vedda celebration, an expression of their view of the world as their forest homeland came into contact with Indian civilization for the first time.

Background

The region of the Kataragama shrine is known as Rohaṇa, now a rather thinly populated area in the dry jungles of the southeast sector of the island of Śrī Lanka. Earlier in the history of the island, however, it seems to have been a major center of civilization, if not the most important center on the island (de Silva 1983; Ray and Paranavitana 1959, 1960, 1973). (The center of modern Śrī Lanka, around Colombo on the southwest coast, was once a malarial jungle, and the ports in the southeast and the northwest were the original centers of civilization.) The dry forests of the southeast seem to have been a habitat of the Vedda hunters, and a few of those ancient tribes still choose to live in the traditional way in these forests.

The elaborate legends of the Indian prince Vijaya, who is thought of as the "founder" of Śrī Lanka, describe him landing on the coast of Śrī Lanka and marrying the Vedda princess Kuveni in about the fifth century BCE. These legends became part of the reconstructed histories of the island written by Buddhist monks in later centuries (Geiger 1912). Vijaya was probably not the first Indian visitor, however, for the distance between India and Śrī Lanka is slight, and there were apparently numerous contacts with both the east and west coasts of South India over a long period. Many of the early contacts seem to have been with this southeast coastal region, and the festival in Kataragama is a celebration of the mythic arrival of a prince-like deity who falls in love with a local girl.

The Festival Site

The physical layout of the festival site in Kataragama is difficult to describe because it is dotted with dozens of sacred places established over many centuries. I will attempt to reconstruct the stages in which the development of the many shrines might have taken place and describe the festival site as a sequence of ever more crowded arrangements. In suggesting these stages, I will create a history of this worship center that will no doubt stir up controversies about precedence that swirl around this great festival event. Such controversies and religious rivalries indicate that one of its important functions is to provide a central forum where all the different religious communities of Śrī Lanka can interact and try to reinforce their role in the island's cultural identity.

Stage one might be thought of as the period before the present site was established. The festival action at that time might have taken place between the Wadahitikande mountain peak, 3 kilometers to the south, thought to have been where an ancient Vedda mountain god resided,[2] and the little town of Sella Kataragama, 6 kilometers to the north along the Manik Ganga River, where the tribal girl/deity Valli first met the prince/deity Kataragama.

Stage two would be when the two essential buildings of the central ritual were constructed, and the festival ritual took on the character of a drama set in a sacred ground beside the river (fig. 2.1). Both buildings are still exceedingly plain rectanglar structures with porches of tree branches, which give them the appearance of forest dwellings. The temple management is uneasy about rebuilding them, especially the one of Lord Kataragama, until, as they say, they have "direct orders from the deity." The two structures are so plain that one cannot use architectural style to estimate their age. The temple of Lord Kataragama, locally called the *mahādevale*, faces south. Three hundred meters to the south (and a bit east) of Lord Kataragama is the temple of the princess/goddess, Valli, which faces north. Just to the north of the Kataragama temple is the great Bodhi Tree, the planting of which in the third century BCE is described in the Buddhist Chronicles (Geiger 1912, ch 19), and just to the west of the Valli shrine is a great Kohomba tree (*Azadirachta indica*) or the local tree in which Lord Kataragama is said to have hid. During the ritual of the festival, Lord Kataragama moves back and forth between these two points, as well as to the nearby river.

Stage three might have been when the great Buddhist *stūpa* (burial mound) called Kiri Vehera was constructed 560 metres to the north or behind the temple of Kataragama (fig. 2.2). This *stūpa* was recently reconstructed and has probably been reconstructed many times over the centuries. However, some sculpture near the *stūpa* dates from before the beginning of the Common Era, and that provides proof that there was a Buddhist *stūpa* on this site at that time. (Buddhists sometimes argue that the *stūpa* was built before the temples of Kataragama and Valli.) Buddhist rulers often controlled this part of southeast Śrī Lanka, as well as the better-known Anurādhapura in the northwest of the island. There are elaborate *stūpas* and monasteries in the ancient capital of this re-

Figure 2-1. Temple of Lord Kataragama Śrī Lanka: "*Mahādevale*."

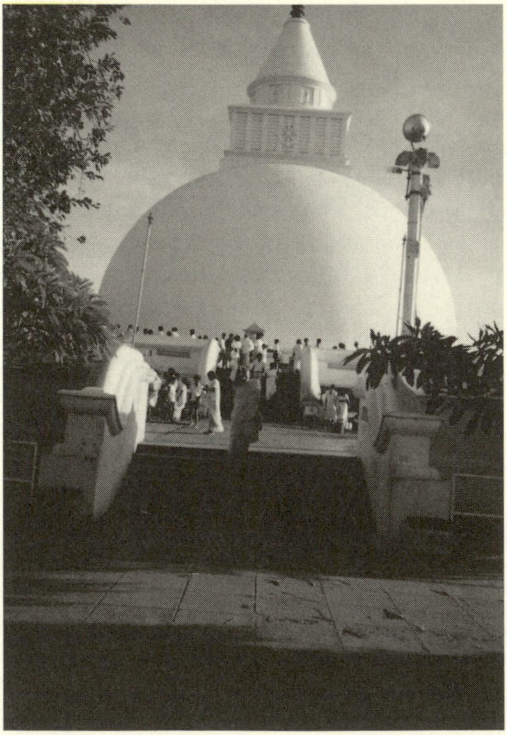

Figure 2-2. Buddhist *stūpa* "*Kiri Vehera*" in Kataragama.

gion, called Tissamahārama, 16 kilometers away from Kataragama. Other ruins of *stūpas* and monasteries are in the forest closer to the Kataragama festival site. Many of these Buddhist buildings were centers of activity over the centuries, and it would be impossible to reconstruct how extensively Buddhist themes interacted with the central ritual of Kataragama in different eras. The soaring white forms of the remodeled Kiri Vehera now provide the worshipers at the festival with an oasis for quiet visits, as well as a base for minor ritual events led by Buddhist clergy.

Stage four involved the building of three memorial shrines for three famous sages from India. Each of these three shrines has over the centuries become the base for a walled compound with its own cluster of buildings, religious specialists, and worship routines. The shrine center closest to the main temple of Lord Kataragama is the orthodox Hindu center in the walled compound just east of the temple. This compound includes a series of grave sites for the ascetics of a small Dasanami monastery, as well as temples to the goddess Tevayanai and Skanda/Murukaṉ in his ascetic or "Paḻani" form. The other two shrine centers are on either side of the Valli temple. To the west of the Valli temple is the shrine compound of Muthuliṅka Swāmi, which includes a temple of Śivaṉ and a small temple of the goddess Kāli. To the east of the Valli temple is a Muslim compound, which includes a number of saints' graves, a mosque, and a rest house.

Stage five might be thought of as the recent years when extensive additional building activity has been going on in Kataragama. Probably around the turn of the century, an orthodox Hindu temple of Ganeṣa was built by a prominent Tamiḻ businessman just to the west of the main temple of Lord Kataragama. It is served by the orthodox Hindu monks who live in the monastery in the compound to the east. Just to the west of this temple is a relatively new Buddha shrine, which includes an image of Viṣṇu.[3] North of the ancient Bodhi tree behind these temples another string of smaller shrines to popular Sinhala deities has even more recently been established. The busiest of these is the shrine to Pattini on the west, but the row also includes shrines of Dedimunda, Saman, and Suniyam beside hers. In recent years, the whole festival site was renovated. Paved roads and sidewalks were constructed, two bridges were built across the river, government offices and a museum were established, and all commercial activity was forced to withdraw to the other (western) side of the river.[4]

The Central Ritual

Unlike most of the temple festivals in the South Indian tradition, this festival's central ritual is easily distinguished from the host of other activities. The preparations begin 45 days before the festival when priests go deep into the forest to cut two sacred trees with identical forked ends. These are immersed in the river for some time and then kept in the Valli temple as their white milk ("like semen") oozes out from the bark. At the beginning of the festival, one is kept in the Valli temple; the other is taken to the temple of Lord Kataragama for the opening ceremony, a ritual act that some worshipers interpret as a marriage proposal from Valli.

The central ritual is a dramatic procession each evening as Lord Kataragama emerges from his temple and rides on the back of an elephant around the circle of shrines within his own compound and then out the south gate of the compound to the temple of the village girl/goddess Valli (fig. 2.3). After a brief "visit" there, he returns to his own temple in a grand procession on the first 14 nights of the festival. On the thirteenth and fourteenth nights, there is a second, quiet "visit" at midnight. On the fifteenth night the midnight visit lasts until the wee hours of the morning and the romantic bond is consummated. On the following morning the hundreds of thousands of worshipers share in the joy as a priest in a swing mysteriously covered with leaves (many worshipers believe the deities are with him) is taken to the river for the "water cutting"[5] ceremony. After he leaves the leaf hut in the middle of the river the crowd surges forward to grab a piece of the hut and to bathe and play in the waist-deep, newly sanctified waters. After the priest returns to the Valli temple, worshipers obtain droplets of bloodied water from the garments of the bridal couple as those garments are rinsed over and over to the great delight of all concerned.

The ancient ritual forms in which this festival activity is carried out occur now only at this festival site. The priestly or *kapurala* family which carries out the ritual now live in a grand modern compound of houses near the festival site, but they are of an ancient Vedda lineage, and the foundations of the houses they lived in just a generation back are still identifiable in the forest nearby. About a dozen priests work in the Kataragama (they say "*mahādevale*") temple and Valli temple, but the important titles are the *mahā kapurala*, or the head priest, and the *devini kapurala*, or the priest who actually handles the box that holds the symbols of deity.

Figure 2-3. Processional elephant in Kataragama, with deity and priest on back.

The main deity, Kataragama, is thought of as a hunter and warrior. In many ways he is the most important ancient deity of Śrī Lanka, and many temples all over the island honor him. There are no images in the temple where his presence resides; the symbol of his presence is a box covered with scarfs. When the priests handle the box, especially during festival time, they are dressed in plain white with tightly bound handkerchief head coverings and handkerchiefs over their mouths and noses. When the box is moved to the back of the elephant, younger priests hold a large cloth canopy around the priests carrying the deity, so that even the box itself is not seen. The role of the elephant is central in the ritual; it is believed that the weight of the deity is so great that the elephant cries in pain. The elderly elephant that carries the deity is well trained. Each day before the procession, it is carefully bathed in the river, adorned in elaborate dress, and allowed to perform a series of ritual actions indicating its own reverence.

The shrine of the village girl/goddess Valli to whom Lord Kataragama's procession goes is comparatively plain. Her temple is now served by a younger brother of the head priest in the Kataragama temple, but this arrangement is new. Traditionally the priesthood of the Valli temple was held by a different family of Veddas. However, they did not have a natural successor some years ago, so the younger brother of the head priest of Kataragama was asked to take over the Valli temple worship because his role in the main temple worship was compromised. He married outside the traditional community, thereby cutting himself off from the main priestly family. The deity in the shrine is understood as a simple Vedda girl who was chasing the birds from her grain field when the deity saw her and fell in love. The most important ritual symbols of Valli's forest heritage are the *ālatti ammas*, or "mothers of light," and the Vedda chief. The *ālatti ammas* are tribal women who serve as representatives of Valli's family; they accompany Lord Kataragama on his rendevous at her shrine. The Vedda chief officially authorizes Valli's marriage after receiving gold coins from Lord Kataragama and then leads the procession of Lord Kataragama to her shrine. The *ālatti ammas* in the festival ceremony are about a dozen senior women from the Vedda community, who wear the distinctive traditional dress of their community and lead Lord Kataragama to the shrine of Valli as a kind of honor guard. Upon returning to Lord Kataragama's shrine each night, they, on behalf of Valli's community, perform a beautiful dance with lights and make offerings to the guardian deities at the back of his shrine. An actual forest-dwelling Vedda chief in traditional loincloth threatens Lord Kataragama with his bow and arrow as the festival procession heads off to the shrine of Valli each night (fig. 2.4) then, after intermediaries plead with him and he receives gold coins, he is satisfied that it is a good match and leads the procession the rest of the way.[6]

The final days of the festival romance are highly erotic, but that eroticism is set within the framework of a traditional bridal family's excitement as it plays host to the visiting groom. Because this "marriage"[7] joins partners who are from two cultural backgrounds, the hosting activity of the bride's side is carefully done, enhancing the mystery and excitement surrounding the groom. In general grooms in India and Śrī Lanka are treated with some of this same excitement and respect, but in this case the mystery is allowed its full development, and the reverence and awe for deity are expressed in their fullest and most emotional form. Lord Kataragama remains a deity who inspires fear, and worshipers keep their vows to him with utmost care. In the symbolism of this festival, Valli, like the human heart, has achieved the most tender of relationships. Neverthe-

Figure 2-4. Vedda chief threatening Lord Kataragama with bow and arrow.

less, she, like all of us, will remain in awe of the wondrous but mysteriously unknowable visitor, and the groom of this celebration is still the transcendent deity from another world.

Medieval Reinterpretations

Because the ancient ritual pattern of the festival remains evident in the rituals carried out by the representatives of the Vedda community, the other interpretations of the sacredness of this site are relatively easy to recognize as later. These reinterpretations are in one sense associated with particular developments in medieval times, but they are put forth by the Buddhist, Hindu, and Islamic communities that still worship at the festival, as streams of reinterpretation intended to influence how the festival worship takes place today.

One of the important patterns of reinterpretation is that associated with the legendary hero Duttagamini, who lived in the second century BCE. He was a prince in the nearby capital of Tissamahārama when the ruler Elara was ruling most of Śrī Lanka. As the later legends tell the story, Elara was an able ruler, but a Tamiḻ, or someone considered a "foreigner" in some quarters. Duttagamini was determined to start a guerilla war against him. Just as he started, someone urged him to get the blessing of Lord Kataragama; he hastily did so and promised to build a temple for the deity if he was successful. The legends eventually make Duttagamini an ardent Buddhist working closely with the monks of certain Buddhist monasteries in the north of the island, but he also attributed his success to the blessing of Lord Kataragama. According to these legends, he is said to have returned to Kataragama town to build the temple, which still stands.[8] In medieval Sinhala myth, Lord Kataragama was one of four deities who protected the island. In places such as Kandy, as we will see in the study of the festival there (chapter 6), a temple of Lord Kataragama is incorporated into a larger system of Sinhala worship. The theological problem of just how one is to understand the place of Lord Kataragama in Buddhist worship remains unresolved. As we will see later, the problem has become even more complex in modern times when, with government help, new Buddhist monasteries, and specifically Buddhist practices, are being encouraged in the context of this festival.

Contact between South India and the southern shore of Śrī Lanka had been constant over the centuries, for Indian mercenaries and civil servants who served the rulers of this region are known. More puzzling, however, is the steady stream of orthodox Hindu and Muslim ascetics from North India who sought this holy place and remained here to die, perhaps because they considered it the most remote holy place one could find within the Indian cultural setting. The graves of these holy men provided the occasion for the introduction of orthodox Hindu and Muslim ritual forms in Kataragama and for the enrichment of the central romantic story of the Vedda tradition.

Whose grave came first is no longer clear, but two quite different worship areas now follow orthodox Hindu practices, as well as the one that houses the graves of the Muslim saints. The best-known story today centers on the orthodox Hindu ascetic Kalyanagiri, who probably arrived during the reign of Rajasingha II, who reigned from 1627 to 1679.[9] Kalyanagiri is said to have been sent to Kataragama by the goddess Tevayanai, whom Hindus of India consider the first wife of Skanda, the second son of Śivaṉ. Kalyanagiri was asked by Tevayanai to find Skanda (Tamiḻ: Murukaṉ) and invite the Lord to return to India. But after 12 years of severe ascetic practice, he had not realized his goal, until one day he went into a trance and realized that the young Vedda boy and girl caring for him were really Skanda and his second or tribal wife Valli. He then decided to stay in Kataragama and worship there, because he had fully realized that Lord Kataragama was Skanda. He later magically carved a *yantra* or mystic diagram of Skanda (which some worshipers believe is in the mysterious box carried by the priests). When the sage Kalyanagiri gave up his earthly body, the local Hindus believe that he turned into a pearl *liṅkam* (*muthuliṅkam*); the *liṅkam* form of Śivaṉ now worshiped in the temple to the west of the Valli shrine. The family of priests who care for this *liṅkam* temple are of a Tamiḻ lineage (although the father of the present generation of priests was a Sinhala), and follow *ākamam* ritual practices similar to those used by most Śivaṉ temples in South India.

The other orthodox Hindu worship center, just east of the temple of Lord Kataragama, is now a monastic *pīta* or "seat," where monks in the Dasanami tradition associated with Śaṅkara have lived for centuries, and where a whole series of graves honor the monastic heads who have died in this sacred spot.[10] The monastic "seat" is something like a throne without legs that is covered with skins. The monks in this particular monastic tradition are said to practice the Dattatreya meditation. The most beloved monk in this lineage is Kesopuri Swāmi or Palkutibawa (Wijayaratna 1987, p. 215),[11] who died in

1898. The incumbents in this ascetic seat perform an elaborate "blessing" of the festival procession of Lord Kataragama each night of the festival as it passes the Ganeṣa temple over which they preside and again when it is about to leave the Valli temple. As indicated earlier, now temples of Tevayanai and Skanda/Murukaṉ in his ascetic form stand just beside the *pīta*.

Like Buddhist worshipers, who must stretch their imaginations considerably to feel comfortable in the ritual traditions of the Vedda-led temple of Lord Kataragama, orthodox Hindu worshipers do not find it that easy either. Some external ritual practices are familiar to orthodox Hindus, in that worship often starts with a broken coconut on the stone in front of the temple and continues by presenting the priest with a basket of coconuts, bananas, betel leaves, camphor, and cash for the deity. But orthodox Hindus then learn that there are no images in the shrines of Kataragama or Valli and that the priests follow many ancient Vedda practices (including making offerings of rice and deer meat, according to some worshipers). Following Vedda tradition, the priests do not utter prayers as Hindu priests normally do; they stand rigidly with arms outstretched diagonally before the curtains that cover the holy inner room. The paintings on the curtains use the standard iconographic form one finds in South India of god Skanda or Murukaṉ with his two wives, Tevayanai and Valli, but Tevayanai plays no role in the local myth or in the festival ritual. Orthodox Hindu worshipers today comment repeatedly about that fact and that there is no reference to the mythic demon, Sura, whom Skanda/Murukaṉ is thought to have slain. Those who are truly orthodox take refuge in the fact that in the orthodox Hindu compound nearby, the worship of Tevayanai and Skanda/Murukaṉ is conducted in a highly orthodox manner.

The Muslim presence at the festival site is said to go back through a long line of saints, among whom the best known are Hoyatu and Kamrai Nabi, the later having come from India along with the Hindu sage, Kesopuri Swāmi, popularly called by the Muslim-sounding nickname Palkutibawa, or "milk-drinking saint." The mausoleums around which the Muslim center is now formed inter Jabban Ali Shah, who died in 1872, and Meer Sayed Alisha Bawa, who died in 1945. This stream of saints came from North India like their Hindu counterparts, but the celebrations that are now part of the festival are led by Muslim communities on the east coast of Śrī Lanka, where mystic practices are still widespread, and Colombo, where Muslims form an important part of modern Śrī Lankan business. The mystical, or Sufi order of Rifai (fig. 2.5), or the Tarik Khadriku Rifairiya, has mystic specialists who put steel points into their forearms and even their skulls, now watched by huge crowds of all religious backgrounds at festival time.

Modern Patterns of Worship

Two major political developments have directly affected the worship patterns of the Kataragama festival in modern times. The first took place in the middle of the last century, when the British colonial government introduced thousands of Tamiḻ laborers into the highlands of central Śrī Lanka to work in the tea plantations developing there. The second was political independence in 1948 and the emergence of a Buddhist political consciousness in the Sinhala majority.

Figure 2-5. Muslim Sufi mystics arriving for Kataragama festival.

The Tamiḻ laborers in the highlands of Śrī Lanka were cut off from their familiar ritual activities at their favorite Murukaṉ and Māriyammaṉ temples in India, and the British tea planters were not keen to see Hindu temples built to accommodate them. The laborers soon discovered that it was only a modest pilgrimage to go to Kataragama for the festival each year. Even though their favorite ritual practices of dancing with a *kavati* on their shoulders (men; fig. 2.6) or a fire pot in their hand (women), walking across burning coals, and swinging from a scaffold with a hook through the skin of their back, were not unknown in Kataragama, their skill in these practices was much greater than that of the local worshipers. With expert Tamiḻ laborers as the primary practitioners, these ascetic practices quickly became central features of the festival in Kataragama. Toward the end of the nineteenth century, crowds at the festival are said to have increased dramatically. Almost certainly, these practices started to draw the larger crowds, and Sinhala worshipers soon began to join in the dances and the fire walking in numbers that astounded the Tamiḻs, who are accustomed to seeing these practices reserved for specialists thought to have superhuman powers. The Sinhalas who flocked to the festival, however, organized dance training in an area near the river and had hundreds sign up for the walk across the burning coals.[12] (Inexperienced practitioners sometimes attempt the hook swinging as well, but most of those who perform this extreme form of asceticism are still Tamiḻ laborers from the tea plantations [fig. 2.7].)

With the festival known for these special ritual practices, the public began to come to the festival without a clear sense of its central focus. A public outcry in far off Colombo arose when a skeptical physician challenged the miraculous claims of the firewalkers and tried to set up experiments that showed that at .3 sec contact time anyone could

Figure 2-6. Renowned *kavati* dancer in Kataragama.

walk on burning coals because a foot would not burn. He was, however, quickly refuted by others who believed a miracle was involved (Kumar 1971). The European television crews, which now regularly visit the festival, focus almost all their attention on these special ritual practices,[13] even though they have at best a passing role in the worship at the heart of the festival. In any case the crowd grew rapidly after these practices were expanded and in recent years has topped 500,000.[14]

With the coming of political independence in 1948, the famous festival of Kataragama became a difficult problem for a succession of democratically elected governments of Śrī Lanka, with their different Buddhism-supporting religious strategies. On one hand, one might be inclined to think that the government would be happy to see a religious celebration in which Veddas, Sinhalas and Tamiḻs all join with equal enthusiasm.[15] On the other hand, orthodox Buddhist monks complain that the Sinhala majority in the country, and especially those in the region near the festival location, are learning a pattern of worship that is more Hindu than Buddhist. The first step the government made to intervene was to take over much of the management of the temple, and, in the guise of "cleaning up" the area, send all the religious entrepreneurs, many of whom were Hindu *swāmis* or *maniyo* (sorceresses), away from the area around the shrines. Premadasa, who took a militantly Buddhist stance as a politician, used his position as minister of public works to introduce a scheme in 1987 called Gam Udaya, or Village Uplift, and used Kataragama as his showcase. The "clean up" of the town of Kataragama, the plac-

Figure 2-7. Hook swinger being lifted into place, watched by curious Buddhist monk in Kataragama.

ing of a stone in front of the *mahādevale* noting that Duttagamini (the legendary Buddhist hero) built the shrine of Lord Kataragama, the new monastic housing and schools for Buddhist monks, and the establishment near the Kiri Vehera of special shelters specifically for Buddhist pilgrims were all intended to give a more "Buddhist" cast to the whole festival. (Orthodox Hindus complained that the forest cut down for these buildings had been the symbolic hiding place of the demon Sura that Lord Kataragama had vanquished.)[16] A government minister now serves as the Basnayake Nilame, or "traditional ruler," who symbolically leads the procession of Lord Kataragama,[17] and dance troops from all over the country are now imported by the government to join in the procession.

With the encouragement of government, a number of specifically Buddhist rituals are given new prominence in the last days of the festival. Two days before the end of the festival, an elaborate loudspeaker system is set up so that all in the vicinity of the Kiri Vehera can hear monks reciting scriptures from a thronelike room in the middle of one of the new Buddhist rest houses. In the middle of the same afternoon, a small procession including Buddhist monks and nuns lead a young "prince" from the *mahādevale* to the Kiri Vehera, but few in the small crowd that follows seem to know much about this procession. A new "bodhi pūja" ritual, which Gombrich and Obeyesekere describe (1988 pp. 384ff.), is also performed the same day for a few wealthy families. And on the next day an elaborate procession is held with a box of symbols of the Buddha. This procession leaves from the Buddha shrine near the *mahādevale* and proceeds to the Kiri Vehera and then back. This procession has an expensive modern electric canopy on the back of the elephant and includes Buddhist monks and nuns and dancers with the more Buddhist styles of Kandy. This explicitly "Buddhist" procession finishes just before the last of the evening *mahādevale* processions is to begin. At present, these specifically "Buddhist" ritual events seem to be confusing the nominally Buddhist public, who have always come to worship Lord Kataragama as part of their heritage. Because they now find themselves obliged to join specifically Buddhist rituals as well, they now have the uncomfortable impression that the other events around Lord Kataragama are more "non-Buddhist" than they had realized.

Far from curbing the drift of the Sinhala public toward Hindu patterns of worship, the actions of the government have tended to "politicize" the whole atmosphere. The Tami<u>l</u>s of far off Jaffna have been publicizing their *pad yatra* or pilgrimage to the festival in recent years, and as they cross the war-torn country, the issue of ethnic differences is highlighted. The Jaffna Tami<u>l</u>s have also insisted on putting only Tami<u>l</u> lettering on the canopy they hold over the elephant carrying the deity; many in the primarily Sinhala crowd commented to me that they found this offensive. Distinctive Muslim voices are also heard more loudly than they once were, and even the Veddas wonder if there are political implications for them in all that is going on. Manik Sandrasagra, the well-known filmmaker, was at the festival in 1990, not only making a film and convincing the Vedda chief that it was in everybody's interest that he personally take part once again but generally lamenting the politicization of the festival and trying to keep the peace between the different rival parties.

Of all the festivals I have studied, the challenges of modernity seem strongest here in Kataragama. Nevertheless, in another sense, no festival is at the same time so pure and so careful in its performance of what appears to be a core ritual form that goes back for thousands of years. This celebration is truly at the "edge" of the forest, and it has probably always belonged more to the forest than the excited worshipers who join in from time to time really know. Buddhist, Hindu, and Muslim leaders have for centuries wanted to make it theirs, but they have not really changed it much. Modern pressures are somewhat different in kind, but they too may prove more ephemeral than they seem. The filmmaker Manik may speak for many in the island torn apart by ethnic strife when he argues that what Śrī Lanka needs is to forget the later divisions and rediscover its roots. This festival still powerfully reminds the Śrī Lankans of the ancient Vedda sense of reverence and the awe that all humans feel when visited by deity. In a profound sense this feeling of reverence is still at the heart of Śrī Lanka's divided culture, and it seems unlikely that worshipers able to grasp that feeling will relinquish it easily, despite the distractions of more modern voices.

Conclusion

Of all the festivals included in this study, only the one at Kataragama has attracted a significant body of scholarship. This scholarship focuses almost completely on the question of how the festival has been affected by changes in Śrī Lankan society in the last century. Some of the studies focus primarily on the political atmosphere that swirls around all aspects of contemporary Śrī Lanka (Pfaffenberger 1979; Swearer 1982), and others focus on the complex anthropological question of why modern Sinhala-speaking Śrī Lankans are attracted to patterns of worship that do not arise from the mainstream of the Buddhist tradition (Gombrich and Obeyesekere 1988; Wijayaratna 1987).

However, worship in Kataragama is an extremely serious matter. Worshipers never lose a chance to explain that some catastrophe occured in their lives because they ignored the deity in Kataragama, or that some miraculous change had altered their life since they had started coming there for worship. Typical of the tone of worship is the story of a family I met once while on a more leisurely trip to Kataragama in the nonfestival season. One of the leading lawyers in the country was there with his wife, her two sisters of marriagable age, and the parents of the girls, who were home on leave from the diplomatic service. The lawyer's wife explained that they were staunch Buddhists but had come to Kataragama for the first time about five years earlier when their mother had fallen sick. Because the mother recovered, the family was now afraid not to come and had taken a vow to make the trip whenever the parents were on leave. The girls of marriagable age especially had come to believe that their hopes for a good marriage dependent on Valli, to whose temple they went regularly. The lawyer was quiet for a time but then began to explain that a year earlier he had made the trip for the first time, on the condition that as a self-proclaimed atheist he could remain in town while the rest of the family went to the temple. When the family returned to the town he could not be found, and he claimed it took two days for a local *swāmi* to bring him out of the trance that had come over him as he sat by the river. The trip when I met them came a year later, at his insistance.

In the worship of Ayyappaṉ at Sabarimala (chapter 1), an ancient local worship tradition has been folded into Hindu practice without incident, because the ideological function of the festival seems to have been acceptably inclusive across South India. Both the deity and the ritual practices remain unique, because the reinterpretation that overlays the local tradition with more widely known myths does not directly affect the practice of the pilgrimage. In Kataragama the religious core seems both intense and true to its ancient heritage, which, as far as one is able to judge, was a popular tradition rooted in tribal culture.

In this case, however, both the argument for interpreting Lord Kataragama as if he were none other than the Skanda/Murukaṉ of Indian tradition and the argument insisting that the deity is the one revered by ancient Buddhist rulers such as Duttagamini have been superimposed on the local tradition in ways that seem to challenge the ritual forms the Vedda ritual specialists have maintained so carefully. Perhaps now only the presence of the Vedda ritual leaders serves to keep the peace in what could be a direct conflict between the claims of the orthodox Hindu and orthodox Buddhist clergy.

In the end, because this is a popular festival, it will likely be the understanding of the worshipers, rather than that of the many priests, monks, sorcerers, and government officials, that will prevail. As long as the worshipers remain as certain as they seem to be at present that they know what Lord Kataragama is like, and that they know what an experience of his visitation is like, they will not be easily swayed by efforts to reinterpret that experience. But concerted efforts at reinterpretation of the religious experience of Kataragama are going on, and some of these efforts have the support of powerful financial interests and others of the even more powerful government. What is amazing, however, is that such efforts at reinterpretation have been so ineffective for so long and that the ancient power of this ritual tradition is still evident. One cannot witness this great festival today without feeling that, in spite of all the excitement, awe still premeates the crowd, a deep reverence brought on by the evidence that a mighty and wondrous deity would deign to visit a simple young woman and her delighted fellow human beings.

3

The Goddess of Koṭuṅkaḷūr

A Festival of the Wild Goddess of Ancient Kerala

Goddess Traditions

One of the most difficult problems for scholars of the religious traditions of South India has been to trace the traditions of goddess worship. The earliest written texts refer to a spirited goddess named Koṟṟavai, and the great epic of the region, the *Cilappatikāram*, is the story of how the heroine Kaṇṇaki came to be worshiped as a goddess. At the other end of the stream of history, abundant evidence shows that goddess worship remains in every village in the region and still stimulates some of the most emotional and satisfying forms of religious life.

The history of goddess worship is difficult because the evidence from the middle period is so fragmented. When the medieval landlords and kings began to build stone temples, they concentrated their efforts on the newly popular cults of Śivaṉ and Viṣṇu. In many cases the locally popular goddess worship was combined with the worship of one or the other of these deities, so goddess shrines were often included in the larger temple complexes. In fact, this practice of incorporating the goddess traditions in larger temple complexes actually obscured the traces of the independent goddess traditions, and scholars have sometimes overlooked the fact that small shrines, where primarily laboring classes worship, sometimes preserve old goddess traditions. Only recently have scholars carefully looked at the many independent goddess traditions preserved primarily in ritual and song.

In Śrī Lanka and in Tamiḻnāṭu, or the eastern side of South India, the independent traditions of goddess worship were revived in the past, and those revivals produced eclectic traditions of goddess worship associated with Pattini and Māriyammaṉ respectively. The origins of the Pattini cult of Śrī Lanka probably lie in the Koṭuṅkaḷūr temple traditions, the subject of this study, but over the centuries in Śrī Lanka they have been carefully interwoven with Buddhist themes and have absorbed other local goddess traditions of Śrī Lanka.[1] The origins of the Māriyammaṉ cult in Tamiḻnāṭu are less easy to identify, but the process by which that cult absorbs other local goddess traditions is still ongoing and is relatively easy to observe (Beck 1981; Younger 1980; and chapter 8).

In the case of Kerala, the local goddess traditions seem to have remained more independent of one another and hence appear to be more deeply grounded in ancient ritual forms. The two most famous medieval temples of Kerala, Guruvayur near Trichur and Padmanābhasvāmi in Trivandrum, are Viṣṇu temples that have not absorbed major goddess traditions. The more famous goddess temples sometimes did see the introduction of male deities in medieval times (as did the Koṭuṅkaḷūr temple where an orthodox east-facing Śivaṉ shrine was attached to the main temple at some point), but the ancient goddess tradition remained dominant. At some point in the history, there must have been an effort to create an eclectic goddess tradition in Kerala, similar to those of Śrī Lanka and Tamiḻnāṭu, for the generic name "Bhagavatī" is now used of almost all goddesses. In Kerala, however, worshipers insist on using the geographical reference as well as the name "Bhagavatī," so the prayers are always addressed to "Bhagavatī of Koṭuṅkaḷūr" or "Bhagavatī of——," and each goddess remains relatively independent.[2]

For South Indians the primary object of worship is as likely to be a goddess as a god. In describing a worship tradition such as Koṭuṅkaḷūr it is important to remember that the central deity is a direct manifestation of ultimate reality. Because worshipers normally refer to her by the generic term "goddess" or "tēvi" (Sanskrit "devī"), rather than by the various proper names found in the stories about her, it is necessary to capitalize Goddess or Tēvi when referring to her as the primary object of worship.

The Story of Koṭuṅkaḷūr

The west coast of South India is extremely fragile. The mountains run north and south and catch the monsoon rains during June and July. The resultant heavy rains produce powerful rivers that flow down from the mountains and create small pockets of extremely rich soil near the coast. As a result, the sea penetrates almost to the mountains in some regions (along what are called "backwaters"), whereas in other regions profitable agricultural crops are grown in the coastal plain. Occasionally flooding or tidal waves dramatically alter the course of a river and the nature of the coastline (Eapen 1983).

Koṭuṅkaḷūr is on the coast at the mouth of the great Periyar River. At the beginning of the Common Era, it was one of the great ports of Asia, known as Muziris, and was visited by ships from Rome looking for the spices from the mountains of Kerala. Jewish traders had settled in the area even earlier, and there are still synogogues in some of the towns round about.[3] By the beginning of the Common Era, many of the local traders were intermarrying with Christian traders from Syria; the "Syrian Christian" churches are still thriving in the towns of the region.[4]

The Cēra kings, who already had diplomatic relations with the North Indian emperor Aśoka in the third century BCE, had their capital in Koṭuṅkaḷūr (often called Vañci during this period). Due to the absence of stone inscriptions, we cannot reconstruct a continuous line of Cēra kings, but we do know much about them in the second, eighth, and thirteenth centuries (as well as the third BCE) and have every reason to believe that they were powerful rulers throughout that period. We do know that in the second century the Cēra ruler, Ceṅkuṭṭavaṉ participated in the annual festival to the Tēvi (Goddess) by placing in her shrine a stone that he had brought all the way from the Himālaya mountains. As part of this celebration, his younger brother, Iḷaṅko Aṭikaḷ, wrote the famous *Cilappatikāram* epic about the heroine/goddess Kaṇṇaki, which I will examine shortly. In the eighth century a prince named Kulacēkara became a hymnsinger and saint in the tradition of Viṣṇu. Shortly thereafter, another prince, Cēramān Perumāḷ, became a convert to Śaivism through his friendship with the famous Śaiva hymnsinger Cuntarar, who was from Tamiḻnāṭu on the east coast but was a frequent guest in the palace at Koṭuṅkaḷūr. The royal temple in honor of Śivaṉ still stands just 2 kilometers away from the temple of Tēvi of Koṭuṅkaḷūr, and the ruins of the palace and an earlier temple to Viṣṇu (Kṛṣṇa) are also nearby.[5]

In 1341 a tidal wave silted in the ancient harbor near the capital.[6] Trade shifted to the port of Cochin 50 kilometers to the south, and the shifting river bed left Koṭuṅkaḷūr on an island cut off from the nearby towns. The town is now quite small, and the fertile soils around are covered with coconut groves and houses. The whole region continues to be one of the most densely populated in the world.

The Local Traditions

Ancient songs, stories, rituals, and even an epic about the Tēvi are associated with Koṭuṅkaḷūr. The songs and stories are still sung and told as part of the festival celebration, as groups sit around a reciter and sing back to him in an antiphonal form the lines he gives them. The dialect of Malaiyāḷam used in these recitations is archaic; Malaiyāḷam-speaking listeners and scholars find that they can understand only a phrase or two in each song. Folklorists and language scholars are now studying these tales, and the general outlines of the stories are reasonably well known.[7]

The Tēvi involved is usually called either Śrī Kurumba, Cīrma, or Kaṇṇaki and is portrayed as independent, resourceful, and temperamental. Her male companion, called Palakhan, Ponmakan, Pālakār, or Palanga, is portrayed as immature, incompetent, and sometimes even demonic. He usually does something foolish, such as venturing somewhere he should not on the advice of his relatives or stealing jewelry. She then has to assert her ingenuity and courage in a dramatic effort to rescue him by dragging him away from his relatives, slaying his enemies, and even resuscitating or piecing together his body.

The social background for this divine persona is the *marumakkattāyam* marriage system of Kerala. For the ancient castes of Kerala, the home, or *taravād*, is passed down from mother to daughter.[8] Male visitors to the *taravād* form *campantams* with a woman for a shorter or longer period of time, but they usually return to their sister's home during the working day and certainly have no role in the long-term management of their "wife's" estate. Because of their relative freedom from family obligations, men in Kerala often served as mercenaries in foreign armies,[9] and women sometimes became impatient with their irresponsible suitors.

The second century epic, the *Cilappatikāram*, written by the prince Iḷaṅko, uses Kaṇṇaki, the traditional name of the Tēvi, for his heroine. The epic is a great piece of literature in many ways. It is not merely a repetition of the local myth of Koṭuṅkaḷūr, but it does provide us with a beautiful variation on that central story. Iḷaṅko starts his story in the relatively distant east coast port of South India, Kāvēripattinam. There Kaṇṇaki, as a young daughter of a merchant, marries Kōvalaṉ, the son of a trader who is at sea. Suitably irresponsible, Kōvalaṉ spends the next few years with a courtesan poet and dancer named Mātavi. Finally, he returns to Kaṇṇaki and suggests that they go to the central trading city of Maturai. Taking her gold anklet into the city to pawn it, while she participates in a tribal festival, he is soon "over his head" in this sophisticated city, and a pawnbroker falsely accuses him of stealing the queen's anklet and drags him before the king. The king quickly executes him. Kaṇṇaki then appears before the king and, by throwing down her anklet so that the red rubies roll out, is able to demonstrate that Kōvalaṉ had not stolen the queen's pearl-filled anklet. The king falls on his sword in remorse, and Kaṇṇaki in a rage sets the city on fire. The tribal women then lead her off to the mountains of Kerala and proclaim her a Tēvi.[10]

In Koṭuṅkaḷūr now the power of this goddess tradition is localized in different ways. Some of the processions originate at a small shrine of Cīrma (many worshipers use the name Śrī Kurumba as well) about a kilometer south of the main temple. At this little shrine, meat and toddy offerings (*cāktam* offerings) are still allowed, and many worshipers argue that this little shrine is the original home of the Tēvi. Just west of the main temple and within the temple compound is another goddess image, now usually called Vasūrimālā.[11] The women of the Nair *taravād* associated with the Koṭuṅkaḷūr temple usually serve in a priest-like role in this shrine, and offerings of cocks are made here (in the "modern" form allowed by the government in which the knife is thrust into a melon and the "blood" to be smeared on the donor is made of turmeric and lime). Inside the main temple is a sealed room with a closed window, which has been taken to be the memorial shrine of Kaṇṇaki.[12] A row of stone images of the Sapta-Mātṛkās, or seven "mothers," faces north, with the Tēvi of Koṭuṅkaḷūr being one among them (third from the east) lined up with the main entrance.[13] Finally, directly behind the stone image of the goddess of Koṭuṅkaḷūr is the primary image of worship, a large wooden image of that same Tēvi with eight arms.[14]

The Bharaṇi Festival

At the beginning of the festival[15] huge crowds of rough-looking laborers descend on the town from all directions. Some come by bus, but most seem to walk into town with the energetic gait of the laboring classes of Kerala, who often walk long distances through wooded groves and along inland waterways to find the shortest distance to their destination. The immediate goal of a newly arrived worshiper in the past had been to offer a cock on the sacrifice stones right in front of the temple. The state government has now made that practice illegal, so the offering now consists of placing a bright red scarf over the stones and then dancing around the pile of scarves as if a sacrifice had been made. Many still do carry a cock as offering, but they now have to throw it live over the wall of the temple, which is closed for the duration of the festival.

Soon after arrival, people meet old friends and make new ones; in a short time the frantic activity begins, and continues day and night for the remainder of the week. Because almost no time is allotted for eating or sleeping, as the week goes on many of the worshipers have a frenzied look. Loosely organized groups of a dozen or so sit around a reciter and sing back to him the ancient songs.[16] When he is finished, most get up and soon reorganize around a central dancer. Following him or her down the road, they bang their sticks together and sing antiphonally. They usually dance their way around the temples and ponds and then go down the road 2 kilometers to the large compound of the royal temple complex. Few enter the royal temple compound itself, but most rest for a few minutes and take a gulp of the buttermilk provided by devotees there before starting back again. Some of these groups include traditional worshipers, who sing songs passed down for centuries in a dialect but reputed to include explicit references to the Tēvi's aroused sexuality and the need for the worshipers to satisfy her. Other groups include primarily teenagers who try to outdo one another in bawdy joking and gesturing. Women do not move freely in the unruly crowd, but many of the groups of dancers include women, who enthusiastically join in the singing within the context of their own group.

As the week goes on, the temple itself begins to look a mess, with turmeric powder all over its copper roofs and banana stalks and broken coconuts strewn everywhere (fig. 3.1). As the week progresses, more and more of the dancers go into trance, and the crowd starts to move from place to place to watch. People often go into trance around the red scarves in front of the temple, as well as anywhere there is a sacred tree, pond, shrine, or image of any kind.

Distinct from this general pattern of worship, yet totally integrated with it, is the activity surrounding the two thousand *veḷicapāṭu* ("light bearers") or sacred specialists, who become more and more prominent in the crowd as the week goes on. These *veḷicapāṭu* have long loose hair, wear a distinctive red dress, and are adorned with heavy brass anklets filled with brass balls and girdles with bells attached; they carry a four-foot long sword with a distinctive sickle-shaped farther end (fig. 3.2). Both sexes are represented, but the majority are female. In their villages they function as sorcerers and di-

Figure 3-1. Closed temple of Koṭuṅkaḷūr, Kerala, with turmeric, cocks, and other offerings thrown onto the roof.

Figure 3-2. *Veḷicapāṭu* lady surrounded by frenzied dancers banging on sticks in Koṭuṅkaḷūr.

viners, but unlike many shaman-like specialists elsewhere, they are attached to the local goddess temples and usually stowe their swords and bangles with the temple priest when they are not in use. Like shamans, however, they do go into dance-induced trances when performing their function as a sorcerer or diviner. Whereas they usually function alone, and there is seldom more than one in a small village, in the context of this festival they arrive, like other worshipers, along with their village fellows and participate fully in the frenzied marches, singing, and dancing. In some cases they are virtuoso dancers and draw large crowds.

During the later half of the week, the *veḷicapāṭu* take on a new role. One by one they take their swords and go to the area near the cock sacrifice scarves, where they dance until they go into a final frenzy and use the sword to slice open the top of their skulls (fig. 3.3). As they draw blood, their handlers rush in to help and lead them to a Nair gentleman from the *taravād* that manages the temple, who sits almost day and night on the parapet wall just to the side of the scarves. They hand him their sword, and he then holds them and rubs turmeric powder into their wound. His assistants take the sword to his house/shrine, where it is kept on an altar over a magic *yantra* diagram until the final day of the festival.[17]

As I mentioned earlier, the temple is closed for the duration of the festival, and the priests take no part in the festival activities.[18] It is difficult now to know how long that arrangement has lasted and what events led to it, but the crowd now interprets it as an indication of the differences of opinion between the Tēvi and the male priests. According to the oft-repeated story, once a whole village of Namboodri Brāhmans lived near the temple, but when they would not satisfy the Tēvi's hunger on one occasion, she

Figure 3-3. *Veḷicapāṭu* dancers cutting their skulls open in front of the Nair man seated on the wall in Koṭuṅkaḷūr.

burned all their houses; since that time no Brāhmans have lived on the island. (The priests who serve in the temple now all make it very clear that they come from elsewhere, although in fact they stay near the temple, and some even have *campantam* relations with women of the *taravād* that manages the temple.) With regard to the festival itself, the story is that a member of the goldsmith caste was irritated because the priests would not let him worship when he was sure the Tēvi was calling for him, so he entered the temple and intentionally touched the image and "polluted" it.[19] Now the central activity of the festival is seen as both a joyous dance with the sexually aroused Tēvi and a defiant taunting of the priests who would protect her from the lower class worshipers she so craves.

The final day of the festival involves a reconciliation of all concerned and an apparent reaffirmation of the cosmic and social order. In a superficial sense, a formal order is restored immediately because thousands of police, who were not to be seen earlier in the week, descend on the town and set the tone for the events of the last day. For those who have been through the exhausting frenzy of the days before, the passion is still boiling. The *veḷicapāṭu* are given back their reempowered swords, and they start a dance marathon that lasts all day. By midafternoon ancient curved temple horns are blown, producing a different mysterious sound, and the dance tempo quickens. With hundreds and hundreds of flashing swords whirling around in the sky, everyone is screaming, jumping about, and exulting. Finally, the Nair man who once sat on the wall emerges from his house dressed as a *veḷicapāṭu* with sword in hand, and the mass of humanity leaps even higher as he leads them toward the temple.

Hours pass, and members of the crowd climb higher and higher onto the small shrines, trees, and parapets of the temple compound. The police use makeshift barriers to hold the crowd away from the area adjacent to the temple. Groups break free and are chased back, while the *veḷicapāṭu* jump about in the area nearer the temple to which they have been assigned. Finally a small frail figure emerges from a secret side door of the temple. He is a member of the ancient royal family and supposedly has been negotiating with the priests and the Nairs to have the temple reopened. Now the police help him up the stairs of the throne in the courtyard of the temple, and as he reaches the podium, he slowly raises the umbrella of his sovereignty, the signal to the crowd that the temple will be reopened. Suddenly the *veḷicapāṭu*, with their swords held high, race around and around the temple at breakneck speed, clearly indicating that while they acknowledge the sovereignty of the ruler, they are sure that their own wild worship has won them this victory and this renewed access to their Tēvi. A day later the temple is cleansed, and the normal worship routines are restored, but all head for home knowing that they have once again liberated the Tēvi and brought her the joyful passion she craves.

Efforts to Contain the Goddess

The ancient, medieval, and modern periods in the history of Kerala are not easy to discern. Because the present society is so sharply divided by a combination of class and religious loyalties, scholars have tended to describe the past as if it contained today's social and cultural divisions. Clearly, Kerala had a highly organized society in the medieval period in which the Nair aristocracy used the tradition of *campantam* relationships to develop elaborate marriage ties with both the royal families and the priesthood and was able to use its military reputation to keep order among the lower classes. The Nair *taravād* that still manages the Koṭuṅkaḷūr temple is a classic case of how this medieval system worked.

The Plapalli and Vadakheda Nair *taravāds*, which now manage the temple, both agree that they derive from one *taravād*, which split a few generations back. In the common medieval way, huge tracts of land were donated to the Tēvi of Koṭuṅkaḷūr (as *jenmi*), and this land has been managed by this *taravād*. Princes of the royal family have regularly had *campantams* with women of the *taravād*, so members of the *taravād* consider themselves related to and economically supportive of the royal family. After the medieval crisis in which the houses of the Namboodri Brāhmans were burned, Atikal priests (lower in status than Namboodris and willing to make *cāktam* or meat and toddy offerings, but still Brāhman) were brought from a village 200 kilometers away; their descendants still serve in the temple. These priests are provided with *campantams* with the women of the Nair family while they serve in the temple, and they live together with these women at the back of the Nair compound (further from the temple than the Nair house). They still describe their "home" as the village 200 kilometers away, where they go when they can. (Recently the government appointed a Namboodri priest to also serve in the temple, and he performs a few of the rituals while trying not to disturb the more traditional arrangements.)

Whereas most studies of the Nairs emphasize their elaborate marriage ties with royalty and priesthood that I have just described, the more complex challenge for the *taravād* that manages the temple in Koṭuṅkaḷūr has been to keep some control over the lower class worshipers. In three dramatic ways, the *taravād* becomes directly involved in the worship of the Tēvi, supporting the tradition of passionate devotion and at the same time gaining some measure of control over the worship practice.

The first example of Nair control over the worship is that women of the *taravād* serve in a priest-like role. This practice is especially clear in the Vasūrimālā shrine west of the main temple, but the women say they also still perform much of the ritual that is less visible in the main temple itself.[20] All the worshipers agree that at one time the women of the *taravād* probably carried out the worship of the temperamental Tēvi by themselves and that the *veḷicapāṭu* were originally all women.[21] By suggesting that ancient tradition, the Nair priestesses are still able to whip up the ancient passion for the Tēvi and at the same time support the cause of the dependent priestly class they employ, with whom they have entered into *campantam* relationships.

The second example of Nair control concerns *cāktam* offerings, or the offerings of meat and toddy that the Tēvi is believed to crave. The pile of red scarves, the cocks thrown over the wall, and the simulated cock sacrifices held in the Vasūrimālā shrine provide plenty of evidence that these kinds of offerings are crucial in the symbol system of the main temple. But worshipers insist that the Atikal priests also continue this aspect of the ritual in the context of the wild processions that pass the Cīrma or Śrī Kurumba shrine at the edge of town. In other parts of India where animal sacrifices are still legally performed, they are quietly offered by certain worshipers to certain deities. In this festival the "issue" of whether one can or cannot make such offerings is part of the ritual itself, and everyone at the festival, and those who are afraid to attend the festival, think that such offerings are central to its character. I did not actually see any animal sacrifices or any offerings of toddy, but worshipers delighted in smearing themselves in blood-like red paint and feigning intoxication. By indicating that the Atikal priests are willing to make *cāktam* offerings, the Nairs keep this issue in the symbolic repertoire of the festival while at the same time limiting its actual practice.

The third example concerns the way in which the Nair *taravād* helps organize the *veḷicapāṭu*. One of the Nairs suggested that the *veḷicapāṭu* tradition was actually a military tradition and that the "swords" were issued to the *veḷicapāṭu* as a knight might issue a sword to a vassal. The Nair gentleman who takes the swords after the skull is cut open has a list of the *veḷicapāṭu* who bring their swords to him each year for reempowerment. He also claims that they are all from the Iḻava or Tiyya caste (below the Nairs in status, but above others) and that they all come from the Palghat region north of Koṭuṅkaḷūr. The way he himself "becomes" a *veḷicapāṭu* on the last day of the festival, and wears the full dress and cuts his own skull as he leads them back to the temple, provides one of the most moving scenes in the festival. At the time, he seemed to me "out of control" with devotional fervor, but these otherwise independent and shamanic religious specialists show him a loyalty and obedience that has a powerfully "medieval" quality.

The containment of the passion of the Tēvi that the Nair *taravād* has been able to achieve is truly remarkable. All over the state of Kerala, the Bharaṇi festival is reputed to be an explosion of wild passion. And it truly is. But the Nair *taravād* that established control over the temple in medieval times continues to use its marriage ties and its dominant role in the ritual to ensure that the passion has direction.

Since 1957, when a democratic form of government began in the state and the lower classes started to elect a series of communist-led governments, the medieval balance has been more and more precarious. Certainly now, only the traditionalism of the festival ritual carries on an arrangement that Nair military tradition once set in place. The Nair *taravād* may no longer feel powerful, but the crowd's ritual expectations would dramatically change if the Nair role were to disappear.

Conclusion

This festival for the Tēvi of Koṭuṅkaḷūr was the most emotionally draining of all the festivals I attended. The passion for the Tēvi was palpable, and the fear of not being able to live up to her expectations was real. While all of my research told me that this ancient tradition had survived because of historical accidents connected to the ancient capital of the Ceras, the worship of those who had come to the Tēvi had a power devoid of nostalgia.

In the cases of Sabarimalai (chapter 1) and Kataragama (chapter 2), the ancient ritual forms are now cherished at least partly because they are ancient and unique. Worship there, too, is powerful and involves extremes of physical exertion and sacrifice, but it would be impossible for a worshiper there to forget that those ancient rituals have now become immensely popular. In Koṭuṅkaḷūr the crowds were as large and boisterous as the island could contain, but no one spoke of a new popularity for this festival. People came to witness the timeless passion and power of the Tēvi. There was no time for priestly ritual, and there was no time for personal petitions. People came to worship, and that is where their energy went.

In retrospect, I think I see more clearly in this festival than in any of the others how South Indians understand reverence. The divine presence in this festival is personal, passionate, and even naughty. Yet it is at the same time awesome in its irritation with human incompetence and frightening in its power. Goddesses like this one are central to many of the other rituals I will examine, but in most cases one can glimpse them only through the maze of other deities and the veils of priestly ritual. Here too the carefully established social network of the Nair *taravād* keeps us from viewing the Tēvi without any social or ritual framework, but the framework is hidden by the power and energy of the worship.

It is actually hard to imagine how this militantly nonliterate tradition of worship could survive in the midst of the sophisticated and highly literate culture of Kerala. The literate culture of Kerala has certainly been fascinated with its nonliterate heart, as one sees as early as the second century in Iḷaṅko's epic tale and recently in Menon's (1959) brilliant research on goddess worship. On the other hand, the sharp social class system of Kerala, even though it has changed at given periods of history, has always left the lower classes with a legitimate right to their own voice. This festival is a chance to see why the whole of Kerala society recognizes the power of that voice. One might reasonably argue that this is lower-class religion, but it cannot be dismissed with a label. It is still a vibrant form of religion, almost certainly a direct descendant of the religious forms Prince Iḷaṅko found so fascinating in the second century.

4

Wandering and Romance with Lord Raṅkanātaṉ

The *Ati* or "Original" Festival in Śrīraṅkam

As a fourth example of a festival in the South Indian tradition that continues to reflect archaic elements, I have chosen the *ati*, or "original" festival of the Śrīraṅkam temple. This festival was the first one I ever participated in, and I was amazed at the time at how fun-filled and chaotic it seemed, and how little the hundreds of priests who serve in that great temple could tell me about it.[1] Many priests and worshipers knew that the festival was referred to in a Caṅkam poem,[2] written between the first and the third centuries, and they were all keen to point out that it is called the ati festival,[3] to set it apart from the dozen or so others now celebrated in this temple. But the many ritual events during the festival obey ancient traditions, and neither the religious specialists nor the ordinary worshipers were sure they could give an adequate account of it.

In interpreting this festival, I have used a somewhat different method from that in the three previous examples; I will try to show how the underlying themes of an archaic festival ritual were reinterpreted in the theological language of a sophisticated Brāhman temple tradition. In each of the three previous studies, an ancient festival tradition has continued to stimulate its own religious response, independent of the temple traditions that have grown up around it; the interpreter need only examine the history of festival practice to recognize the core of meaning there from the beginning. However, a great temple tradition has grown around this festival, and the festival itself is now only a relatively minor ritual event in a vast religious complex. The Śrīraṅkam temple in which this festival is based has over the centuries housed some of India's greatest theological debates, initiated some of its most celebrated ritual forms, and now hosts more than a dozen other festival events. One cannot now piece together an interpretation of this festival that does not involve reflection on some of the main themes in this temple's larger tradition.[4]

Theme 1: Wandering: God's Approach to the World

The geographical setting of this festival is significant. The Kāvēri River runs from west to east through the heart of Tamiḻnāṭu. About half way along its course a great rock to the south of the river projects a few hundred feet into the air. Uraiyūr, the ancient capital of the Cōḻa kingdom, was built to the west of this rock. Śrīraṇkam is the name of the island that sits in the middle of the river just in front of the ancient city of Uraiyūr. It is about 2 kilometers across from north to south and about 8 kilometers long, and parts of the island are regularly flooded during the rainy season.

The legends of the Vaiṣṇava temple on the island, which is also called Śrīraṅkam, are that Vibhīṣaṇa, the brother of the demon Rāvaṇa in the *Rāmāyaṇa* story, who supported Rāma against his evil brother, had accompanied Rāma back to his capital of Ayodhya. In thanking him, Rāma gave him an image of Viṣṇu to worship when he returned to Śrī Lanka. While returning home, he stopped to visit the Cōḻa king and left the image on the island of Śrīraṅkam where he was camping. When he was ready to go on, the image of the deity refused to move from the island and offered to face south so that Vibhīṣaṇa could worship him from Śrī Lanka. This precarious island setting is believed to suit the nature of Viṣṇu, the transcendent deity who temporarily descends into the world in the form of various *avatāras*. In the Śrīraṅkam temple the deity takes the form of an eight-foot long figure sleeping on the island platform (in the sea of chaos) created for him by the coils of the snake, Śeṣa.

In the context of the festival, the image of the deity changes dramatically from the sleeping figure in the inner sanctum to a fun-loving youth, known affectionately either as Nam Perumāḷ ("Our Leader") or as Aḻakiya Maṇavāḷan ("the Handsome Groom"). The crowds that accompany the image on the various trips around the region describe themselves as "going along for the fun" and indicate jokingly that they have no idea where "He" will be going today.

1. The first trip really does seem to be at the whim of the deity, for it involves taking the image 15 kilometers up a partially dried riverbed to the west on a moonlit night. The deity spends the next day in a stone *maṇṭapa* or chapel, while the local village of agriculturalists has a joyous celebration. The central joke of the celebration is that a widow in the village once called to her son "Reṅka," who was shaving by the river, to come and eat a special snack she had prepared for him. The deity, pretending that he had understood her to be calling his name Raṅka, had eaten the snack. Now the villagers gaily call out the names "Reṅka" and Raṅka as they offer one another snacks, delighted that the transcendent deity would at least appear to be playfully dependent on one of the women of their community.

Other than the little chapel used in this celebration, there is no temple of Viṣṇu in this village. The most active temple today is the temple of the village goddess Māriyammaṉ. The other important temple in the village is one of the oldest stone temples in all of Tamiḻnāṭu, a temple to Śivaṉ, built by a princess for her home village after she married into the Cōḻa ruling family.[5] Even though these rival temple traditions are the ones established in the village, the village is now called Jīya-puram or the "Village of the Vaiṣṇava ascetic." This name is explained by local residents to be in honor of the famous Jīyar or Vaiṣṇava ascetic of medieval times, who came from this village and supposedly built the original version of the nearby dam across the river that helps protect the island of Śrīraṅkam (Hari Rao 1961, pp. 114ff.).

2. The second major trip takes place a couple days later and proceeds to the north. It involves crossing the dried riverbed of the northern branch of the river in the blazing noonday sun. On this trip a grand feast is held near another *maṇṭapa* beside the river, hosted by "a businessman from Karnātaka." I was puzzled by this reference to a busi-

nessman from a place about 700 kilometers to the north, until I recalled that the *maṇṭapa* was beside the major trade route from the north and that Viṣṇu has often been the favorite deity of the business community. Karnātaka was also the place to which a number of theologians from Śrīraṅkam fled in times of danger and where even the image of the deity was once taken for safe keeping.

Before returning to the island after the feast with the businessman, the procession takes the image of the deity to a small temple that now houses images of Viṣṇu, Śivan̲, and Brahmā together. According to Śrīraṅkam stories, this little temple was originally built by the Vaiṣṇava saint Tirumaṅkai, who before his conversion was a chieftain operating outside the law on this north shore of the river. He had once robbed the deity of Śrīraṅkam but, having accidentally touched the deity's foot, he was converted and became one of his chief *āl̲vārs* or disciples (chapter 7 has more detail on this disciple).

3. The third major trip turns to the south and involves the deity visiting the Cōl̲a capital of Uraiyūr. While passing through the streets of the capital, the deity is said to fall in love with the Cōl̲a princess, and they spend the night together. While returning to the island in the wee hours of the morning, the deity begins playing with his ring and loses it in the sand. He is fearful that its absence will be noticed by the goddess back at the home temple, and, to the delight of his friends, he insists on sifting the sand until he finds it. Meanwhile in the Cōl̲a capital, the friends of the royal family sit in the marriage hall while the infatuated princess/goddess, Kamalādevi tries to overcome the *viraha pakti* (Sanskrit: *viraha bhakti*) or "love in separation" (Hardy 1978, 1983) that torments her now that the deity has departed.

In Vaiṣṇava theology, part of the function of Viṣṇu during his descents into the world is to define kingship and to "maintain" the righteousness, or *dharma*, of the world. In other parts of India emperors sometimes insisted that they were *aṁśas* or "parts" of Viṣṇu and ruled with his power. The Cōl̲as, however, were generally devout Śaivas and built temples that included the local goddesses as consorts of the cosmic lord Śivan̲. In other words, they defined kingship as a kind of cosmic ordering and generally did not appeal to the transcendent lord Viṣṇu for support. By having a Cōl̲a princess fall in love with the deity in this festival drama, the worshipers affirm that in their view the free-spirited Viṣṇu overrides all political forms, even as he had overridden other social structures when during earlier trips he playfully entered the domains of agriculture and business.

4. Finally, on the fourth major trip of the festival, the deity is taken to the eastern end of the island. There he symbolically visits the goddess Akilaṇṭēśvari, who gives him coconut juice and washes his feet in the sacred waters of the Jampu tree tank. While legends seem to imply that Akilaṇṭēśvari was once an independent goddess much feared by all around, her shrine has, since at least the eighth century, been part of a very famous Śaiva temple, called Jampukēśvara or Tiruvān̲aikkā, which occupies the eastern end of Śrīraṅkam island (chapter 5). There had probably always been some uneasiness about the visit of the image of Viṣṇu to the Tēvi inside this Śaiva temple, but we have a detailed account of the riots that occurred during the celebration of the festival in 1375 (Hari Rao 1961, pp. 139ff.). The Śaiva priests eventually appealed to the Vicayanakaram rulers, and a boundary line was established just west of the Tiruvān̲aikkā temple. The image of Viṣṇu no longer enters the temple and is now carried along that boundary to a *maṇṭapa* near the river, where he receives coconut water offerings.

An Interpretation of the Wanderings

In describing the nature of deity in South Indian Vaiṣṇavism, John Carman (1974) has emphasized the need to balance *paratva*, or a sense of transcendence, with *saulabhya*, or a sense of ease of access. In the wanderings of the deity during these 10 days, one senses the moments when the mood shifts from one of these poles to the other.

In general, one experiences the deity as the initiator of action, free to come and go in the life of the world as he chooses. Along the way business establishments and village headmen have erected temporary shrines called *upāyams*, where they play host to the deity by offering him juice in return for a chance to worship. The priests, however, approach these *upāyams* with a wonderful sense of the deity's impatience and emphasize to the hosts that, even though he may "descend" into their lives temporarily, he must soon be on his way.

Throughout the many journeys, the deity is addressed as a royal figure. He is frequently described as Raṅkarāja (Raṅka the king), and those who accompany him on the trip are said to be doing royal *kaiṅkarya* or "service." Throughout the trips those who carry the image use a special step imitating a "march," and at certain points in the journeying the deity is said to choose to ride a horse and the stride becomes a dramatic "gallop." The image of kingship represented here is not the Cōḻa one, in which kings were proud to have intermarried with many local landlord families and tried to develop an orderly society modeled on the cosmic lordship of Śivaṉ, but a kind of distant grandeur which still maintains the *paratva*, or transcendent, dimension of the divine.

What made the *saulabhya* or intimate aspect of the wanderings believable was first of all the humor of a dramatic actor. The special name for Viṣṇu in Śrīraṅkam is Raṅkanātan, or Lord of the Stage (*raṅka* meaning "stage"). All along the way on these trips, the deity impulsively teases someone, rides off on his horse, decides to start a journey in the middle of the night, or starts to sift sand. On each of these occasions, the temple musicians play appropriately raucous music, and the crowd responds to the actor/deity with firecrackers, peels of laughter, and other expressions of delight. In the persona of an actor, the deity does not really sacrifice the transcendent aloofness, yet he is able to establish many colorful ways of being involved in human life.

As we will soon see, the final test of the *saulabhya* form of contact with divinity occurs when the deity takes the form of a lover. In the context of this festival, the one beloved of the god is the innocent princess, and I have never seen teenaged girls so prominent in any other festival. As worshipers tried to describe the infatuation of the princess to me, they constantly jumped from the story of the Cōḻa princess to the story of Āṇṭāḷ, the orphan girl raised by one of the saints, who naively wore the garlands she made for the Lord until he asked for her to be united with him. Others jumped even further away from the story of the Cōḻa princess to the story of the Muslim princess, whose father had allowed her to play with the image he had stolen from the temple until she fell in love with it. She then returned to the temple with the image when it was recovered, is now united with the deity, and is said to still prepare his favorite Muslim-style *chapati* meal each day. Other accounts of infatuation involved people telling stories from their own lives until they would catch themselves and shift back to theology long enough to summarize by asking "how could anyone resist the beauty of Aḷakiya Maṇavāḷan, the Handsome Groom."

The "wanderings" of the deity during this festival were often interpreted by participants in terms of the classical Tamil̲ concept of "heroism." In the classical Tamil̲ grammar, Tolkāppiyaṉ distinguishes *puram* poems about kings and other "heroes" from the more numerous poems about *aham* or inner feelings, particularly romance. In this poetic tradition, the king is pictured as a colorful free spirit, who makes generous gifts to his petitioners, but is often pursued in vain. In retrospect, one can see that the trips of the deity cover the four directions and involve visits to the four major classes of society (farmers, businessmen, kings, and priests, respectively), but the worshipers prefer to think of the deity as a transcendent free spirit and his island as a precarious refuge rather than a cosmic center.

Theme 2: Romance: The Human Approach to the Divine

Whereas the geographical setting of the temple helped explain the nature of the activity of the deity as he moved off his island and out into the world, the temporal setting of the festival within the ritual calendar explains the focus on romance. The month of Paṅkuṇi (March–April) is considered highly auspicuous because it represents the midpoint of the sun's rising or northward movement. In this period, just after the second harvest, agricultural work is finally set aside and marriage arrangements begin.

The question about the human approach to the divine was raised inadvertently during one of the trips of the deity when he went to the ancient capital of the Cōl̲as, and fell in love with the Cōl̲a princess Kamalādevi. Kamalādevi is now worshiped as a *nācciyār* or goddess, but the worshipers who gather in her temple are praying that they might have her innocence, so they too might "lose themselves" in the love of the Lord. The worshipers emphasize that the deity has already gone (as he must if he is to remain truly transcendent), and they seek through the goddess the tender feelings associated with *viraha*, or separation.

What makes the meaning of viraha clear in the context of the festival is the further discussion of the theme of romance that ensues when the deity returns to his home temple. The conscience of the deity had anticipated the problem, so he insisted that there be no music when he left for Uraiyūr at 3 AM, and he had panicked and sifted sand to find his ring when he lost it during his return. The goddess in the home temple, Raṅkanāyaki, had not asked anything when he returned, so he went ahead with his final trip to the east.

The next day, however, is Uttiram, the most auspicious day of the month for romance, the day Raṅkanāyaki and the deity are expected to marry. On Uttiram morning, he approaches her temple in the northwest corner of the temple complex with due ceremony but finds the door dramatically slammed in his face. When the door then opens a bit and he is asked about the trip to Uraiyūr, he playfully puts his hands over his eyes, his ears, and then his mouth to indicate that he knows nothing. He then gives himself a truth test by first putting his hand into a pot of fire and then into a pot of snakes, without suffering any ill effects, but Raṅkanāyaki shrewdly notes that such tests do not work on gods. When the saint Nammāl̲vār intervenes, the deity acknowledges he has been to Uraiyūr but promises that it will never happen again. As the door slowly opens, he contritely enters, and the marriage proceeds as planned.

The next morning, the dramatic structure is brought full circle as the Wanderer again emerges from the temple of the Tēvi, and goes off on a hectic ride. This time the worshipers pull him around and around the temple in a tiny cart. Once again, the deity is transcendent and beyond the bounds of his romantic obligations, yet at the same time he is providing his own sense of *saulabhya*, or intimacy, with the worshipers he is fooling with.

An Interpretation of the Romance

In Tamil̲ poetry the contrast between the excitement of the mountain girls' illicit love affairs and the more complex commitments of other lovers is clearly drawn. In the context of the festival drama, this contrast is intentionally exaggerated. The innocent princess, like an innocent mountain girl, is caught up by the approach of the Lord, and her infatuation has no complication. Raṅkanāyaki, on the other hand, is a formidable wife, famous for her vow "never to cross her own threshold." She preserves her independence as a deity and never even goes to the inner sanctum of the temple for a visit with Lord Viṣṇu. Like the other goddesses of South India, she challenges the male point of view and insists, as do most married women in the region, that her position be honored even by the "hero" with transcendent freedom.

In terms of the Teṅkalai theology (Srinivasachari 1970), the dominant tradition in this temple, the two forms of romance just described represent the twin cries of the heart as it expresses its devotion to the Lord. On the one hand, the heart is overwhelmed by the gracious action that suddenly brings God right into the midst of one's life. When God approaches us in grace, we are "lost" and have no choice but to "surrender," in what the Teṅkalais call *pirapatti* (Sanskrit: *prapatti*). This was the experience of the princess.

On the other hand, the Teṅkalais argue that there is a proper place for *pakti* (Sanskrit: *bhakti*) or devotion, both before and after the experience of surrender. Before the surrender, the devotee can follow the moral and meditative disciplines that strengthen the soul. After the surrender, the soul should seek the strong and lasting love of a deeper union. In pursuing these forms of devotion, the Tēvi Raṅkanāyaki is not only the model but, in Teṅkalai theology at least, the mediatrix. In the North Indian Vaiṣṇava traditions, in which the Tēvi is called Lakṣmi, she is virtually an indistinguishable part of Viṣṇu. The Vaṭakalai school of South Indian Vaiṣṇavism follows a theology with a similar interpretation, but in the Teṅkalai school, she is considered the highest soul, and therefore an independent mediatrix, whose task is to approach God on behalf of the devotees.

Conclusion

Because of the grandeur of today's Śrīraṅkam temple tradition, it is not easy to imagine the drama that would have been associated with this festival when the first-century poet referred to his distraught lover's face as like the mess on the banks of the Kāvēri River after a Puṅkuṇi Uttiram festival. More than any other, this festival is like a massive picnic, in which the deity is thought to enjoy himself immensely, hiking and galloping about, while his devotees, in the form of lovers, find ways to bind themselves to him.

The deity involved in this drama is no longer, like those in the festivals already studied, one who slays demonic natural forces, but a royal-like figure who effortlessly makes the world go around. In the centuries to come, some of the greatest theistic theology in India evolved within the halls of this temple, as renowned theologians such as Rāmānuja and Vedānta Desika reflected on what the divine presence experienced here.

Whereas the portrayal of deity in this festival drama is rich, it is really the portrayal of the stubborn search of the human heart for contact with the divine, which is the creative genius of the drama. Valli, as the lover of the divine being in the Kataragama festival (chapter 2), is portrayed as a silent and passive partner, but in this story both the "infatuated princess" and the "formidable wife" express their passionate longing with great force.

In fashioning these pictures of a "heroic" deity and a "love-torn" soul, the festival drama eloquently used the classical categories of puram and aham respectively. The four thousand Tamiḻ hymns that the Vaiṣṇava saints wrote in the next few centuries rework these themes with great care and often explained how the classical canons affected their theological thought. The festival drama gives us a portrait of the religious community in which the saint-poets worked. These were not poets simply trying to voice their personal religious experience but the members of a religious community that celebrated its annual festival picnic around a drama that gave life to their deepest theological vision.

Conclusion to Part I

My argument is that the archaic elements in these four festivals indicate that these are old religious traditions that have continued to provide particular varieties of religious experience to worshipers for many centuries. Only in one case do we have a specific ancient writing that seems to refer to the festival, but in each of the other cases the earliest historical evidences in that region are closely linked with themes dramatized in the festival.

The precise age of the festivals is not, however, the most important point. The central motifs of these four festivals match the classical themes in the early literature of the region. The male deities in each case are young and energetic, figures one immediately relates to the classical notion of "heroism." In chapter 1 the young boy/deity Ayyappan̲ controls the natural order and its demonic forces. In chapter 2 the warrior/deity Kataragama falls in love with the village girl Valli and marries. In chapter 3 the impetuousness of Kōvalan̲ and the other male figures almost ruin the relationship, and the Tēvi must make desperate efforts to overcome the incompetence around her. Finally, in the careful balance of chapter 4, the elusive king/deity is brought into relationship only by the extraordinary efforts of two determined devotees/lovers/goddesses.

The four festivals reflect life in four different environments, with different social systems. Ayyappan̲ worship is in the forest, Kataragama's straddles the forest and the dry agricultural areas, Koṭuṅkaḷūr adjoins agricultural and coastal areas, and Śrīraṅkam is in the heart of the largest and most productive river valley. The classical grammar of Tamil̲ specified the kind of deity and the kind of lover a poet might well associate with each geographical area. One would not want to insist that all these correlations seem predetermined, yet there is no doubt that the diversity in the terrain reflects the diversity of the society and its religious expression.

Despite the great differences among these four festival celebrations, one can speak of them as parallel developments reflecting a common social environment. It is highly unlikely that any of them had an impact on the development of the others, but the package of ideas circulating through the societies that gave them birth were sufficiently similar so that someone who grew up in one festival tradition could understand another. In the centuries to follow, the interaction among the different local traditions grew stronger, first as empires developed and kings had some role initiating and participating in festivals, and later when new festivals were initiated by those already familiar with the wider festival tradition. In analyzing the festivals of parts II and III, I have more historical clues than in the case of the four I have already described. These four are, however, among the most revered, precisely because they seem to reach so far back beyond the eras we know so much about.

II

MEDIEVAL STRUCTURES

Before irrigation, life in the lowlands of South India was harsh. The mountains had rainfall and rich tropical forests, but the lowlands were dry, and the coasts provided opportunities for only the bravest fishermen. Agriculturalists in Śrī Lanka experimented with irrigation first, using a technique involving catching the seasonal rains in artificial lakes and then developing sluices to carry the water to nearby fields. Even in the early stages of these experiments, social and political changes quickly followed, and landlords, who controlled the newly enriched lands, reinforced their privileges by aligning themselves with political figures and with Jain and Buddhist monastic leaders who would support their position of privilege. In South India itself, the techniques for utilizing river water took longer, but in the end irrigation there helped develop even grander centers of civilization, especially in the valley adjacent to the great Kāvēri River. In Śrī Lanka these developments were well established by the third century of the Common Era, whereas in the Kāvēri valley the political consolidation in the Cōḻa Empire occurred only in the ninth century. After the Muslim invasions of the fourteenth century, the political structure of society became less stable, even though the influence of the landlords and temples continued.

The four festivals in part II of this study still reflect the structured social and political relations that characterized the medieval South Indian world, with its powerful landlords and elaborate political and religious ceremonies.

The first of these studies describes the Tiruvāṉaikkā temple's festivals on the eastern end of Śrīraṅkam island in the heart of the Kāvēri river valley. Like festival celebrations in Kāñcipuram, Maturai, and Tirunēlveli on other river systems, this festival celebrates the union of powerful local goddesses with the cosmic lord Śivaṉ and reflects a comfortably balanced cosmos and a highly structured social order.

The second study takes us back to Śrī Lanka for a very "medieval-looking" festival established after the ancient capital had moved from Anurādhapura, then from Polunnaruwa, and reestablished itself in Kandy. Perhaps partly because of those two displacements of the capital, the interdependence of the landlords and kings assumes prominence in this festival, and their links with the Buddhist monastic order are explicitly spelled out in the ritual of the festival. Clearly the religious system here incorporates within its ritual a religious tradition of an earlier era.

The third study turns away from the economic and political to examine how one of the greatest religious establishments or temples, Śrīraṅkam (which we have already visited in chapter 4), settled a major theological controversy through a festival. The new ritual form of scripture recitation, at the center of this festival, although not a part of many other festivals, continues to be a popular form of celebration in the Śrīraṅkam temple.

Finally, the fourth study returns to the traditions of the goddesses or tēvis first examined in chapter 3. Here we will see how the people who were not landlords, kings, or priests continued with their own worship patterns, even as they recognized some ritual forms that the other medieval festivals had developed.

Hundreds of other temple festivals are similar to those described in this section. Most are in grand stone temples bearing dated inscriptions of the Cōḻa era (870–1300 CE), and in most cases the festival is mentioned in connection with donations described in those inscriptions. Apparently, the Cōḻa administrators encouraged some degree of uniformity in festival celebrations, because the festivals of the medieval period are similar in basic structure. Almost all are 10-day festivals; they begin with the raising of the temple flag and the cutting of a sapling or the planting of a variety of grains in a pot of carefully mixed soils. In large temples, the daily processions of the deities on different *vāhanas* or carts climax on the final day with the pulling of a grand chariot with long hempen ropes.

Although the worshipers are proud because the local festival is associated with ancient legends about kings or sages, they have little interest today in the social, political, or religious concerns that made the medieval ritual of the region so elaborate. The festival leaders follow the detail of the ritual carefully, but the crowds focus their attention on their own religious concerns and on the dramatic moments when the music or the procession has brought many people into a direct encounter with the deity.

5

The Family of Śivaṉ in the Kāvēri River Valley

The Traditions of the Tiruvāṉaikkā Temple

In this study the "medieval" period begins with the development of irrigated agriculture in the river valleys of South India and Śrī Lanka and ends with the control of the area falling into European hands. Before the development of irrigation, the other regions—the mountains, the coasts, the deserts, and the pasturelands—often figure prominently in the culture. But with the development of irrigation, population became concentrated in the river valleys, which became the centers of civilization.

Irrigation must have been under development for many centuries, but it gained important political implications first in Śrī Lanka around the city of Anurādhapura.[1] Some of the smaller river beds in South India, such as the Tamrapani in the deep south, may also have developed irrigation fairly early, but the major river of South India, the Kāvēri, was formidable, and irrigation there developed slowly over centuries. The Cōḻa dynasty of this region, an imperial power in the ninth century, made the Kāvēri basin the center of a great civilization, which at its peak covered the whole of South India and Śrī Lanka.

In Śrī Lanka the religious institution that went along with the development of the irrigation system was the Buddhist monastery. As the educated elite in the rapidly expanding political empire of Anurādhapura, the Jain and Buddhist monks of the city sought alliances with the different political factions vying for power, with the result that monasteries came and went with the winds of political change. In South India the different families of the landlord or Vēḷāḷa community controlled the institutional life of their region or *nāṭu* and built most of the great temples of the region. Originally many of these temples seem to have been goddess temples, but during Cōḻa rule the best known of the local goddesses came to be associated with Śivaṉ, so the temples are now shared by the Tēvi and Śivaṉ. During medieval times, many of these temples were developed into magnificent stone monuments, surrounded by four or five concentric walls and a number of gateway towers or *kōpurams* covered with elaborate sculptures. The Tiruvāṉaikkā temple (sometimes called Jampukēśvara) is of this type and is located on Śrīraṅkam island in the Kāvēri River.

The Symbol Cluster

As early as the seventh century when the traveling hymnsingers Appar and Campantar visited the Tiruvāṉaikkā temple, the story that has made the temple famous was already well known. In its simplest form the story is that a sage was meditating in a forest on this island and decided to take a Jampu fruit to Śivaṉ as an offering. Śivaṉ enjoyed the fruit and spat out the seed, so the sage picked up the seed, and taking it to be *piracātam*, or the "leftovers" of the offerings that are returned to the worshiper, he swallowed it. When he returned to his meditation, a Jampu tree began to grow out of his head. Śivaṉ was delighted and took the form of a *swayampu liṅkam*, or "self-formed *liṅkam*," the *Appu Liṅkam* or "Water Liṅkam," and came to reside under that tree (*Tiruvāṉaikkā Stalapurāṇa* 1968).

The picture of a sage with a tree growing out of his head is strange indeed, and worshipers took great delight in explaining it as similar to all the other "reversals" in the symbolism of the temple. Normally one might expect "nature" to form the base on which human achievements or "culture" is established, but in this case, the worshipers explain, that relationship is reversible. Then walking over to the *liṅkam* shrine at the center of this vast temple, they point out the equally odd visual scene of a Jampu tree growing right out of the top of a 10-foot high stone structure with only finger-sized roots stretched around the stone and down into the *appu* or "water" that constantly surrounds the *liṅkam*. Still puzzled by the obvious complexities of this symbol system, I walked out into one of the luxuriant coconut groves that now occupy many of the large open areas inside the temple walls, and another worshiper boasted of the rich green everywhere and explained that it was because everything was in balance, for "the Tēvi is our land, and Śivaṉ is our irrigation water."

The Divine Couple

To outsiders classifying temples, this temple would be called a temple of Śivaṉ. To the worshipers, it is usually called the temple of the Tēvi Akilaṇṭēśvari, and two-thirds of all the tickets bought at the entrance are for worship of the Tēvi. Akilaṇṭēśvari is still described as "very powerful," and it is considered dangerous to neglect her worship or to worship her carelessly. Her temple faces east, the orthodox direction for a medieval temple. In a most unusual arrangement, the temple of Śivaṉ is set side by side with hers, facing west, suggesting that the legends that say that her temple was here first and his was built later might well be correct. Her name, which means "Universal Goddess" in Sanskrit, does not have a local quality about it, but I could not discover any references to an earlier name that might have predated her link with Śivaṉ and her general Sanskritization. The "universality" of the Tēvi is given a ritual form at present by dressing her during the forenoon in the "green" of Parvati, the normal wife of Śivaṉ and a symbol of fertility; during the afternoon in the "red" of Lakṣmi, the goddess of wealth; and during the evening in the "white" of Saraswati, the goddess of music and learning.

In Sanskrit myth Śivaṉ is usually portrayed as a recluse dressed in ashes and skins living in the mountains. In the ritual activity of this temple, he is portrayed as a family man, who is tied to the immediate surroundings of the *kā* or grove in which the family dwells and for which he provides the water. His provision of water is taken as a special act of divine favor and therefore as a form of "culture" (in contrast to the local origin and natural rootedness of the Tēvi); in that sense, he is still linked with the original source of the water. The priests are most anxious that one peek into the inner sanctum and see the water that surrounds the *liṅkam* and understand the special miracle that brings this water underground from the Kāvēri River a kilometer away. The Kāvēri River is in turn linked with the holy Kaṅkā (Ganges) River of North India, because when the sage Agastya brought a pitcher of water from the Kaṅkā to the south, the Kāvēri was begun. And the Kaṅkā is divine, because it, in turn, was brought from heaven when Śivaṉ allowed it to fall into the locks of his hair, so that its fall would not destroy the earth. Irrigation comes about through a similarly elaborate linkage of channels, possible only because of the foresight of the Vēḷāḷa landlords and the cooperation and ordered social forms that have characterized the whole society of this region over extended periods of time. The "water" provided by Śivaṉ and the foresight of the Vēḷāḷas should be properly linked, respectively, with the natural "power" and fertility of the Tēvi and with the efforts of the laboring classes who work on the land.

The stories that link the "Mother" ("Ammaṉ") and the "Lord" ("Swāmi") carefully retain a sense of her power, while providing him with some kind of control. In the story that links them with the original symbol cluster, she takes the initiative and goes to the mountains to ask him to teach her "the difference between *bhoga* (enjoyment) and *yoga* (self restraint)." He told her females cannot understand such philosophical matters and suggested she go to the Jampu grove and try to meditate. In anger, she developed enormous power through deep meditation, and her power forced him to come there and join her. Another story suggests that the Tēvi once presided at this location alone. Because she was at that time extremely angry, she often cursed the people with drought or sickness. On behalf of Śivaṉ, the great sage Śaṅkara (an eighth-century philosopher) came there and offered her earrings containing magical *yantras*, or geometrical shapes, with Śivaṉ's power contained in them and built her an image of her most beloved oldest son Vināyakaṉ so she could always see it high above the crowd. Since then, her power has been under control; she uses her still dangerous power for blessing rather than cursing the worshiper. This pattern of interdependence, which recognizes the female as the repository of dangerous natural "power" and the male as able to activate that power with the judicious use of good ideas, is the pattern that Tamiḻ culture used in its understanding of the family (Wadley 1980). In general, it fits with a widespread tendency to link women to "nature" and men to "culture," but it is unique in the degree to which it seeks to establish a close interdependence between them. The three festive rituals I will describe each express that interdependence in a different way.

Festive Rituals

1. One daily ritual in the Tiruvāṉaikkā temple has the atmosphere of a festival ritual. The male priest emerges from the inner shrine of the Tēvi dressed in a *sāri* and playing the role of the Tēvi. Accompanied by an elephant and the temple musicians, he leads a crowd of worshipers to the shrine of Śivaṉ and enters the shrine with a basket of food for the Lord's midday meal. After a suitable time for family intimacy, the "Tēvi" re-

emerges from the shrine and proceeds to worship a cow tethered to the front door of the shrine, just like what would happen in a rural home. As the cow is fed and begins to urinate, the "Tēvi" and the crowd rush to touch the urine and receive its properties of fertility. The "priest- Tēvi" then returns in procession to her own shrine.

2. The 10-day festival, held in the month of Tai (January–February) so as to climax on the *nakṣatra* or star of Pucam, is one of the most widely celebrated Śivaṉ festivals. In Tiruvāṉaikkā the procedure is standard for medieval temple-festivals: the flag is raised on the first day to initiate the festival; on days two through nine processions around the town are conducted with the images of all the temple's deities (one of Śivaṉ and the Tēvi together, one of Akilaṇṭēśvari alone, one of the oldest son Vināyakaṉ and his rarely seen consort Varali, one of the second son Murukaṉ and his two consorts Tevayanai and Valli, and finally one of the mythological "manager" of the temple Caṇṭēśvaraṉ). Now the crowds for these events are relatively modest, and the images, no longer carried, are pulled along on rubber-wheeled trailers that comfortably hold both the *vāhana* or vehicle for each day and the image. The second day is somewhat of an exception. On this day the ṛṣbha or bull *vāhana* appears, a magnificent golden image with an enormous swinging testicle. The Vēḷāḷa family, which sponsors this day's procession, claims to have had the image carved many centuries ago and to have sponsored the worship ever since, because, as they say, it "guaranteed fertility to the neighboring area." It was, however, the final day of the festival that provided the tone of worship for the whole 10 days. On this day everyone in the neighborhood gathers for the *Teppam* or "Float" with the divine family on the "waters" of the temple tank. In a wonderfully relaxed atmosphere, hundreds of local families gather slowly through the afternoon on the stone steps of this ancient tank. Many devise leaf rafts for their bouquets of flowers and food offerings, and young boys swim about, providing excitement for all. As dusk comes, the images are brought from the temple and are placed on a large raft with a temple-like superstructure and a beautiful arrangement of electric lights. As the barge is poled around the tank three times, worshipers crowd forward to send out their offerings. Everyone revels in the security and joy of their own family's company and the corresponding security of knowing that the divine family shares in the peace and order of the whole social system and its environment.

3. If the Tai Pucam festival expresses the stability and solidarity of the society and its harmony with the cosmic order, the Pañcapirakāram Festival, which lasts 40 days during the months of Paṅkuṇi and Cittirai (March 15 to April 25), is the comic expression of the joy of the family's intimacy. This festival is held during the hot season that precedes the monsoon rains, a time for leisure, merrymaking, and weddings before the careful work of preparing irrigation canals and fields begins. This wedding includes all kinds of merrymaking, but the most popular celebration, after which the festival is named, comes on the 37th day, when the clothes and makeup of the deities are reversed, to the hysterical delight of the crowds. The story that explains the occasion for the reversal concerns the creator god, Brahmā, who was so erotically inclined that when he finished creating a beautiful young maiden, he could not control himself and made love with her. The Ammaṉ and Swāmi of Tirunāṉaikkā switch clothes for this festival so that Śivaṉ in female dress can lure Brahmā into chasing after him and then embarrass him by revealing his true self. In the festival setting, the enticement takes the form of an all-

night chase through the corridors of the temple. When the exhausted worshipers have finished the chase, they have also circumambulated the temple five times by passing through each of its five corridors or *pirakārams*. Although conducted with much laughter, this reversal of symbols still provides a joyful expression of the social and cosmic balance around which the temple's worship system has been constructed.

Bhoga or *Yoga*?

While the worshipers of Ayyappaṉ (chapter 1) exerted enormous energy to dip into their subconscious and reach out in faith to something that would help them overcome the fear of the natural order, the worshipers of the divine couple, Akilaṇṭēśvari and Śivaṉ, are involved in a less intense but somewhat more complex search for the right approach to the divine. In this case much of the activity is thought to take place in the cosmic realm, and the worshiper takes a relatively passive role as she or he fits into society's hierarchical interrelationships. Although acceptance or "devotion" is the predominant mood in some sense, the worshiper still must make the intellectual effort to grasp the divine purpose expressed in the societal and cosmic order, and this effort may take a number of slightly different forms.

The alternative forms of worship were formulated by the Tēvi when she went to the Himālayas and asked that Śivaṉ explain the difference between *bhoga* and *yoga*. Both express devotion and a clear religious posture, but one brings to a joyous focus the natural desires for food, physical satisfaction, and enjoyment, whereas the other brings into focus the need for self-discipline and a willful determination to achieve a particular goal. In an ancient story connected with this temple, and alluded to as early as the seventh century, this choice is spelled out most colorfully. Once the *liṅkam* had been established under the Jampu tree, an elephant and a spider each sought to worship it. The elephant's form of worship ("service") was of the *bhoga* type, for he just wanted to provide an enjoyable bath or *apiṭēkam* (Sanskrit: *abhiṣēka*) for the deity, so he carefully brought his trunk full of water each morning and washed the *liṅkam*. The spider, who was more of the *yoga* type, wanted to think of a form of worship that would have a lasting effect, so he built a web over the *liṅkam* that would protect it, especially from the falling leaves and other debris. The problem was that each morning the elephant's worship undid the worship of the spider, and the spider became distressed. Crawling inside the trunk of the elephant, he bit the elephant with his poison, and the elephant fell down dead and crushed the spider to death. As the story is normally told, both types of worship seem to be praised, for the elephant got immediate salvation (and had the temple named after him), and the spider was reincarnated as the great Cōḻa king Kōcceṅkaṉāṉ, who is thought to have built this temple.

In one sense the two types of worship correspond to the two halves of the social structure of this region. The "right hand" castes worked on the land together (even though there were grades of authority and respectability among them) and generally boasted of their fertility, their joyousness, and their physical exuberance. They were inclined to goddess worship, local shrines, and the spontaneous forms of worship such as feeding and bathing the deity. The "left hand" castes were involved in crafts and provided the carpentry, metal work, stone work, jewelry, and cloth for the society. They tended toward self-discipline, vegetarianism, and esoteric worship rituals and were often involved in the construction and support of temples and *matams* outside of the local village setting.

The inscriptions on the walls of the Tiruvāṉaikkā temple indicate that the management committee of that temple shifted dramatically over the centuries from one group of managers and priests to another. The story of the inscriptions is actually complex,[2] but it might be summarized in the following way. The early inscriptions (from the tenth to the thirteenth centuries) all involve land grants, with Vēḷāḷa landlords (a "right hand" caste) either giving land to the temple or buying land from the temple.[3] During the thirteenth century the Cōḻa authority declined, and the emperor of the Hoysala kingdom to the northwest built a "southern capital" a few kilometers north of the Tiruvāṉaikkā temple, so as to assist the Cōḻa rulers, who were his allies through marriage. Inscriptions show that the Hoysala royal family established a couple of *matams* or monastic memorial shrines in the temple and presumably brought in *yogis* or ascetics to live there.[4] After a period of chaos resulting from Muslim armies marching through the area, an inscription tells us that in 1470 four sets of *sthānikas* (perhaps Vēḷāḷas with priestly functions) sold their rights to worship in the temple to someone from a trading center near modern Madras, some 300 kilometers away (*Annual Reports on Epigraphy 1936–7* no. 106). One may presume that this person was a merchant connected with the "left hand" castes, because we know that for the next century the temple was run by an order of celibate ascetics. In 1584 a detailed legal document was prepared by a committee of Vēḷāḷas that describes how the celibate order was dismissed from the priesthood of the temple and a married priesthood of hereditary priests (called Paṇḍita) was appointed (*Annual Reports on Epigraphy 1936–7*, 106 and note on p. 91; Derrett 1971; Mahalingam 1957, 135). The present priests claim to be descended from that family. The vacillation between control of the temple sometimes in the hands of landlord Vēḷāḷas (the "right hand"), and married priests allied with them, and sometimes in the hands of merchants (the "left hand"), and ascetics (*matam*) allied with them, is a fascinating reflection of the *bhoga/yoga* contrast and the two loci of spiritual authority the temple was built on.

For present worshipers the medieval structures of society are somewhat remote, and many feel the choice between *bhoga* and *yoga* really boils down to personal temperament. For them, the choice is formulated most easily in terms of reflection on a well-known story about the two sons of Śivaṉ. Although this story is known elsewhere, it is a special favorite of this temple and is featured in the sculpture of the temple, the modern paintings on the temple wall, and in the focus on it during the festival processions. The story is that Śivaṉ and his wife called their two sons and offered an exceptionally beautiful mango fruit to the one who could go around the world first. The self-disciplined and energetic second son, Murukaṉ, started off at once. The rotund first son, Vināyakaṉ, hesitated for just a moment and then walked slowly around his parents, saying that they constituted the whole universe. He was quickly given the mango fruit; when his brother later arrived, he was most angry and took up the life of an ascetic. As worshipers now tell the story, most of the sympathy is with the heartbroken Murukaṉ, but the moral taken from it is that we must always remember the balance of the two paths, for it is in achieving the balance that we will be able to worship aright.

Conclusion

Even though the crowds that gather for the festival activities of this temple are modest in comparison to those attending the festival of Ayyappaṉ (chapter 1), it would be a mistake to think that this pattern of worship is no longer influential. This pattern is so familiar, and so independent of the worshipers' participation, that the society assumes it goes on and derives comfort from that fact whether they attend or not.

The sense of cosmological and societal balance achieved here was probably dominant during the Cōḻa rule, which lasted from the ninth to the thirteenth centuries. Some features of the cosmological interest developed during those centuries may have been borrowed from the Brāhmans who moved in from the north of India during this period, but much of the love of orderliness that characterized this society was probably the result of a gradual development of an irrigation system that required the careful interdependence of a rather large number of separate caste communities. The Tamiḻ Śaiva hymnsingers of a couple centuries earlier had picked up the warmth and joy in the life of these agriculturalists and had sung about temple after temple as if Śivaṉ were there, even though we know many of the temples had been dedicated to goddesses. The inclusiveness thus expressed in the mythology corresponded neatly with the inclusiveness sought for the expanding social networks, and the result was a confident and joyful affirmation that family, society, and the cosmos were all in harmony.

In the present social setting, discord is more evident than harmony. Nevertheless, two members of the Vēḷāḷa families still attached to the temple are among the most respected leaders in Tamiḻ society (one a high court judge and the other a retired university president turned fundraiser for temple renovations),[5] and many people comment that it is the sense of "harmony" such people represent that is still the only hope for Tamiḻ society, which now seems so embroiled in the Brāhman/non-Brāhman quarrels of the modern Tamiḻ political arena. Certainly the economic control once enjoyed by Vēḷāḷas will not return, but the values associated with the faith in cosmological and societal harmony may resurface in a variety of other ways. Testimony to the respected "middle ground" the Tiruvāṉaikkā temple still seems to represent comes from the fact that other temples seem comfortable "borrowing" from this temple tradition. Thus, the militantly anti-Brāhman managers of the Māriyammaṉ temple nearby (chapter 8) turned to the Tiruvāṉaikkā temple when it needed better educated priests to handle its huge crowds. And in quite the opposite direction, the very-Brāhman priests of the Śrīraṅkam temple of Viṣṇu (chapters 4 and 7) asked the Vēḷāḷa university president-turned-fundraiser of Tiruvāṉaikkā to help them with their renovation, even though he was a well-known Śaiva.

In some sense the system of cosmic and societal harmony expressed in this pattern of worship is the central system through which the others measure themselves. Māriyammaṉ worship in nearby Samayapuram (chapter 8) brings out all the sense of injustice that women in particular feel so pointedly. The social ideal of a closely integrated family is still strong in the area, and many Māriyammaṉ worshipers also come to Akilaṇṭēśvari on their way home and comment that she brings them not only justice but family harmony as well. On the other side, the Viṣṇu worshipers, who revel in the playfulness of a deity with great transcendent freedom and few obligations, recognize that Śivaṉ too enjoys transcendence, but, in the context of South Indian worship at least, his primary reputation is as one who establishes ordered relationships within the family, the society, and the cosmic order. Few worshipers in South India have not visited the temples of each of these deities (as well as those of their Muslim and Christian neighbors). Whatever their primary focus of worship, most are well aware of the other primary worship patterns, and few would not recognize that the temples of Tēvi/Śivaṉ couples provided the undergirding sense of social order that characterized life in medieval South India.

6

Monks and Kings Intervene

The Kandy Perahara in Central Śrī Lanka

The festival described in chapter 5 reflects the worldview of the landlord class in the irrigated river valleys of the South Indian region. In this chapter I present a festival in which a similar landlord view was dramatically modified when monks and kings saw the opportunity to use the festival celebration to express their roles in the maintenance of the society as well. As a result of all the modifications in the festival celebration of Kandy over the centuries, most observers of this still enormously popular festival have just described it as "full of medieval pageantry" and have concentrated on its contemporary meaning. The earlier forms of the festival are, however, still included in the present celebration, and it seems useful to begin the story of the festival by trying to reconstruct their meanings, if only to better understand the intentions of those who tried to redirect that meaning in later centuries.

Phase 1: The Most Archaic Festival Segment

The full festival today lasts for 22 days. Five days of preparation begin on the new moon in the month of Asāḷa (June–July); then 10 days of processions climax on the full moon; and seven days following the full moon are given over to ritual dance, celebrated only in the Alutnūwara temple. This 7-day segment of the festival, called the Valiyak Netum, seems to have the most archaic rituals of the Perahara.

The Valiyak Netum rituals take place in the ancient temple on the side of the hill on the edge of the present city of Kandy. The name of the deity in this temple has changed during the course of history and seems to have originally been Utpalawarna or Upulvan, then Alutnūwara, and now sometimes "Viṣṇu."[1] Upulvan is generally equated with the Vedic deity Varuṇa and taken to be the lord of the sea and, in that capacity, to be the protector of the island of Śrī Lanka.[2] (In later, medieval, classifications of the protector deities, Upulvan is sometimes joined by Saman, Vibhīṣaṇa, and Kataragama, to provide protection in all four directions). The name for the protector deity of the island was changed from Upulvan to "Alutnūwara" or "New City" when the Emperor Parākramabāhu II (1236–1270) moved the national capital to a new city and a new temple he built in Kegalle District. When the capital was later moved to Kandy, the deity bearing that name was installed in the temple on the hill. Many worshipers still refer to the deity in the temple on the hill outside Kandy as "Alutnūwara," but devout Buddhists tend to use still another name, "Viṣṇu," the commonly used name for a guardian deity whose temples are placed beside Buddhist temples or *stūpas* throughout Śrī Lanka.

The rituals of the Valiyak Netum are archaic priestly dances that the present generation of priests do not really understand well. The dances are Flower Dance, Boar Dance, Cobra Dance, Fire Dance, and War Dance (between the Veddas, or the ancient tribal people, and the Sinhalas), and the priests describe them as providing protection against the primordial forces of the forest, which once covered most of the island. These dances appear to have come from a festival tradition that dates to a time before irrigation when Śrī Lanka was primarily a hunting and gathering society. Few of the worshipers attend this part of the festival today, but they all know about it and think of it as a secret priestly ritual that must be performed or there would be grave consequences for the whole society.

Phase 2: The Classic Medieval Festival

Although a relatively small island, Śrī Lanka has had a fairly turbulent political history. As seen in chapter 2, the region of Rohaṇa in the south had its own kingdom much of the time, and the northern capital shifted from Anurādhapura to Polonnaruwa, to the southwest near Colombo, and back to Kandy nearer the center. The *Mahāvamsa* or Great Chronicle (Geiger 1912), written in the fifth century by the Buddhist monk Mahānāma, provides us with a good account of how Anurādhapura became a major center. The region around Anurādhapura is relatively dry, but it does have some rainfall from both the southwest monsoon, which is heavy on the southwest coast near Colombo in July, and the northeast monsoon, which hits the northeast of the island in November/December. When the agriculturalists learned to catch this rainfall in artificial lakes, irrigation for two separate harvests was possible. The Lambakanna and Moriya clans both developed irrigation works in this area; when they emerged as the leaders of the landholding aristocracy, they fought one another for political control for centuries. The Lambakannas had worked with a number of different monasteries in the city of Anurādhapura to legitimize their control for some time, but by the time the *Mahāvamsa* was written, the Moriya clan had come to power under King Dhātusena (460–478), who worked closely with the Mahāvihāra monastery, to which Mahānāma belonged.

In the tenth century, the Cōḻa Empire, based in the Kāvēri river valley of South India, expanded to include all of South India, Śrī Lanka, and parts of Indonesia and Cambodia. The Cōḻas moved the capital of Śrī Lanka from Anurādhapura to the more central location of Polonnaruwa. They built Hindu temples around the country and developed the more elaborate irrigation works of the Polonnaruwa region. We do not have any accounts of festival celebrations in either Anurādhapura or Polonnaruwa, but the earliest account we do have, from 1681, describes the present Kandy Perahara as 10 days of colorful ritual processions, elaborate opening and closing ceremonies, with many political leaders participating, much like hundreds of other medieval temple festivals in the Cōḻa period of the South Indian tradition.

When his ship landed on the Śrī Lankan coast in 1661, Robert Knox was taken prisoner and spent the next 20 years as a kind of hostage/guest of the Kandyan king, who would not let him leave but provided him with food and allowed him to operate his own farm. Other Europeans in that position married local women and blended into the Sinhala society, but Knox remained a bachelor, kept careful notes of his observations, and wrote *An Historical Relation of Ceylon* (republished, 1958) soon after he escaped in 1681. Knox describes the festival at that time as taking place between the new moon and full moon of the month of Asāḷa, with the 10 days of processions involving elephants, drummers and dancers from many regions, and the king and other officers of the state marching at the rear (Knox 1958, p. 151). He describes the festival as in honor of Alutnūwara, the "Maker of Heaven and Earth," with Kataragama and Pattini joining in (Knox 1958, p. 150). Each of these three deities is represented by a "painted stick" carried on the back of an elephant, and there is little doubt that this odd description referred to the *ran ayūdhas* or Holy Instruments of the deities that are still carried today.[3] (The important roles in the festival now played by the Buddhist Tooth temple or Daladā Māligāva and the Nātha temple were not mentioned in his account and clearly were later additions to the Perahara.)

The processional segment of the festival begins and ends with rituals, which have rough equivalents in the temple festivals of South India but are sufficiently different to require description. The opening rituals involve raising the temple flag and cutting a splice from a jackfruit sapling. The priests carefully select the sapling (*kāpa*) deep in the forest, and then they ceremonially bring it from the forest on the back of an elephant. It is then wrapped carefully in cloth; after some days sections of it are planted in pots near the entrances of the Hinduized participating temples (the three from the seventeenth century and the Nātha temple built since), where they are said to ooze semen. The flag and the sapling seem to be symbols of sovereignty and fertility, respectively, and are found in some form in almost all temple festivals. (In the grain-producing regions of South India, the fertility symbol shifts from a jackfruit sapling to a pot of cereals, which sprout during the festival after mixtures of soils and water from different sources in the region enrich them.) In Śrī Lanka the jackfruit tree is still abundant and a natural symbol of fertility.[4] Once the *kāpa* is installed in the temple, the priests circle around and around it and finally tie a ribbon (*Kāpsittavēma* or Tamiḻ: *Kāpukkaṭṭu*) around the tree as a vow binding them for the duration of the festival to the deity embodied in the *kāpa*.

The ritual at the close of the festival is called "water cutting" in Śrī Lanka and takes place during the wee hours of the morning after the last grand procession on the night of the full moon. For this ritual only one elephant, which carries both the *kāpa* and the *ayūdha* symbols of deity, the *randōli* or box of other sacred symbols of both the deity and his or her consort, and the priests of the temple constitute the procession from each of the participating temples. There is no procession from the Tooth Temple of the Buddha, but processions from each of the other temples (including the Nātha temple) proceed to a temple of the Hindu deity Ganeṣa (Vināyakaṉ), a temple that has no other role in the festival. After a brief ceremony in this temple, the bowl of water left there a year earlier is taken, and the joint procession winds out of the city to a special ford or *tīrtha* in the river a couple of miles away.

At the river a fairly elaborate ceremony lasts throughout the remainder of the night. The priests, standing in the shallow water for much of the ceremony, use umbrellas and curtains to shield what they apparently consider a highly charged ritual act from the view of the public. The "cutting" of the water involves slicing through the water with ceremonial swords or sticks and placing the jackfruit splices or *kāpa* into the water. Symbolically, they are reconsigning to the primordial realm some of the divine power that had been part of the mundane world for the duration of the festival. (Village festivals in both India and Śrī Lanka often end in a similar manner with all the apparatus of the ritual thrown into a well or river. Clay or paper images are all consigned to the nearest body of water, but images or weapons, *ayūdhas*, of wood or metal, are usually washed and returned to the temple.)

In Kandy the water cutting ceremony is followed by what looks like a separate ritual, perhaps a remnant from a ritual call for rain, a magical exercise to remind the deities that rain will be needed in the fall rainy season about to begin. For this part of the ritual, the priests empty the bowl of water they brought from the Ganeṣa temple, refill it from the stream, and ceremonially carry it back to the Ganeṣa temple, where it is kept in a special place for the entire year until the next festival.

It is not particularly surprising that in the seventeenth century the two small temples of Kataragama and Pattini in the center of Kandy joined in the festival activity, which Knox thought still centered on the deity Alutnūwara. As seen in the festival description of chapter 2, the base temple of Lord Kataragama in the forest of Rohaṇa has an old tradition. During medieval times the Kataragama tradition spread throughout the island of Śrī Lanka, and Lord Kataragama became one of the protectors of the island. The special steps of the *kavati* dance, which worshipers perform for Kataragama, are now incorporated into the Kataragama temple's segment of the Kandy festival procession.

A somewhat more complex story lies behind the development of the worship of the goddess Pattini.[5] The traditions of this goddess, already encountered in the Koṭuṅkaḷūr festival of chapter 3, were modified somewhat in the process of being introduced to the Sinhala villagers of Śrī Lanka. The important symbol of the anklet remained, as did many of the stories, but the name "Pattini" or "Faithful Wife" changed the emphasis to focus on the patient and forgiving aspect of the Kaṇṇaki story. Worship of this goddess is now almost universal in Sinhala villages, and the Pattini temple's part of the procession focuses on the dances of girls of puberty age.[6]

Knox described the seventeenth-century processions as if they were formal political displays. Drummers, dancers, and elephants represented different regions, and the soldiers and their commanders marched at the rear to ensure that all was performed properly. Knox comments that the king himself normally marched in the procession, but when he had tried to cancel the festival in 1664, a major rebellion ensued. At the time of writing, Knox noted that the king himself was not walking in the procession but was delegating his role to the commander of the army (Knox 1958, p. 151).

This "early-medieval" part of the festival is similar to many others still celebrated in South India in Cōḻa-era temples. In most cases the celebration is more clearly based in one grand stone temple compound, with an associated goddess temple usually in the same compound, but the opening and closing ceremonies and the 10 days of processions are similar to those here. Although there are strong political overtones to all medieval-style festivals in the South Indian tradition, those in Kandy are more explicit than most. In this isolated mountain kingdom, the religious and the political were no longer easy for anyone to distinguish, especially as the next phase in the evolution of the festival developed.

Phase 3: The Eighteenth-Century Reforms

Kīrti Śrī Rājasimha, who ruled in Kandy from 1747 to 1782, ordered a total restructuring of the Kandy Perahara, and we have a contemporary account of that restructuring in the *Cūḷavamsa* or later (literally "smaller") chronicle of the Buddhist community. To explain the intentions of the king in ordering this reform, I provide some background into the complex ties of the Buddhist monasteries with the political structures of Śrī Lanka.

Even though the political history of Śrī Lanka has really been quite turbulent, the three "chronicles" composed by Buddhist monks at the end of three "crises" periods (fifth century, twelfth century, and eighteenth century) have provided a coherent account. The first account, called the *Mahāvamsa* (Geiger 1912), written by Mahānāma in the fifth century, justifies the arrangement in which King Dhātusena (460–478) had entrusted the cultural leadership of the landlord class to the Mahāvihāra monastery in the capital city of Anurādhapura. Inadvertently Mahānāma's story reveals historical clues about alternatives to that arrangement. He refers to the rival political center in Rohaṇa at the south of the island, to numerous Tamil̲ kings, to the rival dynasty of the Lambakannas that had a major hand in developing the irrigation works of the Anurādhapura region and had ruled for some time, and to the other monasteries of Jains and Buddhists that earlier kings had favored. Although the arrangement Dhātusena had with the Mahāvihāra monastery may have been relatively new at the time of writing, Mahānāma still demonstrated the idea that the political system of Śrī Lanka "should" operate in interdependence with the central monastic community of Buddhism.

In the second "chronicle," called the *Cūḷavamsa part I* (Geiger 1953a), the author, Dhammakitti, had the difficult task of maintaining the argument that Śrī Lankan kings "should" rule with the support of Buddhism, even though during the period in which he was writing Cōl̲a kings from South India, who were Hindu, ruled much of the time. In this case the story briefly mentions the Cōl̲as and then focuses on the career of the Śrī Lankan ruler Parakramabāhu I (1153–1186), who restored the alliance of the Buddhist monasteries and the court.

According to this account, the monastic order had fallen into such disorder during Cōl̲a rule that there were not enough monks to perform a proper ordination, and Parakramabāhu's predecessor, Vijayabāhu I, had to bring monks from Burma to reinstate the monastic order. During this state of disarray, the "chronicler" argues, the Buddhist legitimation of the ruler had come to reside not so much in the support of the monastery but in the king's possession of the sacred tooth relic of the Buddha. In the chronicler's view, Parakramabāhu's great accomplishment was that he had gone to Rohaṇa, where the tooth relic had been hidden at the time of the Cōl̲a conquest, and had brought it back to his capital.

The third "chronicle," *Cūḷavamsa part II* (Geiger 1953b), describes the political chaos between the twelfth and the eighteenth centuries, as the great "empires" of the irrigated lands in the north and central plains (Anurādhapura and Polonnaruwa) gave way to a number of smaller kingdoms, the most prominent ones being in the southwest of the island. Eventually one of the rulers of the mountain kingdom of Kandy, which is inland from the southwest coast, Vimaladhammasuriya I (1592–1604), was able to bring the tooth relic to his capital. In this kingdom Robert Knox witnessed the phase 2 festival already described. A century later the festival was radically restructured after a new ruling family took over in Kandy and another revival of the Buddhist order took place.

The first in a series of changes to the religious scene witnessed by Knox occurred, according to the Chronicle (Geiger 1953b, p. 77.46), during the reign of Narendrasimha, who died in 1739. This change involved building the Nātha temple in the main city square. Whereas the Nātha temple has all the same ritual arrangements as the more traditional temples scattered around the city, and participates fully in the opening and closing rituals of the festival (which the Tooth Temple does not), it is more Buddhist in some ways than the other temples or *devales*. Whereas a full study of the Nātha cult within the Buddhist tradition of Śrī Lanka has not yet been undertaken, and ties with Śaivism or the Nātha ascetics of North India might be uncovered, the Buddhist worshipers today link the deity called Nātha with one or another of the Buddhist *bodhisattvas*. (The monks tend to identify Nātha with the *bodhisattva* Avalokitesvara, the embodiment of compassion, but laymen more often say that Nātha is the future *bodhisattva* or Maitreya.) The subsequent reorganization of the festival (about to be described) finally established the primacy of Nātha by placing his procession after that of the Tooth Temple and before the others.

In 1739 the Kandyan kingdom underwent a major crisis. The chieftains of the regions around Kandy, the powerful *radala* aristocracy, were not sure how to proceed when the ruler Narendrasimha died without leaving an heir. The Dutch colonists, who had by this time taken over from the Portuguese in the coastal areas, were tempted to move against the weakened inland kingdom, but they too held back partly because the *salagama* cinnamon pickers the Portuguese had brought from India were threatening to cut off the all-important spice trade from the mountains if their inland refuge was taken away and partly because the alliance of conservative chieftains around Kandy posed no threat to the Dutch control of trade. Unlike the Portuguese, the Dutch had no interest in seeking conversions and no interest in administrative reform, as the British would have when they took over as colonial rulers in 1815. So it was in their interest to allow the conservative chieftains to continue to rule the area around Kandy. Both the Kandyan chiefs and the Dutch were surprised when the brother of Narendrasimha's widow, Śrī Vijaya Rājasimha, declared himself the king in 1739.

Like many Śrī Lankan rulers, Narendrasimha had gone to South India to find a bride with royal credentials. Her family included *nāyakkars* or local governors in South India, but their territory had been run over during the French and British wars, and much of her family accompanied her back to the quiet of Kandy after the marriage. Even the Buddhist chronicle acknowledges that this family of *nāyakkars* were staunch Hindus when they arrived in Śrī Lanka. Once they claimed the throne, however, they recognized their opportunity and restored the old tradition of legitimizing the power of the court by aligning it with the Buddhist tradition.

However, no strict Buddhist monastic orders were left, and the Buddhist temples and monasteries were under the control of *ganinnanses*, who were noncelibate monks. It was not long, however, before a zealous novice, Valivita Saranaṅkara, set out a plan to recruit properly ordained monks from Thailand and undertake a major reform of the monastic order. Śrī Vijaya Rājasimha gave the novice his full support and went one step further by deciding to take the tooth relic out of hiding, build a grand Tooth Temple to house it, and thus provide a focus for the religious life of the kingdom. According to the chronicler, when the officials tried to open the door to the room where the mysterious relic was housed, the key would not work. The king then personally opened it, in joy prostrated before the relic, and then carried it outside so that all the people could see it and worship. In this act was born a new kind of worship experience for Śrī Lankan Buddhists.

Śrī Vijaya Rājasimha's successor, Kīrti Śrī Rājasimha (1747–1782), had a secure throne and was able to accelerate the reforms his predecessor had started. Thai monks were able to arrive in 1753, and now that he was properly ordained, the novice Saranaṅkara was given a new semipolitical title as "Sangharāja," or monastic administrator, which allowed him to control all ordinations in the new monastic structures. Using this power shrewdly, he appointed a network of *goyigama* or landlord-caste monks, who quickly took back the extensive landholdings of the *sangha* and used their influence in support of the king, sometimes against the more conservative *radala* chiefs.

The religious reforms of the *nāyakkars* reached a final climax when Kīrti Śrī Rājasimha drastically restructured the annual temple festival so that it came to be led by a grand procession from the Tooth Temple housing the relic of the Buddha. Here is the account of that reform as seen by the Buddhist chronicler:

> After the performance of a *pūjā* [worship] festival for the lotus-colored patron deity [Alutnūwara or Viṣṇu] and the other deities who were recognized as bringers of *mangalam* [auspiciousness] even in the days of the former rulers of Lanka, he then had a military display organized in which the whole town was made like the city of the gods. He gathered together the people from all over Lanka, and in the town he made the people from different provinces dwell in different places, and provided them each with identification standards. Then he had the *ayūdhas* from the temples of the gods placed on the backs of elephants. He then had the elephants surrounded by troops of drummers and tambourine players and dancers. These were in turn followed by troops of elephants and horses, by Brāhman priests, by people carrying umbrellas and fly whisks, by groups of women and dignitaries, by people carrying swords and shields, spears and other *ayūdhas*, by people carrying banners, by people coming from various regions and speaking a variety of languages, by artists and artisans. With these and many other people he has the elephant surrounded, ordering them himself to go before or behind. Thereupon the King set forth, like the prince of the gods, with great royal splendour and marched around the whole town, with his right side turned inwards [the proper direction for circumambulating a sacred object]. Finally the whole procession returned.
>
> When the King of kings, full of faith and wisdom, was in the habit of holding the Asāḷa festival, he thought he ought also to celebrate a festival for the Buddha. Then he had a canopy embroidered in gold fastened on the back of the royal elephant. Then he had the elephant, whose tusk is as white as the bright moon, decorated with ornaments and surrounded by other elephants whose riders held silver umbrellas and fly whisks and flowers of every kind. . . . Finally the Lord of men placed the splendid sparkling casket of gold in which the bodily relic of the Buddha was contained carefully under the canopy and by strewing flowers made flowers to rain upon it. With shouts of "Hail!", and the sound of shell trumpets and cymbals and the rattle of drums the people celebrated the festival. Good and pious people, their hearts filled with astonishment and admiration, their hands folded before their brow, paid reverence. . . . Then placing at the head the relic, which holds the first place among all things worthy of reverence by gods,

men or demons, he ordered the rest, such as the *suras* [deities] and men to follow. He himself in royal splendour, to the tunes of hymns of praise which promised happiness, set forth in all the majesty of a great king, with great munificence showing men how even thus the King of the gods in the city of the gods celebrates the festival for the relic (Geiger 1953b, p. 99.42–65).

The present festival could not be more faithful to the description here. There are elephants, drummers, dancers, banner carriers, dignitaries, and so on, just as described in the chronicle. The one significant change is that the office of Diyavaḍana Nilame replaces the king at the rear of the procession, but the person holding that office, from the local aristocracy, is chosen in an election among his peers and dresses in the ancient kingly dress. For the four temple processions a similar lay official representing the king was and is appointed with the title of Basnayake Nilame. In a full monograph entitled *Rituals of the Kandyan State* (1978) H. L. Seneviraratne provides a detailed description of how each of the nine *raṭa* (nearby wards of the king's territory) and twelve *disā* (autonomous provinces) met their obligation to send drummers, dancers, and elephants to the festival along with their chieftain, so as to ceremonially signify their loyalty to the king.

In many ways the restructuring of the festival could be described as the work of an ambitious ruler of Hindu background who recognized the power of the traditional festival of the temple deities and used his control of the Tooth Relic of the Buddha to add that to the older celebration of the society and its links with cosmic meaning. What happened as a result of this reform of the Buddhist role in the society is, however, somewhat more complex than even Kīrti Śrī Rājasimha probably envisioned.

First, the Buddhist monastic order was not comfortable participating in a traditional (primarily Hindu) festival. The monastic order, which Saranaṅkara restarted, does not allow its members to actually march in the procession, but as caretakers of the tooth relic, they now play a visible role in the rituals of the Tooth Temple and other arrangements of the festival. (The official monastic order has since split into the two branches of the Asgiriya and Malvatte, but they serve the Tooth Temple in alternate years and play identical roles in the ritual when on duty.)

A vivid ritual reminder of the difficulty the monks had with Kīrti Śrī Rājasimha's reforms and desire to have the Tooth Temple join in the procession of the more traditional deities is evident in one final procession. In this special procession the relic casket is taken to an ancient monastery for a few hours (while the processions of the other deities are at the water cutting by the river). Just an hour after the end of the grand final public procession (about 3 AM on the full moon night), a small procession takes only the relic casket on the back of an elephant to this ancient monastery. This time the procession goes directly to the Geḍigē Vihāre shrine, housed in the monastery now run by the Asgiriya sect. When the procession reaches it, the relic casket is handled by the head monk (not the Diyavaḍana Nilame as in the processions), who sets it on the flower table and reads an official list of all the jewels embedded in the casket. He then puts it in the shrine room, where it can be worshiped until 2 PM the next day. At that time it is taken back to the Tooth Temple in the "Day Perahara" and is followed the last part of the way by the other four processions that have come back from the water cutting. Presumably this quick visit to the monastery acknowledges the authority the monastery still holds over the relic, where it is thought to have been housed before the Tooth Temple was built within the royal compound.

The links between the worship of temple deities and the worship of the Buddha constitute a structural interdependence in Theravada Buddhism about which quite a bit has been written. Some of these analyses (Ames 1964) concentrate on the contrasts between the elite meditative forms of Buddhism and the action-oriented rituals of the minor gods and goddesses. Obeyesekere (1966, 1977, 1978, 1981, 1984, 1988) gives more attention to the major Hindu/Buddhist deities Kataragama and Pattini, but he also does not provide a long-range historical perspective and explain the importance in medieval times of a deity such as Upulvan/Alutnūwara. The Kandy festival provides a rich picture of a structure of interaction that changes over time and allows both the priests of the deities and the monks of Buddhism to claim differing forms of priority in the worship experience of the people.

Today this festival has been affected by government and media interference to a degree not apparent in any of the other festivals I have studied. Even in medieval times the festival had an explicit political role, and the British colonial government, and now the elected Śrī Lankan government, has seen an important opportunity here to legitimize its hold on power (Swearer 1982). The political is, however, not the only theme the festival activity addresses. If the present equation of Sinhala culture, Buddhism, and national government were to fade a bit, it might once again become possible to reflect on Sinhala culture in its historical perspective and realize the variety of symbols hidden within this festival celebration. With the political symbols now so dominant, it is no longer easy to see what earlier worshipers saw in either the ancient forest rituals or the early medieval processions of the gods and goddess. Kīrti Śrī Rājasimha tried to bring the popularity of the older festival symbols into the service of the state and the Buddhist order with which it was allied. His modified festival now serves primarily as a state-sponsored celebration of national identity, but the older symbols, with their rich variety of religious and social meanings, are still present and deeply cherished by many worshipers.

Conclusion

In this account of the Kandy Perahara I have emphasized the important stages in the development of the festival ritual. The two important changes I have tried to identify occurred in the early and late part of the medieval period, respectively. Both changes involved kings, with the support of the landed aristocracy, modifying the festival to assert their views of the proper social order.

The earliest festival cannot really be reconstructed with any accuracy, but the seven days of ritual dances, called the Valiyak Netum, which take place only in the temple of Alutnūwara/Viṣṇu, are a kind of precious museum piece of the past. This part of the festival has none of the political atmosphere of the processions and is an intense engagement with the primordial powers of the forest, as it uses magical drama to neutralize and control those forces. This part of the festival reminds one of the concern with primordial forest power in the festivals of Ayyappaṉ (chapter 1) and Kataragama (chapter 2), but in those cases the festival activity continues to center around a return to those forest settings. In this case, the more formal ritual activities of medieval times, which involved processions of sacred symbols and important social leaders through the major urban centers, have taken central stage but have left the older festival intact, as people say, "lest something go terribly wrong."

In the second form of the festival, the prescribed structure of Cōḻa-era festivals, with their elaborate opening and closing ceremonies and 10 days of processions, is so clear that one is tempted to believe that this form of the festival might well date back as far as the era of Cōḻa rule in Polonnaruwa. Details of the ritual certainly reflect a local Sinhala calendar and taste: the festival preparations start on the new moon, the cutting of the sapling in the opening ritual and the cutting of the water in the closing ceremony are all local features, but the general structure is uniform throughout the medieval period. More research needs to be done to delineate in what sense Upulvan/Alutnūwara is the "god of heaven and earth" in medieval Śrī Lanka, but the central role of the festival in the society Knox describes can hardly be doubted. One can certainly imagine that festival serving to integrate the social order almost as effectively as any of the other medieval festivals one sees in other places.

Finally, the late-medieval style of festival introduced in the eighteenth century went much further than usual in allowing the king to arrange the festival and participate in it. The fact that a king decided on these new arrangements is not particularly surprising, for there were *nāyakkars* or regional kings in South India doing much the same thing at this time (Breckenridge 1978). What is almost unprecedented is that the explicitly Buddhist symbol of the Tooth Relic was included in the celebration. The monks' restrained and distant participation in the celebration has probably allowed this dramatic innovation to work, in that the innovation remains a political act that does not really change the meditative foundation of Buddhist practice nor challenge the unconscious or "deep" structure in which the earlier festival celebration of the deities had taken place.

This festival certainly demonstrates more clearly than most the level of implicit values and social meanings a society associates with its festivals. Looking at the *Cūḷavamsa*'s account of Kīrti Śrī Rājasimha's reform of the festival, one might conclude that he thought he could design it to express whatever values he wanted to impose on his society, and one might conclude that its continued celebration still ties the society in some degree to his value system. Supporting this interpretation is the fact that the *radala* aristocracy in the region continues to see the festival as upholding its traditional role in society; members of this aristocracy still carefully elect members of its leading families to the important tasks of Divyavaḍana Nilame of the Tooth Temple and Basnayake Nilame of each of the other shrines. In recent years many of these festival officials have even been able to use this exposure to secure appointment or election to prominent positions in government. When at the end of the festival these quasi-political figures march to the ancient palace beside the Temple of the Tooth and make a formal phone call to the president of Śrī Lanka to say that all has been accomplished as originally ordered by the king, one wonders if we are watching ritual ceremony or the exercise of real political power.

In a social sense, the past lives on in that the traditional arrangement, in which the procession moved down the street on which the houses of the aristocracy were arranged in an ordered sequence, has been modified only slightly in that now there is a "bleacher" erected right in the royal square that contains boxes for the prominent families, who now enjoy even more public exposure than before. The continued "display" of the dancers, drummers, and elephants from the different regions also conveys the message that the aristocracy of those regions still "leads" the society in its celebration.

Yet for most worshipers something cosmic still takes place when this festival is properly conducted. The specific sign of that cosmic transaction is that the monsoon rains are thought to depend on the ritual of the festival, but for most people the cosmic power is really most evident in the fact that events in their lives go well and the enemies who could harm them are held at bay. In this sense, the festival is a celebration of civilization. Whereas that includes the aristocratic hierarchy in its deepest form, it starts with rituals associated with Upulvan/Varuṇa, the protector of the island, who is especially responsible for the cosmic waters. In spite of the prominence of the social values set forth in this festival, one can still sense a deeper level of meaning in which the primordial powers of the forest and cosmos are acknowledged and respected even as the order of the civilized domain is affirmed.

Looking toward the explicit and contemporary meanings the festival might hold, an outside observer familiar with the recent tensions between the Hindus and Buddhists in Śrī Lanka might think that the "message" of this festival is to be read in terms of those issues. (Some have suggested the festival celebrates the "triumph of Buddhism" and others that it points to a "reconciliation of Hinduism and Buddhism".) Certainly the monk Saranaṅkara had explicit theological concerns at the time of the eighteenth-century reform, and Kīrti Śri Rājasimha certainly had specific political goals as he tried to force loyalty out of the *radala* aristocracy and fight the Dutch threats (which eventually forced him to sign a treaty with them in 1766). There definitely is a touch of Buddhist chauvinism in the festival organizers of today, and one can quickly bring that to the surface if one asks them explicitly whether this festival might help the cause of Sinhala Buddhist nationalism. On the other hand, the atmosphere surrounding the festival is such that it would not seem quite right for monks to participate in the procession, and most of the worshipers intensely involved in the festival see it as a direct encounter with a deity through the *kāpa* or *ayūdha* symbol on which they focus their attention. The monk Saranaṅkara and the king Kīrti Śrī Rājasimha were certainly able to show that dramatic changes in the celebration of a festival could be made and its meaning no doubt modified in the process, but the power of the ancient forms and ancient meanings endures because they continued to be relevant. The explicit concerns of this monk and king were expressed clearly in the eighteenth century, but one should not forget that they had been obliged by the widely understood grammar of meaning in such festival settings to express themselves in that form. Their efforts amounted to a dramatic restructuring of the festival, but the character of the festival remained intact. The deeper meanings others had always found in it seem to continue, even into the politically turbulent Śrī Lanka of today.[7]

7

Singing the Tamil̲ Hymnbook

The Adhyayanōtsava Festival in Śrīraṅkam

Introduction

Whereas the Paṅkuṇi Uttiram festival in the Śrīraṅkam temple (chapter 4), described as the *ati* or "original" festival, is full of mysterious archaic events that no one can account for very well, the origin of the Adhyayanōtsava (or Recitation) Festival of that temple is directly related to a crisis a group of priests faced in the fifteenth century. The *Kōyil Ol̲uku* (Hari Rao 1961) or temple chronicle they produced at that time describes their intentions. There are three other Brahmōtsavas or 10-day processional festivals in the temple's tradition, but the Adhyayanōtsava, which attracts the largest crowds of the year to the temple, has all the ornate pageantry of a great medieval festival of South India.

This festival's central feature is the chanting of the *Nālāyira Divya Prabandham*, or the 4,000 hymns of the *āl̲vārs* or Tamil̲ Vaiṣṇava saints. This ceremonial chanting of the Tamil̲ hymnbook indirectly establishes the authority of the Teṅkalai school of priests, the group that reintroduced a theological tradition associated with the name of Rāmānuja when they restored worship in the temple after the Muslim armies had desecrated it early in the fourteenth century. Notwithstanding the intentions of the Teṅkalai school, the thousands who attend the festival call upon some of the more primitive patterns of worship associated with the temple and incorporate elements from the continually changing worship environment of the surrounding culture.

I hope to demonstrate how the historical consciousness of the Teṅkalai school is incorporated into the overall religious meaning of a popular temple festival. The discussion has three sections: the first generally describes the festival, the second examines the reconstruction of historical events implicit in the festival symbols, and the third asks what kind of religious meaning the present worshipers find in this festival.

The Festival

This 21-day festival falls into two main parts and a 1-day footnote. The first 10 days are called Pagal Pattu or "The Ten Daytimes." During this period the festival image of the deity is moved each day from his inner sanctum at the heart of the temple to a small room in the second *pirakāram* (surrounding walkway). There, in the presence of images of *āl̲vārs* (saints) and *ācāryas* (teachers) and a hundred or so priests and worshipers, hymns are sung. This part of the festival, sometimes called Tirumol̲i-utsava, after the first half of the Tamil̲ canon, which is sung during this period, is generally thought of as not open to the public. As the second 10-day festival begins, the scene shifts dramatically. The northern gateway between the second and third *pirakārams* is opened for the only time during the year. The image of the deity is taken in procession out of this northern gateway and through hallways to the eastern portion of the fourth *pirakāram*, where it is set in the Thousand Pillared Maṇṭapa, designed as a vast *ratha* or heavenly chariot. During this part of the festival, this hall becomes Vaikuṇṭa or Heaven. Because the timings of heaven are the reversal of those on earth, the chanting of the hymns for the next 10 days takes place during the night, and this part of the festival, sometimes called Rā-pattu or "The Ten Nighttimes," is also called Tiruvāymol̲i-utsava, after the second half of the canon, which is recited at this time. The 1-day footnote to the festival is virtually unknown to the ordinary worshipers, for only a few gather as a different family of priests recites the *Iyar̲pā* section of the canon, which consists of almost 1,000 hymns, after the ceremonial return of the image into the inner sanctum of the temple at the end of the second 10-day festival.

The central activity of the festival is the recitation of the 4,000 hymns of the Tamil̲ canon. In the format for the recitation of the second half of the canon, in the public setting of the Thousand Pillared Hall, the images of the *āl̲vārs* and the *ācāryas* are brought one by one from their respective shrines in the temple compound and are arranged along the end and two sides of the rectangle facing the throne of the deity, as if they were participating in a seminar. Then the representatives of the leading Brāhman families of the temple arrange themselves on the floor in front of these images. Finally, the male members of a family of *araiyars* or traditional chanters and actors enter; after requests from the deity and the saints, they begin their recitation, formal chants of the memorized hymns accompanied by a steady beat on tiny cymbals. The three to five male members of the family, ranging in age from about 12 to over 80, stand before the deity and chant in unison. Two or three times during the recitation, one family member recites a full commentary of a hymn while others look on the text and prompt him, and two or three times one family member steps forward and performs a highly formal dance illustrating the theme of the hymn.[1]

The college of *āl̲vārs* and *ācāryas* before whom the hymns are recited is treated like a galaxy of mythological beings who are fed, bathed, and worshiped much as the deity is. The *āl̲vārs* are recognized as the sages who served as the authors of these hymns, and the author of each block of hymns is well known. The legendary tales about each of the *āl̲vārs* are rehearsed repeatedly in conversations as the crowd mills around during the breaks in the recitation.

In addition to the 11 *āl̲vārs*, the company brought to hear the recitation of the hymns includes four others: Tirukkacinampi, the non-Brāhman teacher of Rāmānuja; Rāmānuja himself (who in these contexts is always called Uṭaiyavar or "the Lord"); Kurattāl̲vān, the one to whom Rāmānuja is said to have passed on his spiritual authority; and Piḷḷai Lōkācārya, who was the first head of the Teṅkalai priesthood after this school was supposed to have been clearly distinguished from the Vaṭakalai school. Many other *ācāryas* are omitted, including the great teachers Nātamuni and Yāmuna, who preceded Rāmānuja, and Vedānta Deśika, the great scholar now considered the leader of the Vaṭakalai faction of priests. The selection is a clear indication of the special interests of the Teṅkalai priests, who use this festival to establish a close relationship between the Tamil̲ hymnary and Rāmānuja, the universally acknowledged Śrīvaiṣṇava teacher.

The central role of Rāmānuja or Uṭaiyavar in the *caṅkam* or college of *āl̲vārs* and *ācāryas* that listens to the recitation is emphasized at every opportunity. As the images are brought from their respective shrines, as they are fed, as they are addressed by the priests, and as they are approached in worship, a strict order of precedence prevails. The *āl̲vārs* Nammāl̲vār and Tirumaṅkai, and the *ācārya* Uṭaiyavar, are always called upon first, after which come Periyāl̲vār, Maturakavi, Poykai, Pūtatt, Pey, Kulacēkara, Tiruppāṇ, Toṇṭaraṭipoṭi, Tirumal̲icai, and, at the end the remaining *ācāryas* Tirukkacinampi, Kurattāl̲vān, and Piḷḷai Lōkācārya. When they are arranged on the three sides of the rectangle facing the deity, Nammāl̲vār is in the center of the far end directly in front of the deity, with Tirumaṅkai to his left and Uṭaiyavar to his right. At many points in the ceremony only these three images accompany that of the deity, and they are then seen as the "ministers" of his court.[2] Finally, after all the hymns have been sung and the *āl̲vārs* and *ācāryas* have been returned to their shrines, the image of the deity is taken to the shrine of Uṭaiyavar, so that the deity may thank him for arranging the recitation. There, a well-known hymn, called *Rāmānuja Nūṟṟantāti*, is sung to Rāmānuja. The images of Rāmānuja and the deity are then said to joke about who should be showing respect to whom, after which the image of the deity returns to his inner sanctum.

In addition to giving religious importance to the Tamil̲ hymns, and the *āl̲vārs* and *ācāryas*, the organization of the festival clearly spells out the importance of the hundreds of Brāhmans who serve the deity, as well as the primacy of the Teṅkalai half of the Brāhman company. Although both Teṅkalai and Vaṭakalai priests serve in the temple, only Teṅkalai Brāhmans can receive "honors" in this temple. And even among the Teṅkalai certain priestly lineages claim that Rāmānuja gave them special tasks. Members of those lineages are the first to receive honors, to receive food, or to lead any procession with the image.

As I have said, the arrangement for the recitation is as follows: after the image of the deity is brought to his throne, and the images of the *āl̲vārs* and *ācāryas* are set on three sides of the rectangular courtyard before him, the Brāhmans who serve in the temple enter and arrange themselves in rows up and down the sides of the rectangle, with the leading lineages nearest Nammāl̲vār, Tirumaṅkai, and Uṭaiyavar. Sitting with their torsos bare, their heads shaved back to the crown, and the vertical marks of a Śrīvaiṣṇava on their forehead, the Brāhmans, clearly set apart from the worshipers, are recognized as part of the divine court that includes *āl̲vārs*, *ācāryas*, and Brāhmans together.

When the recitation finishes each day, this separation from ordinary humanity appears even more clearly. A rope is set around the area, and the priests on duty serve food and water in the following sequence: first to the deity, then to the *āl̲vārs* and *ācāryas*, and then priestly families, each called by name. As representatives of each family come forward, they receive *betel* leaves, *tōcais* or pancakes, and *vaṭais* or cupcake-shaped snacks that have been prepared in the large temple kitchen. After the final recitation on the last day of the festival, a huge crowd gathers to watch, as a special Brāhman feast is held in which over 12,000 *tōcais* and *vaṭais* are distributed in the same way, with each family carrying home huge baskets. In this case, the hungry throng is deterred by a stout bamboo barrier through which they cry (to no avail) for a small morsel.

In other festivals of the temple, the Teṅkalai priests and the Vaṭakalai priests appear to be roughly equal in number; when they go in procession with the image of the deity, the Teṅkalais, chanting Tamiḻ hymns, go before the image of the deity, and the Vaṭakalais come behind chanting Sanskrit hymns. This arrangement is widely followed in Śrīvaiṣṇava temples where both groups are represented and likely dates back to the time when the priesthood split into two groups, with the Teṅkalai or "Southerners" wanting to emphasize the Tamiḻ hymns and the doctrine of *pirapatti* or surrender, whereas the Vaṭakalais or "Northerners" wanted to emphasize Sanskrit and the need for devotion or *pakti* (Sanskrit: *bhakti*) manifest in self-discipline. Some Vaṭakalai families in Śrīraṅkam have the traditional right to serve the deity in the inner sanctum, and others have a reputation for great scholarship, but the Teṅkalai lineages have won a series of court tests that have supported their claim to the exclusive right to receive "honors" or *varicai* in Śrīraṅkam.

In this festival, "honors" are a prominent part of the ritual. Each day after the recitation ends and the deity and his court have been fed, the priest on duty (on behalf of the deity) calls out the names of the leading Teṅkalai families. As their names are called, they go in turn to receive from the deity sandal paste, water, an opportunity to wear the deity's garland, and, most important, an opportunity to have the deity's red and gold rope or *parivaṭṭam* tied around their heads, and, finally, an opportunity to have the *caṭakōpam* (a crown-like object with an impression of the deity's feet on it) touched to each of the four sides of their heads. (Other worshipers follow and receive from the deity only the water and sandal paste and a single touch of the *caṭakōpam*.) Even though this same group receives honors in all the festivals, their prominence in this festival, coupled with the fact that the Vaṭakalais do not accept the primacy of the Tamiḻ hymns, means that Vaṭakalais acknowledge this festival as Teṅkalai and attend only a few of the most important events.

Even among the Teṅkalais, the order of precedence is fiercely contested, and the rituals of this festival provide the best opportunity for families to test the acceptance of their respective claims. Ranking at the top now are various branches of the Bhaṭṭar family, which claims to trace its line to Kurattāḻvāṉ, appointed by Rāmānuja as head priest; the Vādula Deṣika family, which lost its role for a time during the Vicayanakaram period but which claims to have inherited the role of temple administrator from their ancestor Āṇḍāṉ, appointed to that job by Rāmānuja; and the Śrīraṅkanāta Jīyar or the ascetic appointed to carry on Rāmānuja's *matam* or monastery in the northern precincts of the temple.[3] Some families have brought court cases to press their claims to precedence before a succession of Vicayanakaram, Nāyakkar, Muslim, and British rulers.

In addition to the status accorded to certain families by the order in which the names are called for "honors," the highest ceremonial honor is accorded when, as a final climax to the whole festival, a senior member of one of the leading families is carried home in procession, dressed in special robes, jewelry, and headdress, preceded by the temple elephant. He is carried on a special platform called a *brāhma ratha* and is generally accorded all the reverence usually reserved for the deity. This honor, which the temple chronicle tells us was once reserved for the head priest, is now accorded to senior members of different leading families, with one Bhaṭṭar and one Araiyar receiving the honor the year I witnessed the festival.

Although the explicit structure of the festival centers around the recitation of the Tamil̠ canon and the accompanying glorification of *āl̠vārs*, *ācāryas*, and Brāhmans, the general body of worshipers pays little attention to this elaborate exercise. Large crowds join the festival only on four special occasions. On two of these occasions, there is virtually no connection with the reading of the Tamil̠ canon at all; one must look to the more primordial patterns in the worship of this temple to understand why they are included in the festival.[4] In the other two cases, the recitation serves at least as a backdrop, for it calls to mind moments of repentance and final liberation in the lives of the two leading *āl̠vārs* and therefore provides the occasion for dramatic presentations of those stories.

The first of these four popular events in the festival is the opening of the northern gateway, which marks the beginning of the second half of the festival. This event, which takes place when the sacred *ēkātaci* star appears, draws over 100,000 visitors to Śrīraṅkam. Many believe it to be a festival itself called Vaikuṇṭa Ēkātaci or "Heavenly Ēkātaci." North and east are the directions of the divine realm, and the ornate gateways of the temples mark the boundaries through which one moves from one cosmic realm to another. In the intensely theistic religious atmosphere of Śrīraṅkam, the deity is, in his ultimate form, distant and transcendent, in spite of the playful forays into the ordinary world made by his processional image during festival periods. The opening of the northern gateway is thus an awesome occasion and provides the worshiper with the only opportunity of the year to literally step out of this world and into the heavenly transcendent realm.

The note of transcendence has always been the primary note in the worship of Śrīraṅkam; many people head back home after stepping through the northern gateway. Yet, a note of joyful delight and romantic intimacy is kept alive by the bathing party in the lotus pond Candrapuṣkaraṇi on the last afternoon of the festival. As a crowd of thousands gathers on the courtyards and towers above the pond, everyone talks about the beauty of the bright winter sun of Mārkal̠i (December–January), and the erotic excitement of the young girls, resembling the hymnsinger Āṇṭāḷ,[5] as they splash in the cold water of the ponds and rivers during this month. As the predominantly female crowd gathers on the stairs leading down to the pond, the priests take hours preparing the image of the deity for his bath, and a few young boys get overanxious and dive from the towers. Finally the image goes into the water, and hundreds of women hasten to get into the water, which has been made especially sacred by the presence of the deity. As their *sāris* mix with the lotus blossoms in the pond, the whole scene demonstrates the deity's *saulabhya* or willingness to make himself intimate and "easy of access," but it also portrays the natural joy, freedom, and innocent eroticism that the Śrīraṅkam temple generally and Āṇṭāḷ's hymns particularly have always held to be one characteristic of the devotee's relation with the deity.

Although these two popular events are true to the primordial patterns of worship in Śrīraṅkam, they have hardly any relationship to the singing of the Tamil̠ hymns. The other two popular events, dramatizations of aspects of the lives of the two most famous of the *āl̠vārs*, are only slightly more closely related to the general hymnsinging format.

On the eighteenth day, the schedule is adjusted, with the procession of the deity to the Thousand Pillared hall starting at noon rather than at dusk. A huge crowd gathers in the large open courtyard of the third *pirakāram* for the dramatic presentation of the story of Tirumaṅkai, the robber *āl̠vār*, who plundered the deity's marriage party but later repented and became one of his faithful ministers. When the image of the deity is brought into the courtyard riding on a life-sized golden horse, the 30 men carrying the image race back and forth to show the deity to be a fun-loving bridegroom. Then small boys carrying sticks aloft race into the enclosure and surround the deity until the image of Tirumaṅkai, as the chief of the robbing party, arrives. Then, to the sound of wild music, the boys surrounding the image of Tirumaṅkai run off with boxes holding the deity's goods. But the deity is said to have whispered in Tirumaṅkai's ear,[6] and the crowd waits anxiously. As darkness descends, the image of the robber is brought back dressed in the white robes of repentance, with his weapons hanging down at his side. As the crowd gathers silently around, the Araiyars sing the famous hymn of repentance beginning with the words *vāṭinenati varuntinen.* Accepting his repentance, the deity immediately makes him, along with Uṭaiyavar (Rāmānuja) and Nammāḻvār, part of his entourage.

On the twentieth day of the festival a fitting climax is reached with the fourth popular event as crowds gather to commemorate Nammāḻvār's attainment of *mokṣa* or salvation. Again the image of the deity is brought to the recitation early, and on his way he is greeted by Nammāḻvār, bare-chested and covered in 12 places with the "Y" marks or *nāmams*, which the Teṅkalai Brāhmans wear on their foreheads. After the recitation of special hymns, the usual format for the nighttime recitation goes on, but on this occasion there is great excitement in the air. Throughout the night the crowd swells. As the recitation of the Araiyars goes on in the Thousand Pillared Maṇṭapa, the other corridors and courtyards of the temple come alive in a more informal way as devotees of Śivaṉ, Ayyappaṉ, Murukaṉ, and Māriyammaṉ, as well as those of Viṣṇu, form circles in which they clap and sing to their favorite deity. By 6 AM the crowd looks uncontrollable, and the priests seem worried for their safety and that of the image, as they carry the image of Nammāḻvār from its usual place to the throne of the deity. As they approach the throne, the deity's feet are said to be placed on the head of Nammāḻvār. At that moment the image of Nammāḻvār suddenly disappears (believed to be absorbed by the deity), and then hundreds of baskets of *tulaci* leaves are poured on the feet of the deity and are then sent off to temples all over India. As Nammāḻvār's image disappears, hundreds in the crowd swoon.

The dramatizations of the repentance of Tirumaṅkai, with its afternoon playfulness, and of the final salvation of Nammāḻvār, in the early morning stillness, set forth the primordial themes of intimacy and transcendence, but emphasize the way they are experienced in the life of the saintly devotee. The crowds find these familiar themes portrayed not in the ritual acts of opening the door and bathing in the pond but in enactments of the lives of model devotees who, like themselves, longed to find the way in which God meets them in their weakness and then transports them into ultimate oneness with himself.

The Historical Quest

For hundreds of years there has been a rift between the Teṅkalai and Vaṭakalai priests within the Śrīvaiṣṇava community. The rift has produced such intense suspicion that even modern scholars find it difficult to write about Śrīvaiṣṇavism without being accused of bias by one side or the other. Most traditional accounts of the origin of the dispute trace it to differing theological emphases among the followers of Rāmānuja, who were based in the temples of Śrīraṅkam (Teṇkalai) and Kāñcipuram (Vaṭakalai) between the time of his death (1137?) and the Muslim invasions (1313 and 1323). When, toward the end of the period, Śrīraṅkam asked the great scholar Vedānta Deśika to come from Kāñcipuram and help with a challenge debate from the Śaiva followers of Śaṅkara, he stayed on and thus possibly raised the issue of which school had the right to serve in the great Śrīraṅkam temple. The formal dispute between the two schools probably started in earnest at the end of the fourteenth century, when worship restarted in the Śrīvaiṣṇava temples of Tamiḻnāṭu after they had been desecrated by Muslim armies and left empty for 50 years. During the restoration, priests from both sects took up residence in most temples, and, with the Vicayanakaram rulers arranging for lavish support of the temples, the test of which group could win the right to receive honors from the temple deity began in earnest.

The heart of the Vaṭakalai argument was that their teaching had the authority of the Veda, the revealed Sanskrit scripture. The antiquity of the argument that the Veda was the revealed authority of Indian religion is not very clear. Certainly Śaṅkara in the eighth century made it the cornerstone of his system of philosophy; from then on, his position stood as one all other teachers had to reckon with. Temple practice was, however, a primitive and eclectic pattern of religious behavior, which, while possibly not out of accord with Vedic revelation, had not been directly derived from the teachings of the Veda. Śaṅkara, although nominally a Śaiva who has been credited with some temple reform, argued that the worship in the temples was directed to the *saguṇa Brahman* or the deity with attributes, whereas the highest level of worship is directed to the *nirguṇa Brahman* or the attribute-less Reality. Śaṅkara's followers have generally left the Śaiva temples to run in their traditional ways and have concentrated on gaining control of the *matams* or monasteries, where the teachings of the master are thought to be properly preserved.

The new emphasis on the authority of the Veda proved to be more complex for Vaiṣṇava temples than it had been for Śaivas. Rāmānuja in the twelfth century had echoed Śaṅkara's theme of Vedic authority, but he had also argued that the traditional Śrīvaiṣṇava literature, called the *Pañcarātra*, was also authoritative and that the interpreter had to follow the spirit of both in interpreting. He had also argued that the philosophy of the Veda held that the soul and the world were in a "qualified way" different from the Lord or Brahman, and therefore that the *pakti* (Sanskrit: *bhakti*) or devotion of the soul expressed in temple worship was not a lower form of religion but the true realization of *mokṣa*. All the Śrīvaiṣṇavas agreed that Rāmānuja's system continued to make temple worship essential, but the Vaṭakalais contended that there should be a greater emphasis on the Sanskrit Veda in the light of the teachings of Śaṅkara and Rāmānuja. This emphasis would give less attention to the Tamiḻ hymns and their characteristic teaching of devotion as abject surrender or *pirapatti* and would allow for a lesser role for the goddess and the saints as intermediaries between the soul and the highest Lord. The Teṅkalais of the fifteenth century recognized the need to acknowledge the authority of the Veda, but they felt that the heart of Rāmānuja's contribution had been that it maintained the traditional system of worship while providing it with intellectual support through the introduction of a particular form of Vedic interpretation.

To demonstrate that their traditional patterns of worship had been set in the context of a renewed awareness of Vedic authority by Rāmānuja, the Teṅkalais had to accomplish three ends: (1) argue that their Tamil̲ hymns were to be understood as Veda, (2) show that the universally accepted Śrīvaiṣṇava teacher Rāmānuja had provided detailed instruction on the recitation of Tamil̲ hymns, and (3) show that the tradition he established had been maintained in the lineages of priests down to the present. To make these points, the Teṅkalai priests organized the festival I have described and started a history called *Temple Chronicle* (*Kōyil Ol̲uku*), which is one of the few documents of sectarian history found in the Indian tradition. I now turn to an examination of that chronicle.

From the fourteenth to the nineteenth centuries, when it was being recorded, the *Chronicle* was a surprisingly detailed and clear account of how the priestly families' fortunes rose and fell, how various kings affected the fortunes of the temple, and how a few disputes on ritual procedures and on relations with the neighboring Śaiva temple were settled. This part of the *Chronicle* can be checked for accuracy against well-known historical events and makes a solid case that the priestly families have been keeping the tradition intact.

For the period before the fourteenth century, the *Chronicle* had to rely on the collective priestly memory up to that point, and the result is a rather inaccurate but revealing reconstruction of historical events. To show the general logic of this reconstruction I shall set down the sequence in which major events are said to have taken place according to the *Chronicle* and the sequence that seems probable to us today in the light of well-known historical events and the inscriptions on the temple walls (table 7.1).

The first notable feature of the *Chronicle's* reconstruction is that the Muslim invasion is inserted between the time of the *āl̲vārs* and *ācāryas*. Although this is, of course, incorrect, it did provide the legendary history with a kind of *pralāya* or interlude of cosmic darkness to explain an older tradition of "lost" hymns the *ācāryas* had to recover. This chronology made it possible to envisage the miraculous recovery of the hymns by Nātamuni as the discovery of the Veda or the "knowledge of the ages," and it also avoided having a gap in the priestly traditions since the time of Rāmānuja. Second, in the *Chronicle* the kings who built the temple courtyards are set in the legendary past (rather than in the two centuries after Rāmānuja), so as to establish the impression that the temple practices known by Rāmānuja are those of the temple in its present size. Third, by setting both the Muslim invasion and the temple building in the pre-Rāmānuja period, the detailed priestly reforms, which take up much of the *Chronicle*, can be attributed to Rāmānuja and can be carried on in direct continuity from his time. And, fourth, by describing the kingly role in later times as "interference" with priestly authority, the danger of the Vicayanakaram court coming out in support of the Vaṭakalai tradition, which placed less reliance on the Tamil̲ hymns and painted Rāmānuja in a different, more scholarly, role, is avoided.

The *Chronicle* seizes every opportunity to underline the special association of this temple with the Veda. In the beginning the story appears about how the temple was buried in sand until a parrot sat over it repeating the following verse:

Table 7-1 Comparison of Chronicle history and "probable" history of Śrīraṅkam temple

Chronicle	Probable
Vimānam or shrine given to Vibhīsana by Rāma and left in Śrīraṅkam at the request of a local king.	From the third to the ninth century *ālvārs* sang at a small shrine.
Vimānam covered by sand and lost.	At an unknown date thereafter the shrine does seem to have been flooded and lost.
Kings recover the *vimānam* and build up the many walls. A north Indian king comes to dedicate the northern gateway (Hari Rao 1961, pp. 7ff.).	By the tenth century the *ācāryas* were using the rediscovered shrine as the locale for their teaching.
Ālvārs or saints praise the great temple. Tirumaṅkai gets the deity's permission to sing in the temple.	Sometime in the eleventh and twelfth centuries Rāmānuja taught there.
Muslim armies carry the image away.	Between the tenth and the thirteenth centuries the Cōla, Hoysala, and Pāṇṭya kings were involved as the temple grew.
Ācāryas or teachers restore the temple. Nātamuni gets permission for the singing of the hymns.	In the fourteenth century Muslim armies carried the image away, and the temple was closed for about 50 years.
Rāmānuja establishes a priestly reform (the discussion of which occupies two thirds of the *Chronicle*).	During the fifteenth and sixteenth centuries the temple underwent a major expansion, and the Vicayanakaram emperors were very involved with temple life.
The priests have carried on ever since in spite of royal interference.	Teṅkalai priests gradually became dominant.

Even as the Kāvēri is the same as the river Vraja in Vaikuṇṭa
So the temple of Raṅka is itself Vaikuṇṭa.
And the Lord Raṅka is none other than Vasudeva
For the Supreme Abode is here in perceptible form.
The central shrine takes the form of the syllable OM
And its towers are miraculously like the Vedas
For here the Lord Raṅkasyi reveals the meaning of OM.
(Hari Rao 1961, p. 3)

Hearing this verse, the *Chronicle* tells us, the Cōḻa king had the temple dug up and began building courtyards.

Suddenly, in the middle of the account of the kings who added to the temple, the *Chronicle* tells the story of how the *āḻvār* Tirumaṅkai induced the deity to listen to some Tamiḻ hymns (Hari Rao 1961, pp. 8ff.).[7] We are told that in the month of Kārtikai (November-December), at the end of a festival in which the images of the deity and his two consorts are bathed and dressed, Tirumaṅkai recited six hymns of Nammāḻvār. He "so infused them with divine melody, and combined them with gesticulations, that the Perumāḷ [the deity] was entirely pleased with him." When the deity asked what he could do to honor Tirumaṅkai, the latter replied:

My Lord, after you have thought about me—a poor householder and your humble servant—in this manner, I lack nothing. Yet, I appeal to you to hear the *Tiruvāymoḻi*, the word of Caṭakōpaṉ [Nammāḻvār], recited along with the Vedas, on the *ēkātaci* day of the

> bright half of the month of Mārkaḻi during the Adhyayanōtsava [festival], and graciously assign it *a place of equality with the Vedas* [emphasis added]. (Hari Rao 1961, p. 9)

The deity agreed and sent an official invitation (*aruḷappāṭu*) to Nammāḻvār, who was in the town of Tirunakari, to come for this recitation. (In the temple ritual of today this invitation to Nammāḻvār to conduct the *Veda-pārāyaṇa*, or "complete recitation of the Veda," is issued in a formal way 1 month before the festival of recitation begins.)

After recounting more building programs, and the Muslim invasion, the *Chronicle* describes the way in which the *ācārya* Nātamuni supposedly recovered the "lost" collection of hymns (Hari Rao 1961, pp. 33ff.).[8] The *Chronicle* explains that the arrangement Tirumaṅkai had made with the deity had been neglected because of "bad days," and the hymns had been forgotten. While visiting a temple in Kumbakōnan, Nātamuni had heard a hymn of Nammāḻvār and had gone to the great saint's hometown to see if he could hear more. The local citizens could recite only a hymn in praise of the saint, so Nātamuni repeated that hymn thousands of times until the saint himself appeared to him in a dream and taught him the hymns of all the saints. Nātamuni then returned to Śrīraṅkam, and, after being installed as head priest in the temple, he set up the festival of recitation and started schools to teach the *Divya Prabandam* or the 4,000 hymns of the saints. Clarifying the arrangements he made, the *Chronicle* says:

> Since the Perumāḷ *had equated the Tiruvāymoḻi to the Vedas* [emphasis added], he also fixed the times of "*upakrama*" and "*utsarjana*" [beginning and ending of the recitation] for the *Tiruvāymoḻi* as the same as those for the Vedas. . . . As the Ṛg and other Vedas had the *śikṣā* and the *itihāsa-purāṇas* as their auxiliaries, so the four *Prabandams* of Nammāḻvār are to occupy the places of the four Vedas [the *Tiruvāymoḻi* equals the *Sāmaveda*, the *Tiruviruttam* equals the *Ṛgveda*, the *Tiruvāciriyam* equals the *Yajurveda*, and the *Periya tiruvantāti* equals the *Atharvaveda*]; and the *Prabandams* of the other *āḻvārs* . . . are their auxiliaries (Hari Rao 1961, pp. 34–5)

In addition to being keen to reformulate traditional stories about *āḻvārs* and *ācāryas* to identify the Tamiḻ hymns with the Veda, the *Chronicle* attributes the complex organizational arrangements of the temple to the *ācārya* Rāmānuja. The traditional account of how Rāmānuja became the Śrīkārya or head of the Śrīraṅkam temple is so well established and overgrown with legend that it is difficult to reexamine it systematically. The inscriptional evidence, however, gives one cause to pause. Although more than 300 inscriptions were carved on the temple walls between the traditional dates for the lifetime of Rāmānuja (1017–1137) and the Muslim invasion 200 years later, he is not mentioned in any of them. Furthermore, the three occasions in which his career is said to have touched upon larger political developments in South India are all difficult to reconcile with the sequence of events in secular history.[9] For my purposes, the crucial facts are that, whereas Rāmānuja is nowhere mentioned in the Śrīraṅkam inscriptions and must have had at best a peripheral role in temple life, the *Chronicle* of the temple, which reflects the views of the Teṅkalai priests of the fifteenth century, portrays him as the authoritative guide to the proper traditions of worship and administration in the temple and, in particular, makes him a diplomatic adjudicator of priestly disputes. Obviously the Teṅkalai priests thought there was a need for a strong symbol of authority to sort out the chaos of disputed claims that arose after the Muslim invasion, when different priestly groups arrived back at the newly reopened temple, each with its own idea of how the worship should be organized. The teacher Rāmānuja, who had probably had some connection with the temple during his lifetime, and who by the fifteenth century was widely renowned, was the obvious candidate to provide this symbol of authority.

Apparently a whole host of problems arose when worship was restored in the late fourteenth century. One problem was that another image was being worshiped by the time the original image was brought back from exile. The *Chronicle* tells us that this problem was settled when a 93-year-old washerman, who had washed the clothes of the image before exile, said that he could "taste" the wash water of the newly returned image and could identify the image as the authentic one (Hari Rao 1961, pp. 30ff.).[10] Another problem centered around the fact that an ascetic named Kūranārāyaṇa Jīyar had performed some miracles and had become so popular that much of the temple worship was associated with his *matam* and the headship of that *matam* had become very prestigious. The *Chronicle* indicates that the leading families started sharing their honors with the head of this *matam* and justified this development by associating this *matam* with an earlier one headed by Rāmānuja (Hari Rao 1961, pp. 114ff.).

Most of the problems were settled by imagining them to have arisen in an earlier era and attributing their solutions directly to Rāmānuja. For instance, Rāmānuja is said to have decided that the priests who use the *Pañcarātra Āgama*, rather than those who use the *Vaikhānasa Āgama*, should be in charge of the ritual (Hari Rao 1961, p. 45). He is credited with a tenfold reorganization of the priests, as well as another fivefold reorganization (Hari Rao 1961, pp. 46ff.). He is said to have decided that the two groups claiming to be accountants should divide the work between them (Hari Rao 1961, pp. 92ff.). But the most delicate question of all was which group of priests should recite the hymns (Hari Rao 1961, pp. 40ff.). This question still vexes the peace of the temple, and its proper solution is crucial to the Teṅkalai claim that the ritual recitation of the Tamil̲ hymns bears Vedic authority.

The historic details of the dispute about who should sing the hymns are not clear, but we understand the general character of the problem as the writers of the *Chronicle* perceived it. One group of priests, called the "Śrīvaiṣṇavas" (this label refers to a subgroup of the priesthood in this context, but the same label is sometimes used of all followers of Rāmānuja), seems to have made hymnsinging their main form of devotion both in and out of the temple. A smaller group of priests, which holds the title of "Araiyar," recites the hymns with a special tune and special dance gestures. This smaller group traces its lineage back to Nātamuni's two nephews, Kīl̲aiakattāl̲vār and Mēlaiakattāl̲vār, whose uncle taught them this special form of recitation so that the collection of hymns would never again be forgotten. This distinction between singing groups, which still exists, seems to have great antiquity. An inscription of CE 1085 records how a commander of Emperor Kulōttuṅka I donated fifty *kalanju* of gold to support five families who would take turns reciting the *Tiruvāymol̲i* and the *Tiruppal̲l̲iyelucci* (*Annual Report on Epigraphy 1892*, no. 61; *South Indian Inscriptions IV*, no. 508). This donation was not for the festival of recitation as we know it today but for a daily ceremony at the time of awakening the deity. Four of the families listed bore the title "Nampi," typical of the special group of Śrīvaiṣṇava priests, whereas one bore the title Araiyar. At that time the two groups were presumably already in existence, but their roles in the ritual were not yet distinguished.

The *Chronicle* explains that the dispute began because the deity himself had a taste for fine music and was so pleased with the performances of Nātamuni's nephews that he gave them the title araiyar, or "royal ones," and the honor of wearing the special turban, cotton, and silk upper garments and garlands that the deity had worn. (These items are still ritually presented to the families of Araiyar during breaks in the recitation.) The Nampis or Śrīvaiṣṇavas apparently were not pleased by the special dignity accorded the Araiyar, and at the time of Rāmānuja, the *Chronicle* notes, the Nampis still held the head priesthood of the temple. Although the *Chronicle* does not highlight the head priest's side of the argument, apparently he allowed the Araiyar recitations only in the outer courtyards of the temple. As the *Chronicle* tells it, Rāmānuja suggested reforms, but "the eloquent high priest of our temple, Periya Nampi, of royal dignity, was making mischief in disregard of Rāmānuja" (Hari Rao 1961, p. 47). Rāmānuja thought of removing the head priest, but the deity had warned him in a dream that Periya Nampi had been in that office a long time. Then, Rāmānuja thought of leaving the temple himself, but his disciple Āl̲vān, already chosen as the new head priest, suggested that Periya Nampi might be interested in studying under the learned Rāmānuja. This arrangement brought a personal reconciliation, and the old head priest later wrote the famous hymn *Rāmānuja Nūṟṟantāti* in praise of Rāmānuja; Rāmānuja in turn gave the head priest the name "Amutan̲ār" or "the immortal nectar." Soon thereafter, however, according to the *Chronicle*, Periya Nampi's mother died, and, because the old fellow was shunned by most of the priests he had to ask Āl̲vān to help with the last rites. This dispute finally settled the matter in the old head priest's mind, and Āl̲vān soon

> received the hereditary office of the high priest, and the right to read the *purāṇas* in the temple, as gifts from Periya Kōyil Nampi, and also the document registering those gifts. These he handed over to the *matam* [the monastic institution Rāmānuja had established in the temple compound]." (Hari Rao 1961, p. 48)

This apparent takeover of priestly prerogatives is not so simple, however, for the old priestly lineage, which took on the name Amutan̲ār, still exists and has fought for its rights over the centuries. The *Chronicle's* explanation for the continuation of this line is that when Rāmānuja saw the aging Periya Nampi wandering about, stripped of all priestly privileges, he took pity on him and said: "The learned Amutan̲ār should not remain idle like this." He then took a copy of the 1,000 hymns called the *Iyaṟpā* to the image of the deity and "obtained the divine command that Amutan̲ār should recite the *Iyaṟpā* Thousand [in the traditional way inside the sanctum of the temple] and that all the honors due that day to the Araiyar were to be done to him" (Hari Rao 1961, p. 53). The *Chronicle* then concludes the discussion of singing rights with a chart showing when the Araiyar are to perform, when the Amutan̲ār, and when the "Śrīvaiṣṇavas."[11]

Even though the *Chronicle's* reconstruction of 700 years of temple history is told from the perspective of the fifteenth century, and makes for a somewhat shaky historical record, it provides a revealing account of the meaning the fifteenth-century priests attached to the ritual chanting of the Tamil̲ hymns in the Adhyayōtsava festival. There are four significant features of their interpretation. First, the deity authorized the hymns to be sung "along with the Veda" at the request of Tirumaṅkai. Second, the canon now used is not the product of a period of *pakti* (Sanskrit: *bhakti*) devotionalism that was gradually passed on but the result of a miraculous recovery of 4,000 hymns by Nātamuni. Third, Rāmānuja, whose philosophy is founded on Vedic knowledge, authorized the singing of the hymns and gave detailed instructions on how the singing should be conducted. Last, the special reciters or Araiyars, who trace their lineage to the nephews of Nātamuni and were specifically authorized by Rāmānuja, are the priestly vehicle through which this reciting is raised from the level of general hymn singing to Veda, or sacred knowledge.

Whether historically valid or not, this interpretation, in terms of the religious options available in the fifteenth century, brought the Teṅkalai branch of Śrīvaiṣṇavism into the mainstream of Hindu orthodoxy. Pressure to conform to an orthodox pattern had begun with Śaṅkara in the eighth century, had increased as a result of the Muslim challenge, and was pushed hard by the Vicayanakaram rulers, who revitalized Hinduism in South India after they came to power in the late fourteenth century. The most important theological criterion of orthodoxy was the formal acknowledgment of Vedic authority. For the Teṅkalais this criterion was a problem, because the Vaṭakalai sect, their traditional rival within the Śrīvaiṣṇava community, had always given more attention to the Sanskrit Vedic hymns than to the Tami<u>l</u> hymns. By developing an interpretation by which the Tami<u>l</u> Canon could, at least in a formal way, be recognized as "Veda" and take a central role in the ritual, the Teṅkalais were conforming to the requirements of the new standards of orthodoxy.

The *Chronicle* spells out the theological purposes the Teṅkalai priests associated with the reciting of the Tami<u>l</u> hymns in the Adhyayōtsava, but the religious meaning of the popular religious festival in which the recitation takes place might well reach beyond this narrow priestly concern. In a final section, then, I examine the question of what constitutes the overall religious meaning of the Adhyayōtsava festival.

The Synthesis

As a westerner, I seriously considered the parts of this festival providing historical meaning. I talked with the Araiyars and other priests about their lineages. I took my hymnbook to the recitations and tried to recover some of the original spirit of the *ā<u>l</u>vārs* hymns, and I asked priests and laymen about the claim of the *Chronicle* that the recitation was Vedic. Although people were interested in the historical component, and my questions almost reawakened some dormant disputes, people seemed to wonder if I were missing the larger framework of meaning. Watching the crowds swell into the many thousands for the popular events, but shrink into only hundreds for the recitations, I realized that the majority of the worshipers did not attend the festival to reinforce the position taken by the priests of the fifteenth century. I needed to ask what meaning the festival had for these people in a new way.

After I had thoroughly studied the "*ati*" or "original" Brahmōtsava festival of the temple (chapter 4) and saw how its structure of meaning revolved around the poles of transcendence and intimacy, I reexamined my notes on this festival and recognized why certain events were so popular and how the popular events and the recitation are linked in the overall meaning. The largest crowds attend the opening of the northern gateway and the bathing in the lotus pond, two ritual events that symbolize the emphases on transcendence and intimacy.

In the first instance, the gateway symbol has profound significance because of the elaborate cosmology that makes north and east the directions of the gods. The Brāhman houses are clustered along the northern river bank of Śrīraṅkam island, and many rituals focus on the auspiciousness of the north. The temple's unusual south-north axis is much talked about. The busy southern entrance with its bazaar and bus stand is often contrasted with the silence and holiness of the north, where the gate is usually closed and the *matam* or monastery of Rāmānuja is just outside the gate. The yearly opening of the northern gateway has come to symbolize the worshiper's opportunity to enter the transcendent realm.

As I have already pointed out, the symbolic bath in the lotus pond derives its meaning from its associations with time. Late December is the coolest time of the year when the daily bath in the river becomes not only a necessity of life but an exciting adventure, which includes considerable splashing and frolicking. For a Hindu, the ritual year corresponds to the stages of the day, so that late December corresponds to the beginning of the day, when the sun has just started its northern course out of the southern hemisphere, even as the daily visit of the sun has just started with the approaching dawn. This time, which corresponds to roughly 5 AM, is the appropriate time for the daily bath, which, along with the taking of food, is considered the most essential part of the daily routine. For the deity to share in this is a sign of great intimacy.

In the course of the festival, the polarity between transcendence and intimacy appears over and over, almost like a musical theme. A mini-festival around this polarity is created for those who come only for the gateway opening, by including in the ceremony the humorous story of Viṣṇu's transformation into the attractive young goddess Mōhinī in order to seduce the demons who had stolen the immortal nectar. The enactment of the Mōhinī story strikes a note of playful intimacy, which provides an appropriate contrast to the solemnity of the gateway opening. In a similar juxtaposition, the intimate lotus-pond bath is set just before the all-night vigil leading to the saint Nammāḻvār's entrance into the realm of *mokṣa* or transcendence.

When the fifteenth-century priests, for reasons of sectarian self-interest, introduced the recitation of the *āḻvārs'* hymns into this festival, they wisely used this basic polarity of transcendence and intimacy, deeply embedded in the popular religious imagination, and inserted their concerns within that framwork. They did this at a popular level by associating the *āḻvārs* with this schema through the dramatic presentation of incidents in the lives of Tirumaṅkai and Nammāḻvār, and they did it with the recitation itself by making that recitation both an austere evocation of mysterious words and a joyful feeding of the company of priests who are the earthly embodiment of the divine words.

The contrast between the personalities of Tirumaṅkai and Nammāḻvār as set forth in the dramatic presentations is sharply drawn. Always impulsive, Tirumaṅkai, the robber baron, robs even the deity until he is led to repentance. The deity shows his willingness to descend to the depths of the human situation by contacting Tirumaṅkai at the moment he is robbing the deity. Nammāḻvār, on the other hand, has almost no earthly personality. He is portrayed as a saint already covered with the *nāmams* or marks of devotion, and his subsequent achievement of *mokṣa* becomes a symbol to the worshiper that the ultimate destiny of his soul is to enter a transcendent oneness with the divine.

The meaning of the recitation, too, is inserted into this polarity, even though the psychological connotations of the basic polarity and the sectarian purposes behind the introduction of the recitation initially reflected two different realms of meaning. The idea of Veda came to be an embodiment of the symbol of transcendence. To some extent, this is the meaning of Veda in all of medieval Hinduism, for, as Louis Renou (1965) has shown, the content of the Veda was not studied or followed; it was the formal authority of Veda that was acknowledged by the later tradition. In this festival the association of Veda and transcendence is brought out by having the holiest section of the recitation, the *Tiruvāymoḻi* of Nammāḻvār, recited in the hall of the heavenly *ratha* to which the deity proceeds when he goes out the northern gateway. To further this association formal openings and closings for each recitation and great reverence shown to the reciters, emphasize the mystery of the recited words.

The recitation is associated with the other pole of intimacy by the sudden shift from the formality of the recitation to the earthly joyousness of the following food distribution. The food distribution, like the distribution of honors, acts as an important historical link by recognizing the prominent priestly families as the names are called out, but it also symbolizes the divine presence intimately associated with the daily life of the Śrīraṅkam community. The Teṅkalai priests of Śrīraṅkam have never shied away from the image they project as they engage in these public feasts. They are as proud of their reputation for excess weight (and, more recently, their shrewd performance in civil service jobs and capitalist investment) as they are of their reputation for the faithful performance of the traditional ritual. For them the weight and the shrewdness are this worldly evidence of the presence of God in their lives.

Outside the structural framework of transcendence and intimacy, the tedious reciting of 4,000 hymns and the nuances of the Teṅkalai/Vaṭakalai rivalry would have little religious significance. However, once this polar structure is introduced into the festival through the primordial rituals of opening the gateway and bathing in the pond, a pattern emerges. In the light of that structure, the contrasting stories of the saintly Nammāḻvār and the robber Tirumaṅkai fit neatly together and the recitation becomes a means of reminding the worshipers that the Veda is the manifestation of the transcendent deity, and the feeding and glorification of the priestly lineages is a reminder of the intimate links the divine has with this earthly locale.

Over the centuries, as this festival has been faithfully performed, the sectarian purposes set forth in the *Temple Chronicle* have faded, but the religious meaning behind the sectarian dispute remains alive in the composition of the festival. This evidence of the encounter of historical event and structural pattern of meaning indicates that the impact of the first is not lost when meaning is redefined in a festival celebration. An outsider might read the *Chronicle* and try to argue that this whole festival was designed as the priests' attempt to persuade the masses to legitimize their version of a reformed temple ritual and their version of the importance of their lineages. I have argued that the structure of transcendence and intimacy is a more basic pattern of meaning than the priestly disputes, and that it is the separate rituals of opening the doorway and bathing in the pond that set the festival within the larger framework of meaning. Once this framework was established, the special issues that arose in the fifteenth century could be introduced into it, and ideas such as Vedic authority and priestly privileges, which arose in that context, could be included in the larger context of meaning. If this interpretation is correct, I suggest that this is not so much a festival legitimizing a sectarian claim as a primordial religious structure proving flexible enough to incorporate within it special concerns that arose as a result of a particular crisis in medieval history.

8

Dance and Trance in the Presence of Māriyamman̲

The Festival of Māriyamman̲ of Samayapuram

As we saw in chapter 5, the medieval landlords in the fertile river valleys of South India built stone temples for Śivan̲ and tried to incorporate local traditions of goddess worship into the new temple system by attaching a temple of the goddess to the temple of Śivan̲. In the example in chapter 5, the goddess Akilaṇṭēśvari maintained an independent worship tradition. For many South Indians the worship of the goddess remained completely independent of the Brāhmanical tradition of the stone temples, and for many of those goddesses (usually called "Amman̲ or "Mother") the primary form of worship was the festival. When I was traveling around South India, I was often asked what I was doing. When I replied that I was studying religious festivals, many people assumed I meant Māriyamman̲ festivals. They seemed to assume that her festivals were the heart of that tradition and would start to tell me how they had gone into trance, or had found healing, at her festival.

It is probably now impossible to find out how Māriyamman̲ became the most prominent of the independent goddesses during the medieval period. Because she was not favored by landlords and kings, her temples are usually not made of stone and therefore do not bear the inscriptions that would allow us to reconstruct their history. We know that when the western missionaries arrived, they found large numbers of her temples, and more have been under construction ever since. There are now hundreds of important Māriyamman̲ temples, and most hold a major 10-day festival (fig. 8.1).

Many of the Māriyamman̲ temples are village shrines, and this identification with the village is often made explicit by referring to the temple and the deity as "Māriyamman̲ of . . .". Sometimes where there has been a quarrel in the village, a second Māriyamman̲ temple might be erected, and the two temples are then identified with the group of castes that supplied the money for the construction. In an article entitled "The Goddess and the Demon" (1981), Brenda Beck has studied the annual festival of one of these small village temples. The festival described here takes place in the village of Samayapuram, but Samayapuram is right on the edge of the large city of Tirucirapaḷḷi, and its festival has become a huge festival that now reflects the urban concerns of the city, as well as the village concerns more typically associated with the worship of Māriyamman̲.

Figure 8-1. Chariot of Māriyamman̲ at an old royal temple of Pudukkōṭṭai, just south of Tirucirapaḷḷi. (Courtesy of Dick and Joanne P. Waghorne)

The Festival

Samayapuram lies 10 kilometers to the north of Tirucirapaḷḷi, the second largest city in the state of Tamiḻnāṭu, located right in the geographical center of the state. As one leaves the city on the main highway going north, one first crosses the two branches of the great Kāvēri River that surround Śrīraṅkam island; then one passes the intersection from which major highways turn east and west along the northern bank of the river. Finally, one proceeds north along the highway that eventually reaches Madras 320 kilometers away. The city of Tirucirapaḷḷi is crowded and the traffic on the highway is heavy, but the area on either side of the river is rich green irrigated land, used as either rice paddies or coconut and banana groves. Eight kilometers north a spur road leads off the main road and proceeds about 2 kilometers to the east, where it stops at the modest Samayapuram temple. On Tuesdays, Fridays, and Sundays, the most important days for worship, this 2-kilometer stretch of road is jammed. On other days the road can be ghostly silent, for there is no permanent town or village in this area today; all the hostels and other buildings that line the road are in some way related to the handling of the crowds that visit the temple. The temple, still relatively modest, is constantly under renovation to increase its capacity to handle the vast crowds that now come to worship there. In addition to the main temple, there are a half dozen recently built small shrines to other deities. The irrigation channel that runs nearby has been fitted with steps so that it can serve as a sacred river for bathing. In addition, bathing still takes place in the old bathing tank near the highway, where the remains of an ancient palace and temple complex built by the Hoysala kings of Karnāṭaka in the thirteenth century (they were trying to bolster the declining fortunes of the Cōḻas with whom they were related through marriage alliances) can still be seen.

During the second week of April each year, this 2-kilometer stretch of road, plus another kilometer or two down the main highway toward Tirucirapaḷḷi, becomes a sea of humanity with hundreds of thousands camping at the side of the road. A stream of people pour along the road to the temple before taking their places somewhere along the side. The hostels nearest the temple are owned and used by caste groups that come every year, but most groups just squat wherever they can find space. Nearer the main road, sweet stalls, wild animal cages, and freak shows are set up. On the main highway itself, thousands from tribal hunting societies set up camp and cook what the vegetarians closer to the temple believe to be squirrels, cats, dogs, and small pigs.

The basic pattern of worship is that a worshiper will take a vow (*viratam*, Sanskrit: *vrata*) some months before the festival to worship in a particular way at festival time. Worshipers make these vows in the face of a crisis in their personal lives. Often the crisis involves the health of children or the longing for children, but sometimes it involves other problems with disease, the loss of income, fear of sorcery, and a more general anxiety about "enemies" in the extended family, in the neighborhood, or in the workplace. Once the vow has been made, it is thought to take on a power of its own, and nonfulfillment would involve severe penalty. Most vows involve months of fasting and sexual abstinence, shaving the head and putting on bright yellow clothes, taking an exhausting walk from home to the temple area, and finally dramatically "dancing" along the crowded roadway to the temple. The dance takes many forms. Couples carry newborn babes in a yellow cloth hammock suspended on sugar cane stalks. Some women, elderly people, and small children carry only a small pot on their heads filled with the deity's favorite *margosa* leaves. Many carry a cock for offering. Middle-aged women carry large pots of burning charcoal, usually dancing wildly and careening in and out of the crowd at the side of the road. A few vow-keepers have undergone a special ordeal and have a weapon penetrating their tongue or their cheeks. Young men often have a shrine-like structure or *kavati* built around them and anchored to their skin by 30 or 40 wires. Skillfully dancing along through the crowd with feathers, flowers, and weapons all flying about, these shrine-carriers stir the crowd into "oos" and "ahs" of reverence. Finally, the heroic champions of the worship are the "hook swingers," who come along the road suspended from a long boom and held by a hook through a muscle in the back.[1] Holding a child up to be blessed by one of these heroes, as they are swung about above the crowd, provides the richest benefit of all.

As the more heroic of these vow-keepers make their way along the crowded roadway, they have a whole group of people assisting them, much as handlers assist a prizefighter. Usually one person dances gently ahead, leading the party through the crowd. Then come the drummers, who set a beat consistent with the spirit of the vow-keeper. Then come one or two other people holding up the vow-keeper, who is often in a semiconscious swoon. Others follow, carrying the water constantly thrown over the vow-keeper and the fuel for the firepots, and so on. The movement of the worshiper is usually sporadic. Standing in the midst of the crowd in the blazing summer sun, eyes glazing over, he or she seems for a time to collapse into the arms of the handlers, until, suddenly, the body stiffens and the worshiper, as if possessed, points ahead, and the party goes off at a run. Where the dancing is vigorous, there is a less evident sense of dependence on the handlers, but in this case the supranatural state of mind is equally evident in the wild directions the dance takes. As the dancers enter the presence of the deity, they stuff small metallic "eyes," "arms," "legs," clay "babies," cocks, money, jewelry, and "letters" in the direction of the offering box and then go into a final burst of dance, which often ends in a total swoon. (Handlers and more professional recovery teams are sometimes involved for a considerable time in bringing the most severe cases back to consciousness.)

In the inner sanctum of the Tēvi or Amman̠, the atmosphere is actually surprisingly quiet. The drummers, the handlers, and sometimes even the dancers have been stopped some distance back, and only the moans of those recovering from their swoons are sometimes heard. A few worshipers go up as close as they can, and a few others have kept aside offerings of food or of flowers (more appropriate for a Brâhmanical temple), which they hand over to the priests.[2]

Before long the worshipers go out one of the back doors into a whole new phase of the worship, the identification of the "power" that the Tēvi has given them. The central feature of this phase, in contrast to the energetic "dance" of the first phase, is the "trance" of possession, which allows some of the worshipers to become mediums for the others. For many of the worshipers, the possession is a brief moment directly following the swoon in which they feel that they have the answer to their own immediate "problem" and claim to be "healed," to be "free" of an offending evil spirit, to know the course of action they are to follow, or whatever. When the voice in the possessed person continues to speak in an unearthly hoarseness, however, a crowd quickly gathers around, and individuals begin inquiring of the spirit about their own problems. In one moving example I witnessed, the possessed person was a woman in her midthirties, who was dressed in an ordinary middle-class sari, but she was able to dance about in butterfly fashion for hour after hour while an eerie voice spoke through her to individual after individual in the large crowd that gathered. In this case the woman had probably never found herself in this role before and had all the attributes of someone in the state of hysteria. In other cases the person in the trance is a semiprofessional, who has offering boxes and a firepot or pot of *margosa* leaves to consult, and the voice from the Tēvi has more of the quality that would be associated with fortune tellers in other settings.[3]

When people eventually make their way back to their family and caste group, somewhere along the side of the road, the "messages" of the vow-keeper's experience are shared more widely. Sometimes the trance state continues, but in any case the newly empowered vow-keeper, and his or her caste fellows, eventually start to reflect on the implications of this new empowerment for their return to society. Usually the special sensitivity of this time of renewal continues for a few days, and the group stays at the side of the road revering those still "dancing" along the road. Finally, with a touch of sadness the caste group takes up its few possessions and wends its way back into society.

The Social Meaning of the Festival

The social meanings in a Māriyamman̲ festival are amazingly transparent. The worshiper takes a vow alone, but the vow is almost always related to a social problem, it involves one's family and caste fellows in lending support, and one acts within and on behalf of one's social unit in every dimension of the worship procedure. As one passes by recognizable caste groups and caste houses in dancing down the road, one speaks to each of those other social units of one's pains and problems, as well as of the hopes and dreams that bring one to the Tēvi. As one later waits and watches while others express their problems and their dreams, one once again recognizes the larger social meaning that only the Amman̲ has the power to set right.

In the village temples the social meaning of the festival is fairly straightforward. In an article in 1959, Louis Dumont described the social structure of a Tamil̲ village in terms of the division of responsibilities among the three deities: Aiyanār (possibly linked with Ayyappan̲), a male deity with large horses who never entered the village but protected it in his shrine to the north of the village; Māriyamman̲, whose shrine was at the heart of the village and who dealt mainly with disease and fertility; and Karuppaswāmi, a black deity serving as Aiyanār's servant and particularly worshiped by the castes of lowest status. Brenda Beck (1972), in her study of a village in the Koṅku area in the west of Tamil̲nāṭu, pointed out that even though all women in a village might take part in some of the ceremonies before Māriyamman̲, they did so as caste units, and it was the women of the landholding caste who led off the ceremony and understood the temple to be for them and those who worked with them on their land. For the villagers of the dry plateau areas of Tamil̲nāṭu, life is harsh, with infrequent rainfall but frequent disease. Many of the worshipers explain the etymology of the name Māri-y-amman̲ as "Rain-Mother," based on the word "*māri*," or "rain," and explain the festivals in April as pleading with the Amman̲ not to be angry with people for their failings and to go once again into the Kerala mountains to the west and bring back the rain in time for the rainy season in June. More immediate than drought, and more specific in the life of a particular family, was the problem of disease. The missionaries who first observed Māriyamman̲ worship were indeed so often told that offerings to her were to ward off smallpox that they described her as the "smallpox goddess" (Whitehead 1921). Whereas that kind of functionalist label was probably never an adequate account of what Māriyamman̲ meant to her worshipers, it is particularly inappropriate today when smallpox has been eradicated, and few worshipers even remember that she was ever closely associated with a concern about that particular disease.

Villagers in the dry areas of Tamil̲nāṭu have long felt that a hot-tempered goddess was responsible for the rise and fall in their fortunes, as they fought to cope with the harsh reality of survival in such an environment. As early as the grammar of Tolkāppiyan̲, which probably predates the Common Era, the dry regions were spoken of as presided over by an angry goddess, and the quality of life as lonely survival. Those features still characterize life as the worshipers of Māriyamman̲ see it today.

Most interesting about the Samayapuram festival is the way these underlying social attitudes are preserved and reinterpreted in the more urban context in which this festival is held. Because of its central location, Tirucirapaḷḷi has been a major city throughout Tamil̲ history. But for a variety of reasons rulers have usually chosen to develop their imperial dreams from somewhere else, and the city has survived only by providing the crafts (carpentry, blacksmithy, and weaving) needed by the vast hinterland of agriculture that spreads out from the city on all sides. The original home of the Cōl̲a dynasty was in the ancient core of the city, then called Uraiyūr, but when the Cōl̲as started to develop imperial ambitions in the ninth century, they built a new capital 50 miles to the east in the richer part of the Kāvēri delta, which had been developed by then, thanks to the irrigation provided by the dam at Tirucirapaḷḷi. In a similar way the British and French armies fought for control of the strategic fort of Tirucirapaḷḷi for almost a century before the British won, but when they later set up their own administration, the British operated out of their original trading post in Madras and centered the modern development of education and commerce there. Tirucirapaḷḷi was once again left behind and had no choice but to continue as a vast craft workshop.

The people of Tirucirapaḷḷi have to a great extent continued in the craft with which their caste was originally associated, and they are generally unusually proud of their caste lineage. I spent much of my time at the festival in the hostel of the weavers of Tirucirapaḷḷi; they were extremely proud to have come to the same location for 99 years and were busily making plans to build a larger building by the coming year. The logic with which these people view the world is the same as that of those of village background; they attribute the harshness of their fate to unspecified "enemies" who cut off the flow of well-being in their direction and curse them with barrenness, disease, and other forms of unexpected misfortune. Nowadays "unexpected misfortune" often means the loss of a job, and the "letters" to Māriyamman̲ now explain exactly who the enemies in the workplace are with whom the worshiper is having difficulty (Diehl 1956).

In the political atmosphere of recent years, the "enemy" has taken on an even more specific character, and the pleas to Māriyamman̲ often sound like a class stuggle against the Brāhmans and all the privileges they represent. The wider movement of anti-Brāhmanism started elsewhere in the state at the turn of the century, but its impact on life in and around Tirucirapaḷḷi has been particularly intense. Dating from early in the

Common Era, when Uraiyūr was still the Cōl̲a capital, two of the most famous Brāhman temples in South India were established on Śrīraṅkam island (chapters 4, 5, and 7). Although they are of roughly equal size and each had periods of royal support and great prosperity, the Śrīraṅkam temple of Viṣṇu received an extra measure of support during the Vicayanakaram period from the fourteenth to the seventeenth centuries and continues to have about 3,000 priests connected with it. These Śrīvaiṣṇava priests responded most enthusiastically to the opportunities for education and government service under the British, and the anti-Brāhman movement was directed against them in particular. Most of these Brāhmans live and work in Madras, but some still visit Śrīraṅkam each year to fulfill their temple duties there, and many ask for transfers or plan their retirement so as to maintain Tirucirapaḻḻi as their home area. Although most of the people in Tirucirapaḻḻi do not have much direct contact with Brāhmans, their general resentment toward Madras, with its concentration of education and power, is expressed in terms of strong support for the anti-Brāhman movement; when this anti-Brāhman sentiment takes more specific form, it is directed toward the priests of Śrīraṅkam, who are reputed to represent a great concentration of special privilege.

In recent decades this rivalry between Brāhman influence and power and anti-Brāhman politics has taken a number of interesting forms. In an ironic twist of fate, the Brāhmans of Śrīraṅkam have recently been given an indirect role in the management of the popular Samayapuram temple. Although the provincial government is now headed up by a non-Brāhman party, the Ministry of Hindu Religious Endowments decided to centralize its work in the Tirucirapaḻḻi area by managing the nearby temples out of one office in the Śrīraṅkam temple. This arrangement led to the government managers forcing the Samayapuram temple to make three major administrative changes, to bring it more into line with the practices of the Brāhman temples. One change was that the poorly educated non-Brāhman priests who traditionally served the temple were dismissed, and Śaiva Brāhman priests, who have no background in Māriyamman̲ worship, were hired. A second change was that the festival of Māriyamman̲ began to include processions of a small festival image in various *vāhanas* or carts just as the Brāhman festivals do, even though worshipers tend to give these processions minimal attention and continue with the dance into the sanctum of the main deity. The third change was that the huge offerings of the Samayapuram temple were pooled with those of the deficit-prone Śrīraṅkam temple with its expensive ceremonial. Even though these administrative changes tended to introduce Brāhmanical elements into the Samayapuram situation, the ideology of the Samayapuram festival became more and more openly anti-Brāhman, and the size of the festivity was seen by Brāhman and non-Brāhman alike as a public display of the strength of the non-Brāhman movement.

In a brief one-day festival of Māriyamman̲ later in the year, the festival image of the Tēvi is actually brought defiantly from Samayapuram to the bank of the river at Śrīraṅkam (Younger 1982a). Although this may once have been an innocent medieval ritual, and still involves a quiet handing over of a *sāri* to Māriyamman̲ by the priests of Śrīraṅkam, it is now a highly politicized event in which the non-Brāhman political parties figure prominently. The temple authorities in Śrīraṅkam temple ask the great crowd to walk the two miles around the temple to get from the bus to the riverbank, yet many defiantly tuck their sandals into their bags (technically polluting the temple with the leather) and push their way on into the Śrīraṅkam temple corridors that provide the shortest route to the riverbank. Although both sides limit themselves to muttered threats of defiance and no violence ensues, there is no doubt in anyone's mind that the non-Brāhmans now hold the upper hand and that they see the Tēvi of Samayapuram as their heroine.

Who Is Māriyammaṉ?

One of the amazing aspects about the Samayapuram festival is that so little is said about the Goddess. Time after time I was told in answer to my inquiries that "she is Māriyammaṉ . . . you know . . . she is very powerful." This reluctance to speak about Māriyammaṉ seems to mean that she is almost too close to her worshipers to be spoken about. She represents in some way the Society on behalf of which she acts and is in that sense always "Māriyammaṉ of . . . ."

Whereas Māriyammaṉ is "the Society on behalf of whom she acts," she is not its lowest common denominator. She is thought of as a hot-tempered fighter, one who is used to disrespect and is prepared to stand up to it. In a certain sense she is thought of as like the oppressed and angry women who try to eke out a living for their families from the harsh environment of dry-land agriculture. These women are notorious for their sharp tongues (and filthy language), as they tell their landlords and all other men around them how much they resent the hardships they labor under.

The temple image or *mūrti* of Māriyammaṉ is that of a beautiful young woman with a fair complexion. She normally sits with her right leg tucked under her left thigh and her left leg dangling over the stool. She is not pictured with children, but some village festivals portray her as temporarily having been married to a male who turned out to be a demon and had to be killed. In the program for the Samayapuram festival, three severed mustached heads are pictured at her feet. Repeated questions to many worshipers produced no specific names for these figures but did elicit a general indication that they represented her "enemies." Her upper right hand carries a bloodied dagger, so that one is in no doubt that, despite of her gentle demeanor, she always wins.

The stories I was told when I asked about the character of Māriyammaṉ did explain how she could be both gentle and ferocious at the same time. One of the stories was borrowed from Sanskrit myth and concerned the mother of Paraśu Rāma. She was reputed to have been so virtuous that when she went for her daily bath she was able to come home carrying water in a big ball on her hand, while her *sāri* flew over her head drying. One day an especially attractive angel-like *gandharva* flew by, and she stole a glance. The ball of water immediately collapsed and her *sāri* fell down wet. Her husband asked their son Paraśu Rāma to cut off her head. As he swung his sword, her low-caste servant girl clung to her, and he cut off both heads. He then pleaded with his father to allow him to bring his mother back to life; having gotten permission, he hastily replaced the heads and switched them. Māriyammaṉ is the one with his mother's head and the servant girl's body (another etymology sees "*māri*" as meaning "switched"), and she therefore is both perfectly virtuous and hot-tempered.

Another story I was offered as an explanation of Māriyammaṉ comes out of Tamiḻ folklore and religious history. Kaṇṇaki was the virtuous wife of Kōvalaṉ (chapter 3). She waited patiently when he went off to live with a courtesan, and when he rejoined her she let him take one of her anklets and pawn it to make ends meet. When, however, the pawnbroker falsely accused her husband of stealing the queen's anklet, and the king had him put to death, Kaṇṇaki turned into a different being. She then stood brazenly before the king and flung her other anklet to the ground, breaking it to show that it contained her rubies and not the queen's pearls. After having gone on to burn the city, she left for the mountains of Kerala, where she came to be worshiped. Scholarly histories have traced the worship of Kaṇṇaki in Kerala (and in a transformed form in the goddess Pattini of Śrī Lanka, chapter 6) and not in Tamil̠nāṭu, but the worshipers in Samayapuram often mention Kaṇṇaki and certainly saw Māriyamman̠ as also in the tradition of that patient yet furious Tēvi.

Conclusion

Although I enjoyed many of the festivals I attended and felt challenged with the difficulty of explaining features in others, I found the festival of Māriyamman̠ of Samayapuram the most moving. I thought a great deal in the months that followed as to why it seemed so moving, and I could only conclude that it seemed to have a naked honesty that challenged my own humanity. Here were people dealing with life-and-death struggles with infertility, disease, unexplained bad fortune and generalized disrespect. They defiantly called on a primordial power within their own being and took a vow that set in motion a claim on the personification of that power in the form of the Tēvi. These were human beings, but human beings dealing with supercharged energy or "power," power that they recognized they could not understand, but also power they realized they could not live without.

In this atmosphere the Tēvi was not a theistic being, comparable to the male deities who receive "prayers" or other forms of "devotion," but she was a mysterious station of energy, a "transformer" who took the energy brought to her in the "dances" people performed as they approached her and supplied them with the answers or the empowerment for a return to society in the "trances" or possessions in which her power was once again released. Worshipers asked about any phase of this exchange replied with a description of *śakti* or "power." The western scholarly vocabulary is suddenly at a loss to explain a religious experience so different from the devotional one that fits with the theistic male deity to whom one offers respect. How does one describe this flow of power that seems on the one hand to be so rooted in everyday experience yet sets in motion primordial energies that our cerebral vocabulary is not accustomed to describing? There are, of course, other examples of this type of religious experience (Haitian sorceresses and Korean female shamans, for instance), and an adequate vocabulary may someday emerge, but let us recall the contexts in which the worshipers in Samayapuram described the "power" of Māriyamman̠.

One context clearly involved warning. She is "powerful," One had better not forget that, or one could get hurt. The early missionaries, picking up this theme of warning, had described Māriyamman̠ as a "bloodthirsty" goddess who produced "fear" in the "darkened mind" (Whitehead 1921). They took literally the statements that she "caused smallpox" or she "caused drought." Listening to the worshipers, one can understand those statements being made, but they must then be interpreted in terms of a total worldview, in which affliction is imposed on one's experience by one's enemies. But in an ultimate sense, it is one's own responsibility, for one must have neglected the Tēvi or her power would have been working on one's side. In this worldview, one never deals with impersonal "circumstances of life," "fate," or even "*karma*," but one deals directly with personified power, whether in the control of the enemy or transformed for good by the Tēvi. There is no neutral ground, and the awareness of the Tēvi starts with the warning that if one neglects her, one is powerless in a world run by power.

In another context, one hears about her power in terms of promise. "Don't you know there is a source of power available?" This is not cheap power. One cannot go to her at the last moment or to find out one's fortune in order to know how to act. The acts of worship, which start with the vow and culminate in the dance, carry the total energy of one's being into the power center of the Tēvi, and leave one with nothing, without a fall-back position. The "empowerment" that follows is miraculous, both physically (at one moment someone has collapsed in exhaustion but is soon back on her or his feet possessed of a new personality) and mentally (the new being does really seem to see the universe, and his or her own particular responsibilities, in a totally new light). The empowerment is at the same time a reinforcement of the specific social person who took the original vow; thus, it contains a strong element of continuity along with the miraculous newness.

Nietzsche argued that prayers defined in a Christian sense negated one's responsibility and created an inappropriate passivity. Whether he would have been more pleased with all dimensions of the Māriyamman̲ cult is difficult to know, but certainly the relatively poor and oppressed persons who go to worship Māriyamman̲ in this festival do not appear passive. They walk away with a renewed understanding of the nature of their oppressors and a renewed sense that there is power available to keep up the fight.

Conclusion to Part II

Even though the four particular festivals described here in part II are quite different from one another, that should not be allowed to hide the fact that during medieval times there were forces that led to the standardizing of festival celebrations. During this period many celebrations in temples of the same size became rather similar to one another. In the minds of many South Indian people today, the phrase "temple festival" would naturally be associated with one or another of the medieval-style celebrations.

Among the four festivals described here, the first, in chapter 5 on Śivan̲ and the Tēvi, and the last, in chapter 8 on the independent Tēvi Māriyamman̲, represent the standard patterns. The political involvement of the Kandy Perahara (chapter 6) is certainly unique in a number of ways, but it still reminds us to suspect that direct political involvement was probably a part of other festivals during medieval times, even though in most other cases the political role has not been retained in the ritual to the same extent. The priestly involvement in the Śrīraṅkam festival (chapter 7) is also unique, but it too reminds us to look for suggestions of priestly initiatives in the ritual arrangements of medieval-style festivals.

Between the types of festivals portrayed in chapters 5 and 8 it is not easy to say which might have developed from the other. The newspaper-reading public would probably think of the festivals of Śivan̲ and the Tēvi as the standard type, mainly because the grandest of these festivals in Maturai, Kāñcipuram, and a few other places are reported in the press and are included in tourist brochures and other discussions of medieval culture. There is something in the view that medieval South Indian culture achieved a grandeur in the wealthy river valleys of the region, and that the festivals in the great stone temples of the river valley regions reflect that grandeur. Those festivals give us a picture of the influence of landlords, merchants, and kings on temple building, and of artists, ascetics, and priests in refining the cultural forms that produced the exquisite sculpture, music, and ritual expression we associate with the medieval era of South Indian life.

In the history of religion, however, one might argue that the festivals of goddesses like Māriyamman̲ represent the most basic type of South Indian festival and that the festivals in the grander stone temples of the river valleys built around the goddess festival pattern and a more elaborate ceremony. In the goddess festivals of the medieval type, the connections with the festivals described in part I are more natural, in that both deal with the control of primordial forces. Māriyammaṉ, like the Tēvi of Koṭuṅkaḷūr, can be furious with those who neglect her as she fights the scourges of disease and drought. In the temple festivals of Śivaṉ and the goddesses, one also sometimes finds reminders of old goddess ritual in the healing and exorcism rites associated with the goddesses, but they seem almost hidden from view by the processions and other ceremonies.

As I have already noted, it is very difficult to date Māriyammaṉ temples, because they have so few inscriptions carved by kings or landlords, but there are hundreds of Māriyammaṉ temples in every part of the South Indian region. They are also almost the only temples found in the regions of the world to which South Indians traveled in the nineteenth century "diaspora" (chapter 12). The pattern of Tēvi worship one sees today appears to be an old one that predates the period when historical changes were recorded. If we accept the idea that the style of festival celebration one sees today at Māriyammaṉ temples—with people taking vows or *viratams* to worship the Ammaṉ at festival time and then involving themselves in strenuous forms of worship and ecstacy—appears universally in South Indian cultural areas, then we can see how the more formal festival celebrations were elaborations on that basic style, made possible because of the resources under the control of medieval landlords, kings, and priests. The festivals of Śivaṉ and a Tēvi did not really drop the emphasis on controlling primordial forces, but they did highlight marriage as a socially managed balancing of primordial forces. As other festivals emphasized the social balance of political figures or priestly skills, medieval festivals became celebrations of the elaborate culture humans were capable of—even as they still struggled with the primordial forces that threatened the established social order.

In part III I show how these standardized medieval patterns of temple festival activity unravel a bit. Landlords, kings, and priests are no longer the only voices prepared to say how they would like to see a festival pattern modified, and the newer voices seeking to use this popular cultural medium to express themselves have much more diverse interests than did the three powerful sectors of medieval society. Although the landlords, kings, and priests were not really free to violate the assumptions that made festivals such a powerful force in South Indian life, they worked closely together to try to tie the medieval festival to their interests, while simultaneously encouraging the festivals as the central expression of the whole society and its values.

III

MODERN FORMS

The six festivals described in this section are quite different from those described before because one can identify the individual, group, or institution that organizes the festival. Often the popularity of a festival means that it is beginning to develop in directions that the organizers did not intend, but we have some sense of the organizers' intention and can include that in our evaluation of the meaning of the whole experience.

The first three examples (chapters 9, 10, and 11) are celebrated in India, whereas the last three (chapters 12, 13, and 14) are celebrated in "diaspora" settings outside of India where large numbers of Indian immigrants have settled. Two of those from India (chapters 9 and 10) actually take place in Christian institutional settings. Although these two festivals seem much like goddess festivals to the many Hindus among the worshipers, the Christian organizers try to introduce Christian elements into the festival ritual. (It was tempting to consider including some festivals located in Muslim settings as well, but the issues involved in the interaction of Hinduism and Islam really need a more extended treatment.) Chapter 11 shows how a reform movement in a rival temple in the village stimulated the owner of the temple to try to develop more modern ritual forms for his festival.

In the diaspora settings, the challenge for the organizers of festivals is to find a way of initiating a festival celebration in the new environment that triggers people's memories of earlier festival experience but at the same time meets local needs. The festival of the goddess that one finds in Guyana, for instance, seems a faithful transfer of mid-nineteenth century Māriyammaṉ festivities to a new setting, but it has also evolved into the central ritual form of the popular "Kālī-Mai" cult (chapter 12). The *Kavati* festival of South Africa was also probably a faithful reflection of Murukaṉ temple festivals at the time the laborers went to South Africa, but as the descendants of the workers moved into the suburbs of the city of Durban, they developed their own ways for bringing their delicate socio-political situation to the attention of the deity (chapter 13). For the festival celebrants in Toronto (chapter 14), the focus is still on establishing a faithful version of the festival heritage that reflects their differing memories. Only time will tell whether their enthusiasm about this project will develop into a religious experience with a unique and powerful meaning.

9

Healing Mother Vēḷaṅkaṇṇi

Hindu Patterns of Worship at a Christian Shrine

By far the most successful of all the newer festivals is the one at the shrine of Mary in the fishing village of Vēḷaṅkaṇṇi on the east coast of South India.[1] Many of the fishermen along this coast became Roman Catholic in the sixteenth century, and the shrine in this village seems to have developed a legendary reputation fairly soon thereafter. The Roman Catholic authorities have had a difficult time keeping up with that popular reputation ever since. Today the reputation of Vēḷaṅkaṇṇi Ārōkkiyam Mātā (Vēḷaṅkaṇṇi the Healing Mother) is such that over a million worshipers join in the festival that culminates on the ninth of September each year.

The Festival

The festival is structured much like other South Indian festivals, with 10 days of frantic activity, processions of images, and ecstatic worshipers longing to glimpse the deity. Because the crowd now overwhelms the small fishing village where the festival is held, some of the worshipers' initial excitement comes from the questions about physical survival on everyone's mind soon after arrival.

Probably at one time the festival included primarily members of the coastal community. The fishing villages up and down the coast are densely populated, and the major coastal city of Nākapaṭṭanam is just 12 kilometers away. At some point in the history of the shrine, its reputation spread inland, and now the vast majority of the worshipers come from the huge reservoirs of landless laborers who work on the crowded rice paddies of the Kāvēri River's vast delta. As news of the huge crowds spread in recent years, the catchment area has grown still further and now includes some curious Catholics from Madras (Ce<u>nn</u>ai) and other cities. For the agricultural workers, the largest group of participants, the festival starts with a bus ride over hundreds of miles of twisting roads, in a bus jammed with three or four times its capacity. During the first half of the 10-day period, buses arrive bumper to bumper throughout the day and night, as the population of the little village swells from five thousand to what the police estimate to be over a million. The people packed into the buses appear to be the poorest of the poor, people who do not normally leave their local area even to go on pilgrimages to the great Hindu temples. Frightened, in spite of the large group of relatives they travel with, the bus riders endure nervous sickness and vomiting, and the bus parking lot is full of conductors and drivers trying to clean their buses while the police urge them to get back on the road to make room for those pouring in.

At the pilgrimage site, a fever of frenetic activity begins. Government-placed water taps are everywhere, but toilet facilities are almost nonexistent, commercial food supplies minimal. Eventually most groups move toward the less crowded southern end of the village in search of a shrub around which they can camp and get a tiny bit of shelter from the scorching sun. A few thousand find accommodation on the ground in thatched shelters near the shrine; only a few hundred (probably many with Catholic connections in places such as Madras) are accommodated in a church-run hostel. Many more ignore the need for food and sleep and begin immediately a feverish round of worship activity.

At first, the layout of the festival site is hard to understand. The bus parking lot is perched at the edge of the village, and its customers find that they have to head for the shrine through rows and rows of thatch-covered temporary shops. Eventually they spot the huge white modern church (built in 1975), which they could see from the bus, and head in that direction. But their uneasiness grows when it becomes obvious that the crowd is not focused at the church entrance. Only after some awkward questions and some backtracking are people able to find their way around to the back of the church, where the miracle-working little shrine of Mary faces the sea.

Once the worshiper has discovered the sacred shrine, the whole area between the shrine and the sea suddenly appears to be a normal festival site with familiar knots of busy worshipers moving hastily from barbers to coconut or chicken sellers, to circles of dancers, and then to the exorcists around the huge flagstaff. The great blue flag flapping in the sea breeze and making a huge shadow in the festival area becomes the focus of attention, and new worshipers follow the example of others and touch the long hempen ropes, which trail 50 feet out from the flagstaff, to their foreheads and other ailing parts of their bodies. Once they discover the flag, the whole scene comes into focus. Here they are beside the sea with all its mystery and power, and there in that little shrine is the Ārōkkiyam Mātā or Healing Mother who performs miracles. The excitement quickly reaches fever pitch.

For many, the action of worship begins with a total shaving of the head. Rows of barber shops near the shrine shave men, women, and particularly children, who want to offer their hair to Vēḷaṅkaṇṇi. Probably 20 percent of the worshipers make this their first offering, an offering made only at certain special Hindu temples. The next step, in which almost everyone participates, is to bathe at the beach to the north of the shrine, where one can usually walk far out in the shallow water. Few of the worshipers seem sure of what they want to do about these unfamiliar experiences of shaving the head and bathing in the sea. The sea bath especially is a problem, for in South Indian folklore the sea is a place of danger, and many villagers have never seen it before. Anxiety hangs heavy in the air as people move back and forth to barber and sea, watching others and trying to resolve their doubts.

After the shaving and the sea bath, the worshipers buy offering materials to supplement those they might have brought from home. Chickens and goat kids can still be bought in an emergency. Coconuts, bananas, incense, packets of rice or gram, sweets, flowers, and candles are all on sale. People eventually join the kilmeter-long lineup to see the image but often rush out only moments later to buy more materials, visit some small shrine on the wayside, or run to the flagstaff when the flag is moved up and down at 15-minute intervals. Back in the lineup, the crowd within a few hundred yards of the shrine starts to rush like the water approaching a waterfall. Many by this time are dancing, falling, or tugging at their clothes. A hundred yards from the shrine, the crowd unexpectedly finds itself inside a tiny auxiliary shrine; people hurriedly worship the image of the saint there, much as they would a Ganeṣa image at the entrance to a Hindu temple. At the entrance to the shrine itself, bodies press solidly against one another until the pressure seems unbearable, and everyone struggles to raise his or her offerings or child aloft. Young men at the entrance snuff out all candles and push the crowd along. After another set of doorways, the Mother and Child image appears in view high above the crowd, and folded hands reach up in worship as a delicate sound of "ah" fills the air. Young priests sprinkle the crowd with holy water as it progresses through the hallway. As some young men are pushing the crowd to either side of the central shrine room, other young men take flower garlands to be touched to the feet of the image before being returned. Still another group of young men receives other offerings as worshipers turn toward the side rooms, and then the worshipers follow, as the offerings are taken into the side rooms and placed on huge piles of similar offerings.

Once outside the shrine again, the worshipers move off for more activity. Shops sell colorful pictures of the Mother and Child and of the shrine. Others sell necklace charms, *yantras* or psychosomatic diagrams, and charts of the zodiac. The loudspeaker plays lilting music in which "Vēḷaṅkaṇṇi" is repeated over and over and invites people to booths where they can hear stories of people miraculously healed or get the magazine of such stories, entitled *Vēḷaṅkaṇṇi Calling*. In the new two-storied church to the rear of the shrine, masses are constantly being said in both the upper and lower sanctuaries, as crowds mill around and people sleep at the back of the sanctuaries in one of the few shady spots. At the front of the sanctuary, as a relatively small group gathers, the priest explains over and over that only Catholics should take the wafer. Outside, although the priests at the confessionals have almost no customers, the seller of holy oil is usually busy, and the "museum" that houses physical evidence of past miracles is also packed.

By evening, the anxious activity of individuals and small groups takes on a more organized pattern as all seek the best spot from which to witness the evening procession of the images and decorated carts as they proceed around the worship complex. Here the activity is less frenetic as the worshipers wait with hundreds of thousands of their fellows and know for the first time on this scale the larger solidarity of festival experience. As the moment for catching a glimpse of the images comes, a new tension fills the air and the crowd surges as one in expression of joyous excitement.

All through the festival, the loudspeakers plead with people who have finished their worship to return home on the thousands of buses leaving empty. Few leave, for as in any festival of the goddesses, the ninth day is considered sacred, the time when her power will peak. Finally, on the evening of the ninth day, the flow of packed buses starts in the other direction, as a tired, hungry, and hopeful mass of humanity reluctantly heads back into the constraints of village life.

Miracle Stories

Watching the ritual action of this festival, one could be excused for thinking it was a Māriyammaṉ festival. Worshipers stumbled into the santuaries of the church and asked in irritation, "Where is the Ammaṉ?" Many showed frustration at my "stupid" question about how this Tēvi differed from the Māriyammaṉ in their village temple. I was amazed that many who were interviewed moments after emerging from the shrine remembered nothing about a child in the arms of the Tēvi. They were sure she was, like Māriyammaṉ, "alone" and "very beautiful."

One element that makes the Vēḷaṅkaṇṇi festival different from those of Māriyammaṉ is the role miracle stories are starting to take in the celebration. It is difficult to discover the origin of this feature of the festival. It is not something that is prominent in other South Indian festivals. The original idea of the "miracle story" may have started with the three stories featured in the "official" literature (see next paragraph), but the majority of the nonliterate worshipers I talked with did not know those three stories and had quite a different style of story in mind. They almost always replied that they had heard stories of miracles and usually offered to recount one for me or refer me to a relative or a village acquaintance who had heard the story from another relative or acquaintance. The hope of hearing more stories or seeing a miracle was certainly one of the major motives for coming to the festival.

The three miracle stories that appear in all the booklets and "official" literature about the shrine do not have a South Indian flavor and are really quite similar to stories connected with shrines of the Virgin Mary across the world (Turner and Turner 1978). The first story is about a shepherd boy who was on his way back to the home of his master with a pot full of milk when he stopped at the tank of water in the village of Vēḷaṅkaṇṇi to have a drink of water. While resting under the banyan tree beside the tank, he had a vision of a beautiful mother and child, and the mother asked him for some milk for the child. He hesitated, fearing what his master might say, but eventually gave her some milk. Rushing home, he sought to explain the missing milk to his master, but the master found the pot full to the brim. Together they rushed back to the water tank and bowed to the ground in worship. Later they built a small shrine on that spot and called the tank Ampā Kuḷam, or Tank of the Mother.

Unlike the first story, which appears to be set in a time before the arrival of Christian missionaries, the second one is set in the sixteenth century after Christian churches had been established in the city of Nākapaṭṭanam. This story is about a widow and her son, who was lame from birth. A small thatched hut was constructed under the banyan tree by the tank so that the boy could sell buttermilk to passersby suffering from the heat of the day. One day a beautiful lady with a boy child approached and asked for buttermilk. The lame boy provided some. Then she ordered the boy to go to a specific Catholic gentleman in Nākapaṭṭanam and ask him to build a chapel on this spot for her. The boy explained that he could not walk, but she ordered him again. Trying to obey, he found that he was healed, and he ran off to the city with joy. The chapel was built, and the lady came to be called Vēḷaṅkaṇṇi-Ārōkkiyam Mātā, or the Healing Mother of the village Vēḷaṅkaṇṇi.

The third story involves Portuguese sailors who were on their way from China to Śrī Lanka and became lost in a storm. Praying to the Virgin Mary, they were eventually shipwrecked on this shore and led to the little thatched chapel by fishermen. The Portuguese sailors then built a brick and mortar chapel near the spot where they were shipwrecked, and they presented Mary with the Chinese porcelain plates that still form the backdrop of her image. Their shipwreck took place on September 9th, so now the festival is timed to climax on that date each year.

The miracle stories I heard people tell did not continue with the grand mythic dimension that characterizes the "official" stories. They were, in fact, surprisingly mundane and included the sudden appearance of much needed jewelry or money, the disappearance of skin diseases or internal bleeding, or the rediscovery of "lost" relatives. The most common of all had to do with the two "family" problems of South Indian society, the finding of a proper spouse and the overcoming of infertility. At first, I thought these stories sounded as if they involved problems Māriyammaṉ was capable of handling, so I asked again and again why these people had come to Vēḷaṅkaṇṇi. They insisted there was a distinction between the two "Mothers"; and after I had listened to a number of accounts of the distinction, some differences did start to register with me.

The first distinction was that these "miracles" Vēḷaṅkaṇṇi performed were personal and even secret blessings given to the petitioner alone. In the village context, Māriyammaṉ had "power," so she knew who had neglected her worship and who was trying to harm others with sorcery. The much feared drought or dry season diseases were under her control; with the proper vows and rigorous forms of worship, villagers could appropriate her power. Māriyammaṉ was called "mother" or "*amma*" in Tamiḻ like all goddesses, but along with other "independent" and fierce goddesses, the name always appears with the masculine ending "ṉ" to reflect the full divinity of this subgroup of goddesses and to remind everyone that they are dangerous. The name "Mother" in the case of Vēḷaṅkaṇṇi is the Sanskrit form "*mātā*." Although it is also commonly used in Tamiḻ to mean "mother," worshipers were often sure there was an important distinction between these two forms of address. In their minds, Vēḷaṅkaṇṇi was a "mother", who is much like the generous, sweet-tempered person who does "miracles" to solve the petty and personal problems of her infant children.

The second aspect of the "miraculous" dimension of Vēḷaṅkaṇṇi (that I had to have explained to me a number of times) is that she has an infinite range. After the "seacoast" and the "Portuguese" were mentioned a number of times, it began to dawn on me that, as a Mother who had come from across the sea, Vēḷaṅkaṇṇi had a wider range of influence. The fact that she transcended Hindu, Christian, and Muslim distinctions might make her less "powerful" in specific contexts, but it also allowed her to care for children anywhere with an easy grace.

Finally, the "miraculous" nature of her actions were thought to have a finality and security about them, which some people tried to explain in terms of the triumphal way she held her son and the royal brocade clothes they both wore (fig. 9.1). An Ammaṉ such as Māriyammaṉ represents the feisty underworld that stands up to oppressive

Figure 9-1. Vēḷaṅkaṇṇi and Child on festival chariot in Madras (Ceṉṉai). (Courtesy of Dick and Joanne P. Waghorne)

authority figures and dangerous forces in nature, but her power must be renewed constantly and always works from the bottom again the next time. A Tēvi like Śivaṉ's consort Pārvati bears children and enjoys a nice mother/son relationship with her sons Vināyakaṉ and Murukaṉ, but she does not get to establish them as cosmic lord or king. Vēḷaṅkaṇṇi is able to have it both ways: as a mother, the cries of even the weakest child about the most petty problem seem to reach her, and as her flag flies over the sea and she stands triumphantly with her son, one has the sense that she reigns over all and her miraculous blessings cannot be taken away.

The miracle stories add an interesting dimension to this festival not found in others I have studied. It is as if this festival moves beyond the sociological framework so obvious in other festivals and opens to a new voice or a new festival medium, which allows the worshiper to believe that some intractable problem can be solved or some wild dream might yet be fulfilled.

Conclusion

Now that the festival of Vēḷaṅkaṇṇi has emerged as the largest 10-day South Indian festival (the one associated with Ayyappan̲, while larger, is spread over 51 days),[1] it raises interesting questions about the whole festival tradition.

Does the different composition of the crowd in this festival indicate a weakening of the role of endogamous caste communities in South Indian society? It appears that worshipers to Vēḷaṅkaṇṇi come from a somewhat wider geographical area and that, in the way petitions are formulated, the petitioner is expressing personal need not limited to the traditional castewide problems of draught, disease, and social disrespect. The distinctions here are not sharp and clear, of course, because the geographical area from which any festival crowd comes is always changing, and all petitions to goddesses involve some personal dimension.

Two features of the crowd at the Vēḷaṅkaṇṇi festival might explain what appears to be less of an interest in traditional caste concerns. If the largest block of worshipers really is from the fishing communities, landless laboring communities, and thieving communities so numerous in the area nearby, we know that those groups have always been disdainful of the hierarchical arrangments of the landlord-controlled areas further inland. And, if an increasing number are coming from cities such as Madras (Cen̲n̲ai), they would be operating with redefined caste groupings, where caste affects marriage and residence but not usually employment, religious inclination, or health services; this would give their sense of social identity a different quality.

Because of the weaker social caste interests of these two subgroups within the Vēḷaṅkaṇṇi worshiping community, it is probably wise not to draw any general conclusion about a broad weakening of the role of endogamous caste groups in the festival traditions of South India. The social dimension of the festival seems somewhat different from that evident in more traditional festivals, but the social dimension of the other festivals I will examine in part III is actually quite prominent. Other special features of Vēḷaṇkaṇṇi might identify its unique character.

In the context of the Vēḷaṅkaṇṇi celebration, does the ritual action of the festival or the "new" framework of "miracle story" take precedence? The evidence at the moment seems contradictory. Attendance at the festival continues to grow despite the extremely difficult physical circumstances the large crowd itself creates, so one must assume that most worshipers believe that being part of that ritual experience is important to their contact with the divine. On the other hand, the miracle stories are quickly transporting the Vēḷaṅkaṇṇi experience to other places. There is now a major festival of Vēḷaṅkaṇṇi in Madras, or Cen̲n̲ai (Waghorne 1997) (see fig. 9.2), and I also discovered one in Chatsworth outside of Durban, South Africa. In addition, a rather different style of organization is used in a major cult that has developed not far from Vēḷaṅkaṇṇi around a woman regularly possessed by Mary (MacPhail 1993). These new developments rely heavily on the "miracle story" as the vehicle in which the

Figure 9-2. Lighted chariot of Vēḷaṅkaṇṇi in a festival celebration in Madras (Ceṉṉai). (Courtesy of Dick and Joanne P. Waghorne)

Vēḷaṅkaṇṇi religious phenomenon is now packaged, and many of those who meet it in such contexts may not feel the need to attend the festival. Only time will tell whether these other contexts for worshiping Vēḷaṅkaṇṇi will lead to a decline in the festival itself, or whether these more urban developments will take one direction, and the fishermen and landless laborers will return to a more traditional style of festival celebration at the revered seacoast shrine.

Finally are the sustained efforts of the "official" church to direct the development of this popular celebration likely to succeed? This is not the first time an "official" voice has tried to redirect a popular festival. In each of the festivals studied, the effort has been made. In the first four studies of part I, the festivals had probably been revered for a long time before the efforts to reinterpret them were made; the most the reformers could hope for was to contain the enthusiasm and link it to some related religious or political theme. During the medieval period, the economic and political power behind the "official" temples was enormous, and in that context many older festivals were probably altered to fit in with the temple's religious style. But even in those contexts, the authorities seemed to recognize the validity of the cultural direction that had emerged from the mass of the people, and the festival structure remained visible, even with the imposed modifications.

Some religious authorities within the Roman Catholic hierarchy have wondered if the whole Vēḷaṅkaṇṇi phenomenon is a "Hindu" intrusion into Catholic space, and most have at least tried to forbid the possession states and exorcistic practices associated with the worship. The hierarchy's most intrusive effort to redirect the whole ritual experience came when they ordered the building of a massive modern church back to back with the shrine of Vēḷaṅkaṇṇi in 1975. That building still does not fit well into the festival celebration, and the effort to have Mass constantly said in those noisy sanctuaries seems to continue the clumsy show of authority involved in the original building project. The more recent efforts to discipline the Catholic clergy attracted to the possession cults that are springing up has been even less successful, because it forces those involved to conduct the cult ritual in secret and lends it a mysterious reputation, which it might not have developed on its own.

The church has been more successful in redirecting the energy of the festival in its efforts to control the production of booklets of miracle stories. These stories have given Vēḷaṅkaṇṇi a different style of popular religiosity, which goes beyond the confines of the festival tradition. Because the church authorities are actively involved in spreading the stories, they have some control over the theological framework in which they are expressed.

As with all the "new" festivals described in part III, I have more questions about the future of the Vēḷaṅkaṇṇi celebration than about those described in parts I and II. The sociology of this festival is different from those described before both because the worshipers arrive from near and far and feel they know little about others they see there and because the church authorities can influence that sociology significantly in announcements about the conduct of the festival. The ideological side of the festival is also different because the flow of miracle stories, especially the production of written accounts of those stories, directs the festival away from the traditional multivocal celebration, wherein the mass of worshipers leads the way, and pushes it toward a more hierarchical religious event, wherein institutional authorities direct and control theological thought. Experienced church leaders realize that neither the sociology nor the ideological character of the miracle stories is easy to redirect in such a popular religious form as a festival, but the possibility for major redirection seems greater in this "new" religious setting than in a more traditional one.

10

The Window Opens in Mannarkat

A Vision of Mary in a Syrian Christian Church of Kerala

One of the most surprising of the festivals I discovered in South India was the festival of Mannarkat, which takes place in the compound of the Jacobite Syrian Orthodox Church of Saint Mary. Even the priests describe the worshipers at the festival as "mostly Hindu," but a great many of the old Syrian Christian tradition also find the unusual mixture of worship patterns in this festival at the heart of their experience of the divine.

The Setting

Central Kerala appears to have developed later than either the areas to the north around Koṭuṅkaḷūr (chapter 3), where there was a seaport and extensive land tracts, or the areas to the south, where smaller kingdoms were established first near modern Quilon and later near modern Trivandrum. In Central Kerala, the sea water penetrates much further inland, and the large sea-water lakes extend all the way to Kottayam. Kottayam is really the beginning of the foothills to the mountains. As one moves east, the lowlands soon rise higher and higher until they become part of the Western Ghat mountain range, which rises as high as 10,000 feet and is still thickly forested. At some point in history, Kottayam became the trade center of Kerala and took over control of the export of spices and other forest products from the mountains.

Kottayam is often described as a "Christian" center, because it houses the major seminaries and bishops' residences of some of the Syrian Orthodox churches. However, the Syrian Christian developments of Kottayam are really secondary developments; much earlier and much larger Christian centers existed in the region around Koṭuṅkaḷūr before the center of trade shifted to Kottayam. The church in Mannarkat, for instance, has a clear tradition about its origin, which suggests that 15 prominent families decided to move from Koṭuṅkaḷūr to Kottayam. Upon arrival in Kottayam, they had a vision of Mary, telling them that she wanted them to establish a new settlement in Mannarkat 10 kilometers further inland. Exactly when this shift from the northern settlements to the Kottayam area took place is difficult to determine, primarily because it involved a shift in economic arrangements with little or no recorded political involvement. The best guess is that it was probably after the period of imperial glory in the thirteenth century, but probably before the period of Portuguese occupation and large-scale conversion to Roman Catholicism in the sixteenth century.

Mannarkat is really not a town or village but a region. The people there describe it in terms of the medieval arrangement of *karas* or settlements, and Mannarkat people are proud of the unity that has always been maintained in its 28 *karas*. Within the region of Mannarkat there are now four religious centers. The smallest is a Viṣṇu temple, which now consists of a couple of small, fairly modern, buildings on a much larger ruin. A few Nair families nearby sponsor an R.S.S. (Hindu revivalist organization) training program for young boys in the temple compound and use militantly sectarian language, hoping one day to raise enough money to "restore the Hindu heritage" by rebuilding this temple. A somewhat larger temple site is the Śivaṉ temple at the other end of the region, which is an exquisite example of a medieval Kerala temple. It has a low copper roof, a tightly closed wall around a small compound, and a 12' by 12' wooden shrine, facing east. A family of Verriers, high-status Nairs who perform management and semi-priestly roles in many Kerala temples, now treat the temple and its extensive lands as a private possession. (They explained that the last petty ruler of the 28 *karas* had asked their ancestors to "take over" the temple because he was no longer able to "protect" it.) The temple is now normally locked, but the members of the family still perform daily rituals there and employ a teenaged Namboodri priest, who has a small house in their compound next to the temple compound.

The two main worship centers of the region, called by Hindus and Christians alike the "twin sisters of Mannarkat," are the temple of Bhagavatī and the church of Saint Mary. The temple of Bhagavatī is a relatively large structure set at the edge of a large compound where a variety of festival activities take place. The temple tradition seems rich with history. A door on the north side of the east-facing temple is said to provide an entrance for Bhagavatī of Koṭuṅkaḷūr (chapter 3), whose power is thought to reside in this deity as well. A small stone image of Bhagavatī, said to have been literally brought from Koṭuṅkaḷūr, sits in a small shrine outside of this entrance. On the south side of the temple is a shrine at the edge of the thickly forested square where a Yakṣi, or frightening female tree spirit, lives. This shrine is the focus of much intense worship. Farther into the thick forest is a shrine where food offerings are provided for the cobra snakes that live in the little forest. Beyond the forested square is a lovely old rambling *illam* ("monastery" or "priests' home," depending on how one interprets the tradition) of the priestly family called Thanniyil Illata. This family clearly considers itself to be Brāhman; the men wear sacred threads, but it makes no claim to be Namboodri. The present senior member, T. N. Vasudeva Elayathu, is accepted by the government as both the Managing trustee and head priest of the Bhagavatī temple. The worship in the temple is a vibrant version of the Bhagavatī tradition found throughout Kerala. The Verrier family that runs the Śivaṉ temple brings a garland each evening to Bhagavatī on behalf of Śivaṉ, an act that the Bhagavatī priests interpret as indicating that their temple is considered the main temple for the 28 *kara* region.

The largest religious center of the region, however, is the church of Mary. Worshipers leaving the Bhagavatī temple after prayers at dusk often visit the church of Mary on the way home, and I have more than once been taken on a "tour" of the church by eager Hindus anxious to show me their familiarity with this somewhat different tradition. (These close links between the Christian worship traditions and those of others in the area are not unique to this church. The festival of Saint George about 8 kilometers away, which traditionally involved a huge cock sacrifice, is also well known for its blending of Hindu and Christian religious activities.)[1]

The Syrian Orthodox Tradition

The Syrian Orthodox tradition of Kerala begins with the legends saying that the Apostle Thomas came to Kerala in the first century (Brown 1956). Although these legends are plausible, the evidence for them is not as strong as that for the traditions speaking of a Syrian trader, Thomas of Cana, who brought Syrian families to Kerala in the third century and set up a permanent trading post. By the eighth century, the Christian residents of Kerala were the dominant force in trade, and the king issued them (and some Jewish settlers as well) copper plate edicts saying that they alone would have certain specified privileges such as carrying umbrellas, trading in certain ways, and so on. With the emergence of Islamic power in Syria, the links with the home church became tenuous, and the community became more and more integrated into the local culture.

In the sixteenth century, when the Roman Catholics arrived with the Portuguese adventurers, they discovered this highly respected Christian community and got permission from Rome to allow them to keep all their traditions and enter the Catholic church as a unit. Within a few years, however, the Portuguese bishops who were sent to the area offended some of the leaders of the community, and the leaders declared themselves separate from Rome. The result was highly confusing, because a few parishes stayed with Rome (now called the Syrian and Caanite parishes) along with the large number of fishermen converts (now called the Latin parishes), but the majority broke with Rome and became the Jacobite Syrian Orthodox Church.

In the nineteenth century, the latter church underwent a number of further splits. First, a group influenced by the European missionaries called for reform and set up a branch of the community now called the Mar Thoma Church. At about the same time, the rediscovery of the tiny Syrian Orthodox Church, still carrying on in Damascus, again split the church between those who wanted to reunite with Damascus and those who wanted to continue as a local and autonomous tradition. Generally, the Kottayam parishes wanted to remain autonomous (now called the Orthodox Church), whereas the older parishes near Koṭuṅkaḷūr wanted to reunite and are now called the Jacobite Syrian Church. The Mannarkat church was actually awarded to the Mar Thoma group in a court case of the nineteenth century, but some of the local families who traced their roots to the Koṭuṅkaḷūr area zealously maintained those links and have been able to keep their church within the Jacobite Syrian tradition. As a result, among Syrian Christians this particular parish is unusual in that it is not linked to the locally dominant Orthodox Church tradition, but to the tradition strong in the Koṭuṅkaḷūr area and obedient to the patriarch in Damascus. In that sense, this parish is not typical of the Christian traditions of Central Kerala, and both Hindus and Christians agree that its festival represents an older tradition when the two communities joined more often in common worship than they do today.

The Festival

To the average Hindu worshiper coming from elsewhere, the festival of Mary would seem quite like a festival of a Tēvi. The crowd of 200,000 noisily mills about, in this case for eight days. At a bazaar of 30 to 40 shops, small metallic "arms," "legs," "eyes," and "babies" are for sale, so that the worshiper may place them in the offering box and indicate exactly where the healing touch is needed.[2] Barbers shave many heads. There are bathing tanks, with separate tanks for men and women and a queue to avoid overcrowding. People dance and go into trance, and exorcists expel evil spirits, much of this latter activity taking place around the giant stone cross near the church entrance, just where a flagstaff would be in a Hindu temple (fig. 10.1). People race back and forth to the Bhagavatī temple a kilometer away. Some of the exorcisms are done there, and some people sleep in the relative quiet of the compound there.

The Syrian Orthodox priests see the festival somewhat differently. They describe it as a "second Lent," and characterize the crowd's presence in the compound as a time of "fasting" and "self-discipline." They assist the church authorities in selling holy oil and candles and regularly emptying the steel offering boxes, which the crowd filing through the church continually refills. Most important, in recent years the priests encourage the

Figure 10-1. Exorcists around cross in front of Mannarkat church, Kerala.

crowd to worship before the relic of the girdle of Mary. This girdle, which she is said to have dropped down to the apostle Thomas as she rose to heaven during her Assumption, was brought to Mannarkat only in 1982 by the patriach of Antioch (in Syria) and all the East, H. H. Moran Mar Ignatius Zakka I. Now that this relic is displayed at the front of the church, the crowd files through the church to view it, and some go into trance on the oil-covered marble floors. Throughout the 8-day period, the Jacobite Syrian version of the Orthodox Mass (two hours) is said six times a day, with more and more priests and bishops participating as the festival proceeds. On the final day, the catholicos of the East, H. B. Baselius Paulous II, the supervisor of the bishops and the most holy figure in the Jacobite Church of Kerala, presides.

The central and distinctive features of the festival are the grand procession, which takes place on the sixth day in the afternoon, and the opening of the window, which takes place on the seventh day at noon. The procession involves the carrying of a thousand huge colorful umbrellas which are rented out by the church office (fig. 10.2). Sociologically, this is still a powerful symbolic event, because everyone in the society knows that the umbrella could be carried only by Christians in medieval times. The umbrella of sovereignty is important in the ceremony of all the royal houses of South India and Śrī Lanka, but in the eighth century the king listed it as the most prominent of the 72 privileges he was granting exclusively to the Christians and Jews. For practical reasons, the people of Kerala all now carry umbrellas to use against both the rain and the sun, but the old privilege is still known. In today's revolutionary atmosphere of Kerala, some Hindu participants in the festival also rent umbrellas and join in the procession. To many along the 12-kilometer path, however, the procession still symbolizes the privileged position the Christian minority enjoy in the region.

The opening of the window is, on the other hand, an uncomplicated moment of devotion in which all share. The seventh day is a time of high excitement long before dawn. All through the previous night exorcisms were being conducted at the Great Stone Cross. Before the light dawns, the first Mass is sung and the church is jammed to the walls with people who know how difficult it is to get a place later for the opening of the window. Those who thought they could come later soon begin to crowd into the companies of persons who cluster near the side entrances. From the rear entrance far into the distance past the stone cross, crowds gather, imagining that they too will be able to glimpse the window. The music of two dozen clergy singing the Mass in unison mixes with the buzz of the crowd and the occasional shriek of an evil spirit. An hour before noon, the wait becomes almost unbearable. The mind of each one seems already focused in preparation. Finally, the window opens near the peak on the front wall of the church, and everyone (including those trying to be observant anthropologists) melts into one mass of tearful ecstasy. Before long, people peel away in silence. As I went back to the shops at the bazaar for a picture of the open window to confirm my unstable sense impression, I discovered that there are no pictures of the window as a matter of policy. My memory, and that of those who would talk about their memories (many refused to), was that the window contained a picture of a standing Mary and a prominent baby, predominantly blue with some pink. I have, however, sometimes wondered if I really saw anything, for the experience was in a stunning degree a mystical one, in which that which we all saw was truly transcendent, something we experienced much as an "other," a "mysterium tremendum," to use Rudolph Otto's famous phrase, something I am still a bit in "awe" of.

Figure 10-2. Umbrella procession of Mannarkat Christians, Kerala.

Conclusion

The Mannarkat festival could be interpreted as a Christian imitation of a goddess festival or as a Christian celebration overrun by its own popularity. What is probably more accurate historically is to see it as a natural product of religious life typical of an earlier era, when the sharp distinctions of religious affiliation introduced by the missionary movement from the West were not yet known. Carried on in the present, it is a religious form severely criticized from the Hindu side by the R.S.S., from the Christian side by the teachers in the seminaries of Kottayam (who even forbid their students to attend it).

Because it was composed of elements borrowed from a number of traditions, the festival probably always had a somewhat flexible structure. The recent innovation involving the worship of the relic of the girdle is no doubt an unusually forceful example of a new voice, but it too is only slowly "fitting in," as worshipers reflect on the way the experience of the window is tied to that of the girdle, both related to the Assumption in some degree. On the other hand, other new voices are also "speaking up" more forcefully, as the poor of the region (in a state with a Marxist government) no longer defer to the traditional "leaders" of society, and more and more consider Mary to be "their goddess." Priestly efforts to limit the activity of the exorcists no longer go unchallenged, and the social tensions now current in all of Kerala society are also evident in all aspects of the festival, as people claim their right to a bath, to an umbrella, to a front row in the church, and so forth.

Uniting all the language of the festival is the transcending experience of the window. Suddenly, as one reflects on the experience of the window, the symbols of healing, exorcism, and relics are all transformed. In the end, this is really not a festival of an angry goddess who assists the worshiper in the fight against disease and black magic but of the confused voices of children who believe that their Mother ultimately transcends all their woes. In the window, suddenly one realizes the unity of the Mother and the Son, the cosmic mother and the triumphant son. In this symbol one experiences the totality of the divine in a way that allows the different religious traditions, and the different fears and longings of the human spirit, to unite.

11

Can Śivan̲ Be "Re-formed"?

The Changing Festival Patterns in the Village of Murukapul̲a

The Village

Murukapul̲a is a suburban village on the main rail line about a half hour north of Trivandrum in southern Kerala. Even the owners of the many new houses usually have some ancestral link with the region, and in most ways the culture of the village is a richly layered story that goes back for many centuries.[1]

The history of the village is intimately related to its special geographical setting. It sits on the mainland facing the "backwaters," or narrow sea inlet that divides the fertile and crowded coastal plain from the mainland in the southern half of Kerala. It has been, therefore, for many centuries an important trade link between the mainland and the densely populated coastal strip of rich paddy or rice land. From Murukapul̲a, one can cross the backwater by ferry to the crowded coastal plain. Evidence of the sophisticated medieval culture of that coastal plain can still be found about a kilometer from the ferry around one of the most famous of the ancient Śivan̲ temples built by the Venād kings (Sarkar 1978).

In Murukapul̲a itself, a host of religious structures serve its diverse population. Three of those (not a part of the festival story here) must still be mentioned to indicate the fascinating history of the village. One of these is the pair of old mosques in the heart of the village. The story of the mosques would now be difficult to uncover, for even the newer of the two is no longer well maintained or part of a self-conscious tradition. The central location of the mosques indicates, however, that Muslims dominated coastal trade in this area as early as the tenth century, and Murukapul̲a was as far inland as the seagoing Muslim traders could reach. The largest religious establishment in Murukapul̲a is the huge Roman Catholic church that looks out over the backwater. This huge church was built at the time of the major conversion of coastal fishermen to Roman Catholicism in the sixteenth century, and Roman Catholics of the fishermen caste are still the second largest group in the village, even though many are now educated and work in the city of Trivandrum. The third religious establishment of historical importance is the Śāstā (Ayyappan̲) shrine in an enclave of Nair caste houses on the edge of the settlement. Murukapul̲a has long been primarily a trade center, so the only members of the

Nair landlord caste in the area lived on their estates outside the village. Over the centuries, the leading Nair family employed a Namboodri priest for its private shrine to Śāstā and worshiped there. In recent years the shrine has been opened to the public and is now described by the sponsoring family as the only center of "orthodox Hindu practice" in the village.

The major focus of worship in the village is a large open square containing a number of temples and small shrines built over the centuries. Worshipers are careful to point out the foundations of former worship centers now in scrub land on the edge of the compound, so the history must be even more complex than the present generation knows. Even the structures still used in worship tell an elaborate story.

What would appear to be the oldest surviving focus of worship in the square is a decrepit, but lovingly maintained, wooden temple of the Tēvi. The two rooms of the shrine look like an inner shrine and an anteroom facing east. Directly in front of this shrine, but at some distance, is a tamarind tree, under which is an ironwork fence surrounding a sacred spot that is now only a stone slab. Some worshipers told me that this sacred spot, ritually considered outside the compound, is the traditional place for "Untouchables" to worship. (They also said that the foundation of a ruined building somewhat further away in the scrub was where another temple, perhaps of the fishermen caste, once stood.) This sacred spot under the tree is directly in line with the door of the Tēvi's temple, and in a certain sense her worship area seems to extend out to this point.

The most impressive building in the square is a Śivaṉ temple to the side of the Tēvi's temple and facing north. This concrete building has a concrete wall around a small compound of its own. Two priests, one local and one a Namboodri Brāhman brought from elsewhere for the festival, work here and go to the Tēvi temple for the rituals to be performed there. These priests also keep custody of the *veḷicapāṭu's* (diviner's) sword (chapter 3), but the local *veḷicapāṭu* has free access to it and has a busy schedule.

The present "owner" of the whole temple square is Mr. Prabakaran, who runs businesses in Trivandrum and Singapore as well as locally. He is of the Iḻava caste and boasts that the first in the reforms of the temple square took place when his father bought the property and built the Śivaṉ temple.

The Iḻavas

The majority of the population of Murukapuḻa is Iḻava. The Iḻava community constitutes as much as a third of the population in many regions of Kerala, but their ritual and social status is almost impossible to define. They were traditionally not allowed to worship in major Brāhmanical temples, such as the large Śivaṉ temple just a kilometer away from Murukapuḻa on the coastal plain. On the other hand, they were not enslaved to Nair landlords, as the Pulaya and Paraiya castes were, and were traditionally considered the specialized cultivators of coconut groves, who could make reasonably independent agreements with landowners. One explanation of this unusual status is the suggestion that the Iḻavas were originally brought from Śrī Lanka (the traditional name for Śrī Lanka was "Iḻam") to work in the coconut groves, with the result that they did not really fit into the prevailing status categories.

The traditional religious practices of the Il̲avas are as difficult to reconstruct as any other aspect of their tradition. Many modern Il̲avas insist that they were traditionally not Hindus. In an earlier study of the Bhagavatī temple in Koṭuṅkaḷūr (chapter 3) I noted that in Koṭuṅkaḷūr Il̲avas play an important, but somewhat tangential, role. There they are the majority of the *veḷicapāṭus*, who play diviner roles in the different villages and come to the Koṭuṅkaḷūr festival for a renewal of their power. In Murukapul̲a the Il̲avas play a more central role, and the worship patterns one now sees in the sacred square at the center of the village are under Il̲ava control.

The history of the temple square in Murukapul̲a, before it came into the hands of the Il̲ava family that presently owns it, is not clear. In most Kerala villages, one could assume that the temples were owned by a Nair family and that the worship would shift from a focus on a Tēvi to a focus on Śivan̲ as the Nair family came under Brāhman influence during medieval times. Something like that pattern could have occurred in Murukapul̲a, but because the number of Nairs was so small (and a major temple of Śivan̲ only a kilometer away), it does seem possible the Nairs were not involved in the Murukapul̲a temple square. In that case the ancient Tēvi temple in the central square, which still has no image and a simple ritual, might derive from an early form of Il̲ava religion.

If the Tēvi temple originally belonged to the Il̲avas, the traditional festival arrangements appear to have linked it with the shrines nearby where the "untouchables," or Pulayas and Paraiyas, worshiped and probably also with the former shrines of the fishermen castes (these fishermen shrines were abandoned once the fishermen caste was converted to Roman Catholicism). If the Śivan̲ temple in the compound goes back one generation and was built, as claimed, by the Prabakaran family, then it represents a dramatic shift in the Il̲avas' religious and social strategy. Rather than sharing the religious environment with the lower castes in the village, as they had in the past, the development of the Śivan̲ temple, with its Sanskritic ritual tradition, moved the Il̲ava worship pattern in the direction of the Nair and Brāhman religious pattern found throughout Kerala in late medieval times. For some Il̲avas, caught in the unstable middle of Kerala's social heirarchy, this kind of "Sanskritization" of their religious tradition seemed a natural form of social mobility. Other Il̲avas, however, disagreed and followed the lead of Narayana Guru, a reformer who arose within their community, and argued that the central concern should be to keep their community together and try to find a new religious direction on their own.

Narayana Guru

Early in this century a most remarkable religious leader arose within the Il̲ava community. As a youth, Narayana Guru turned away from the temple rituals of his local village and traveled widely, living an ascetic lifestyle and seeking religious understanding. He eventually became a schoolteacher and then a religious reformer. He urged Il̲avas to give up drinking the local intoxicants, having elaborate wedding ceremonies, and worshiping the more traditional images involving bloodshed and violence, as well as the Sanskritic images involving priestly rituals. What he advocated was education, simple marriages, a careful attention to family duty, and the development of a new religious system involving only newly written prayers and priests from one's own community. His teaching powerfully argued that God was one and humankind was one, and there should be no distinctions between religions or castes. In practice, his message was taken up almost exclusively by Iḻavas, however, so that although it sets forth a universal message, it is in fact a reform movement within the Iḻava community.

During his travels, Narayana Guru visited Murukapuḻa a number of times, and the reform movement that developed in the village at that time is still vigorous. Narayana Guru's reformers eventually chose to build a separate new temple of their own a short distance from the traditional temple compound. Their neat little temple is directly administered by the reform movement, called the S.N.D.P., which Narayana Guru started. Regular worship rituals are held in this temple, with a mirror serving as the symbol being worshiped (an idea suggested by Narayana Guru). The leaders of this reform temple see themselves as a "modern" alternative to the temple compound and even try to interest their educated Muslim and Christian neighbors in the worship. In practice, however, this reform temple's ritual also seems to be moving in a "Sanskritized" direction (including the recent introduction of a Śivaṉ *liṅkam*), as the more sophisticated Iḻavas with contacts outside push for worship forms they have seen elsewhere.

For the Iḻavas of the village, it is a real challenge to figure out where to worship. The temple associated with the S.N.D.P. reform appeals to the modern among them, largely because this reform movement has given their community political leverage and considerable public respect. On the other hand, the old temple square is associated with Iḻava leadership in the village, and its more traditional forms of worship continue to thrive. Most Iḻavas worship in both places but are especially attached to the festival traditions of the temple square, which everyone seems quite fearful of neglecting.

The Festival

The festival in the temple square, held in early March, forcefully reasserts the older village traditions and in a sense structures itself in open competition with the other religious options that have entered the village over the centuries. In the spirit of the celebration, Muslims, Christians, Nairs, and Reform Iḻavas all find it impossible not to join in the celebration, because it presents itself as a nonsectarian religious celebration in which the most ancient rituals blend with the "Sunday school picnic" activities of the children, modern drama troupes discussing Iḻava identity, and the most recent films with religious themes.

For the most part, the ancient rituals seem to be held at auspicuous moments in the middle of the night. The most elaborate ritual is a cock sacrifice held in the northeast corner of the compound. The Namboodri priest is not present for this ritual, and the other regular priest (an Iḻava without a sacred thread) assists an older priest (with a sacred thread), who comes for this ceremony alone but once served this temple and now serves a Kāli temple on the other side of the backwater. First, the two priests mark 3 grids of 16 blocks each by tracing powder squares on the ground. The central grid is said to represent Kāli, and those to either side lesser deities. Plaintains, flowers, and other offerings are then placed in each of the 48 squares, and the senior priest then says mantras and sprinkles water over each square. Next, lighted wicks are placed in each of the squares. Finally, the priests sit in front of each of the three grids in turn and perform the three cock sacrifices. The cock sacrifice involves taking a 10-gallon pot and, after a certain number of prelimary prayers over the large curved knife, making a sharp cut into the pot. (The priest now cuts a large melon, and the simulated blood is made of turmeric and lime, because the state law no longer allows animal sacrifices.) The "blood" is then smeared over the squares and then over the priests and worshipers, before the pot is excitedly overturned and all involved start dancing. The ceremony then turns to the ritual beheading of the demon Taruka, whose head is often pictured in the Tēvi's hand or sitting beside her. (In this context the "beheading" involves the priest using the knife to dramatically cut a plaintain tree in two.) Finally, the priest takes one of the torches set at the entrance to the enclosure in which these rituals take place and throws it over his shoulder to the north, thus sending the spirit of the Tēvi back to Koṭuṅkaḷūr, 300 kilometers to the north. Only about a dozen persons watch this ritual today, and virtually no one from the large crowd watching dramas in the pavilion 50 feet away pays any attention to the ritual. Nevertheless, most people interviewed the following day had seen the ritual in years past and argued that it was the heart of the festival.

About 4 AM, there is a ritual with a rather different emphasis in the enclosure where "untouchable" worship was traditionally reputed to take place. The preparations for this ritual center on a large fire pit that burned for many hours. Three laypersons (two men and a woman), who had been prominent among the large group dancing around the fire, suddenly dance over to the temple of the Tēvi, where, as they described later, they "take on her spirit." By the time they return to the fire, a huge cauldron of oil (about four feet in diameter) is warming up on the fire. The dancing then gets more and more wild, until one of the three central dancers starts going into a trance and is soon followed by the other two. People begin to approach one or another of the dancers and to offer garlands, currency, or other offerings, hastily received by the dancer and then taken off by their assistants. Eventually the oil starts to boil, and the dancers start to splash themselves with the boiling oil and rub it all over their bodies. One of the dancers then leaps into the boiling pot of oil for a time, then the pot is overturned, and all around dance on the oil-covered ground. The crowd of a few hundred are all in ecstasy by this point, and a mad pushing and shoving takes place as everyone seeks to touch those who continue to dance in a total trance. Finally, the dancers calm down a bit, and a relatively orderly queue approaches them one at a time, making requests involving their personal lives. The majority of the crowd is clearly of the "untouchable" caste heritage, but it is difficult to say if I̱lavas also join in. At dawn, the ceremony ends with the dancers returning the spirit of the Tēvi to her temple and rubbing the sacred oil from their bodies all over Mr. Prabakaran, the "owner" of the temple square, and his family.

While these ancient rituals are enacted with relatively small audiences, somewhat more modern and entertaining forms of religious activity also go on throughout the night. One activity said to be "new" was a wagon pulled through the village with a small generator and a stunning display of neon lights. On the wagon were professional male and female actors in attractive costumes who rowed a boat and sang songs honoring the Tēvi. (Boat races on the backwaters are a famous sport in the area.) Those not in the temple square saw this display as it came past their homes. A second form of religion-related entertainment was the dramas performed throughout the night in a carefully set up *pandal̠* or tent-like structure in the temple square. These dramas had many comic and political features, but in some parts they were mythological and religious as well. Finally, there were feature films playing in the theater that faced the temple square. All in all, the village was alive with a religiously stimulated energy, and people of all religious persuasions were touched.

The activities of the final day of the festival involve a modernization of older worship patterns in an explicit way. The most important activity of the day is the "hook swinging" performed by about a hundred boys. Hook swinging is an ancient form of festival worship and usually involves one or two carefully conditioned professionals, who have a hook placed through a muscle on their back and are then suspended from a great boom, while members of the crowd present them with offerings and make petitions (chapters 2 and 8). The arrangement with the boys in this festival seems similar in that they take a vow to swing on the hook and then sleep on the ground in the compound of the Śivan̠ temple for a week. During this week, a couple of adult trainers arrange for simple meals and times of yogic exercise and generally put the boys (said to be between 8 and 12 years old, but the five or six "stars" are obviously older) through a group initiation. On the morning of the day for hook swinging, the boys are reunited momentarily with their mothers, who take them one kilometer away to the Prabakaran family home. There the mothers dress the boys in elaborate silken *dhotis*, garlands, face paints, and crowns. Photos are taken all around, and the boys line up to make a two-rupee offering to the family sage who sits in a shrine in the yard, rather like a deity with a *triṣūl̠a* or three-pronged spear of Śivan̠ on one side and a *vel̠icapāṭu* sword on the other. (Ten girls also got dressed up for this part of the ceremony in what everyone thought was an appropriate innovation.) Finally, a decorated elephant is brought, and the boys and girls parade off to the main compound with their families following along.

Back at the Śivan̠ temple compound, the boys receive their number and turn by turn have a white cloth carefully tied around their waists. The hooks are slipped through this white cloth, and three boys at a time are lifted onto an extra long boom (double the length I had seen in the traditional hook swinging), which is of modern construction and pivots up and down handily. Fifty noisy young people then pull them around the compound while the crowd shouts in excitement. Sometimes the boom is stopped in front of the Tēvi's temple, and with the boom partially lowered, a baby is placed in the arms of the boy suspended from the boom. The prayers offered in this situation are thought to be especially efficacious. (As far as I could see, the girls participated only in the procession, not in the hook swing.)

The festival closes later that same night with a lovely procession in which thousands of girls and young women dressed in white carry small trays of burning camphor lights around and around the village. This ceremonial ending is finally followed by a massive fireworks display that finishes about 4 AM.

Conclusion

To a westerner unfamiliar with the conservatism of the festival traditions of South India and Śrī Lanka, it would be tempting to compare this festival with the fall fair of North America. There is some merit in emphasizing the innovative and organizational component when one interprets this festival, for it is quite unusual in the degree to which one can see the hand of the Prabakaran family in many of the activities. What is fascinating, however, is the way the initiatives of the family are limited to traditional forms of worship, even though those forms are given radically new religious content.

What one could easily forget about this festival is that it now serves as an ideological rival to the S.N.D.P. temple nearby. The S.N.D.P. temple claims to use no traditional ritual and to proclaim a message based on reason and universal relevance. In the evolutionary categories set out by Habermas (1976) in his studies of the history of human discourse, the S.N.D.P. is operating in the "third stage" of evolution, wherein religion is a kind of ideology or statement of universal principles. The Prabakaran family decided to take on the challenge of this new-style temple nearby, and they chose to do it by reaffirming the traditional rituals of the temples in the square. In the process, they have made the traditional system equally ideological, for it too now includes an appeal to universality and wraps the traditional message in some decidedly modern packages.

One of the oddities of this new packaging of symbols is that the ritual that was probably once at the heart of the festival, the cock sacrifice, is now almost totally marginalized, with almost no one in attendance. It is still important in one sense, in that it allows the argument that this is the "traditional" festival of the village, and people still seem to be quite alert to the fact that such a ritual is important in making the celebration a festival. The "untouchables'" trance ritual, on the other hand, although still probably performed in a fairly traditional way, seems to be newly vital, because it now serves as a symbol of the all-inclusiveness of the festival. Roman Catholics present at this ritual trance wondered about its efficacy and expressed a fascinated surprise that they could feel comfortable being there. The fact that the Prabakaran family wiped oil from the "untouchable" dancers all over themselves may be an old family tradition, but it is, nevertheless, an explicit ideological symbol of universality in the way the present head of the family understands it. Thus, these rituals, which in themselves Habermas would classify as part of the "first stage" of discourse, when rituals were understood "magically" as automatically efficacious, are in the present context serving double duty. In the context of the current ideological debate, they have become abstract ideological symbols that at the same time provide solidarity with the past and solidarity with the other castes of one's village.

In the traditional theistic settings of the large medieval temples, where hook swinging was common, it was an optional form of worship, intended only for those who wanted to please the deity with this extreme form of mortification of the flesh. In Habermas's evolutionary scheme, this would be the "second stage," in which a reciprocal exchange between the divine and the human was the basis of the language of worship. In the newly established format of this festival, the meaning of the ritual is much more appropriate to the ideological setting of the "third type," for these boys are being taught the self-discipline involved in belonging to their social unit of Iḻavas, and the message is much the same as that which the youth wing of the S.N.D.P. tries to teach in its activities. What is amazing about this "mass hook swinging" ritual is that the language or form used is so ancient, yet the content of what is learned is so modern. In the same way, the traditional female form of worship had been to carry an earthen pot filled with a camphor or charcoal fire. Again, this was done by isolated women in fulfillment of a vow and involved a measure of mortification of the flesh. By having thousands of women carry attractive trays of camphor lights together in the dark of night, the act becomes an expression of social solidarity, even a joyous exhaltation of the purity (the white) of the domestic (the trays) domain.

Whether Mr. Prabakaran's challenge to the S.N.D.P. will be successful, and a traditional style of festival will be present in this village 50 years hence, one cannot at this stage know. One might argue that he has gone too far in the direction of manipulating a popular form of religious life, and his innovations will die with him. We do know, however, that other festivals have been changed quite drastically in the past, and the changes have eventually blended into the continuing form of discourse. The limits within which one can make innovation will be known only when tested. In this setting, Mr. Prabakaran seems to be testing close to the limit.

12

Dance and Trance in a New World

A Māriyamman̲ Festival in Guyana

Between 1838 and 1917, shiploads of laborers left Madras and Calcutta for a place then called British Guiana on the northeast coast of South America. There they were "bonded" for five years on "indentured" contracts to work on one of the sugar estates along the coast. Although there was provision for them to return to India if they wished, few did, and many of their descendants continue to work on the sugar estates. About a generation ago, the Indian workers began to move out of the estate barracks and into the small settlements bordering each estate, where the freed African slaves had settled before them. Now the Afro-Guyanese and the Indo-Guyanese live together in the settlements, crowded between the coast and the sugar estates.[1]

Scholarly interest has focused on the way these laborers were recruited and the conditions in which they lived and carried on their culture in this new environment (Jayawardena 1963, 1967). During the first three decades, equal numbers of ships arrived from Calcutta and Madras,[2] but later on the numbers from Calcutta or North India increased. In the end, four of every five laborers came from North India (Smith 1959). As long as they lived in the barracks on the estates, the North Indians and South Indians spoke their own languages of Hindi and Tamil̲ respectively, and had two complete and separate sets of rituals.[3] South Indian rituals for the naming of a child, a wedding, and a funeral are all still very distinct, as is the style of the South Indian *pūja*, but the festival celebration is the best known of the South Indian rituals of Guyana.

When the Indo-Guyanese moved from the estates to the nearby settlements, where the Afro-Guyanese had already lived for a couple of generations, they started to share in the "creole culture" already established there. The schools and churches set up in each settlement by the missionaries had proved popular with the Afro-Guyanese, and the Indo-Guyanese, while more hesitant about the church, also went to the schools. Within a generation, the Indians in the settlements lost their use of the Indian languages, except for ritual settings where these languages continue even today in the music and ritual vocabulary. After the move to the settlements, the Brāhman leadership among the laborers from North India chose to distinguish the North Indian rituals clearly from the non-Brāhmanical traditions brought from South India. Guyanese today tend to think of the South Indian traditions and the North Indian traditions as different from one another. Although the North Indian Brāhman priests have tried since the 1930s to achieve the same status as the established Christian clergy in the British colony, the South Indians gradually came closer to the less privileged segments of the Afro-Guyanese community.[4]

The South Indian religious tradition of Guyana involves the worship of the Tēvi Māriyamman̲ (chapter 8).[5] Māriyamman̲ is the best known of the many goddesses of South India, and her worship in the late nineteenth century was generally carried on by part-time non-Brāhman *pūjaris* (Whitehead 1921), some of whom came to Guyana as laborers. The nineteenth-century rituals of animal sacrifice and possession states are still central to the worship of Māriyamman̲ in Guyana, and the Tēvi is thought of as providing healing, relief from evil spirits, and a dangerous but beneficent presence in the life of the devotee. Her images or *mūrtis* in Guyana were until recently made of wood and usually have four arms, with the right hands usually holding a knife and a trident, and the left hands the head of a mustached male demon and her hourglass drum or *utaki* (fig. 12.1). For the sake of communicating with the North Indians in the population, the Tēvi is often referred to as "Kāli" in public discussions, but the lolling tongue of the Indian Kāli is not seen in the images of Guyana,[6] and in the worship itself the Tamil̲ name "Māriyamman̲" is generally used to describe her.

In addition to the central shrine dedicated to Māriyamman̲, the "Madrasi" (to use the local description) temple compound in Guyana has at least five other shrines (fig. 12.2). Just outside and to the south of her east-facing door is Maturai Vīran̲,[7] a heroic figure with a horse (and sometimes a dog), who faces the doorway and is described as the "protector" of the Tēvi. To her north and a bit behind her is a shrine for

Figure 12-1. Old hand-carved image of Māriyamman̲ (center) in Canefield, Guyana.

Figure 12-2. Compound of small shrines in Canefield, Guyana.

Caṅkani Kaṟuppu,[8] a black deity and the master of the land, sometimes called Dee Bābā. He has a 12-foot rope whip over his shoulder, and priests on his behalf give ritual whippings to devotees who request them. Opposite Caṅkani is Munīsvaraṉ, a pure white deity associated with the moon and the ocean, whose devotees go into a trance by gazing at the moon.[9] The last essential shrine is the Nakura or the "empty" shrine, reserved for the Muslims who worship in the compound and sometimes even marked with a crescent moon and star or the statue of a Muslim gentleman. Finally, in an effort to tie their worship with that of the North Indian traditions, most Madrasi temple compounds include on the north side an area for what they call the "Hindu" gods, and there they usually include Gaṇeṣa, Kṛṣṇa, Hanuman, and Śivaṉ.

The present generation of South Indian religious leaders has had to make some difficult choices.[10] In 1956 one of the *pūjaris* or temple priests, Kistama Rajagopaul from the Miss Phoebe, Port Mourant, temple, was impressed by the reform movement stirred up by the Arya Samaj missionaries among the North Indians in his settlement and tried to "reform" the South Indian temple ritual, specifically arguing that the temples should no longer perform animal sacrifices. Only a few of the temples have followed his example.[11] In the 1970s another popular *pūjari*, Jamsie Naidoo, whose followers were mostly North Indian or Afro-Guyanese, began using English rather than Tamiḻ in the ritual and began allowing lay persons, including women, to play a role in the possession states central to the worship. He also added a few other shrines of locally popular deities to the temple compound. A fair number of temples have now moved in this direction.[12] The different efforts at reform have also had an interesting "backlash" effect, and some of the other temples have now become conservative, or very keen about preserving a pure line of tradition back to the first ancestors who arrived from India. I describe a festival in one of this last group of conservative temples.

The Festival

Most of the settlements on the Guyana coast have Madrasi temples of their own, even though many are less than 2 kilometers from one another. Although they all hold Sunday worship, like all religious institutions of Guyana, and the *pūjaris* are busy with rituals of naming, weddings, and funerals, as well as the weekly services, the primary religious event in each temple is an annual 3-day festival.[13] Whereas the religious specialists and the crowds tend to come from far and wide for these festivals, and there are reports of crowds growing into the many thousands, the festival is primarily an event for the settlement. North Indian Hindus, Muslims, Indian Christians, Afro-Guyanese, and Amerindians in the vicinity are all expected to be involved to some extent in the religious activity of the "Madrasi Big Pūja," as the festivals are called. The festival under discussion is held at Canefield, where some Madrasis were given a place to move their image of the Tēvi 60 years ago when the New Dam settlement was displaced during a reorganization of the sugar estates.

For the members of the Madrasi temple of Canefield, the preparation started a month before the festival. The preparation involved making repairs, and repainting the seven buildings of the compound, and planning for the food, bedding, and ritual clothes for the 20 visiting ritual specialists. It also involved locating the three different kinds of drums, knives, pots, tree branches, and leaves needed in the worship. Ritual needs (tender coconuts, mature coconuts, camphor, *campara* or spice powder, incense sticks, limes, bananas, etc.) must be provided for more then a hundred distinct worship events. Offerings of numerous cocks and goats are provided for the sacrifices. Most important of all, the young men who would become possessed[14] by the Tēvi must be prepared so that they would be able to dance through the settlement with her *karakums* or pyramidal pots of flowers on their heads.

On the first day of the festival, the ritual specialists prepare for the moment that evening when the presence of the Tēvi will first be felt. All involved have abstained from meat, alcohol, and sexual contact for a week. The senior priest or *pūjari* (in the festival I witnessed, the *pūjari* was the head priest from the reputably "oldest" Madrasi temple of Guyana in Albion) performs a full *pūja* or worship of all the 10 images at noon and 6 o'clock and takes the opportunity to instruct the young men, who will later be possessed, on details of the ritual. His closest associate, usually called the "interpreter," because at the height of the ritual he interprets the ecstatic "orders" of the Tēvi through the head priest (which are in Tamiḻ) to the supplicants, spends the day checking every detail of the preparations with the local committee. The drummers test the drums during the preliminary *pūjas*, make adjustments, and cook the meals. The young participants are taught how to make the all-important wand of *margosa* (neem) branches and leaves, which the head priest will use to exorcise evil. Finally, after dark, but under the nearly full moon, the priest leads the nervous young men down to the sacred stream where they all bathe and carefully build the *karakums*. First, they place *margosa* branches in the brass pots, weave flower garlands through the branches, and top the pyramid

Figure 12-3. Priest putting camphor flame on his tongue to test his possession state; *utaki* drum is held by the interpreter in Guyana.

with a lime to ward off evil. When the interpreter calls into the *utaki* drum to the Tēvi, the drum begins to vibrate, and the senior priest throws a pot of saffron water over himself (to cleanse impurity) as his legs begin to tremble. Gradually he goes into a bob-and-weave gait that will not leave him for the rest of the complex ritual. He then takes small blocks of burning camphor from the tray before him and holds them in his hand and mouth, as a test to see if the trembling really represents the presence of the Tēvi (fig. 12.3). Now all the religious specialists, and many in the crowd nearby, begin to feel the arrival of the Tēvi and start to dance. The young participants especially find this experience frightening, and they have to be helped back to their feet for some time, until they seem to learn the dance rhythm of the Tēvi. The *karakum* boys also take the fire test. After the *karakums*, which now contain the presence of the Tēvi, are placed on their heads, they dance about in a step that has a strangely feminine quality about it. The haunting sound of the large open-faced *tappu* drums controls all thought and movement, and then at about a 15 to 20-minute interval they pause while the goat skin drums are reheated (to tighten the skin) in the grass fire started nearby. During this pause in the drumming, the dancing goes on at a quieter pace, and then as the drumming resumes, the rush of emotion is back again. The dance goes on until the wee hours of the morning, when one would expect exhaustion to have long since set in. Finally, the priest and the *karakum* boys lead the way back to the temple and return the presence of the Tēvi to the image.

Much of the second day is taken up with the 50 young men, who are in some way involved with the ritual, milling about the compound making ritual preparations. This is clearly an initiation exercise for the *karakum* boys and others of their age who assist them. Much of the day they are sent on minor errands and taught some of the finer points of the ritual. The senior men from the local organizing committee, as well as the visiting ritual specialists, all teach them about drumming, the preparation of ritual foods, and ritual apparatus of various kinds. A constant oral instruction goes on as stories of the different deities are recounted, and stories of *karakum* boys of the past who violated ritual regulations and suffered severe paralysis or death are rehearsed. At 8, 12, and 6 o'clock full *pūjas* of all the deities are performed, with the head priest handing responsibility for minor parts of the ritual to others who have earned the privilege and will need the protection and blessing of the deity in the night rituals.

At 8 o'clock, the head priest goes into the shrine of the Tēvi and initiates the central ritual of the festival. A moment later a dozen ritual specialists—all of South Indian background—are busily scurrying around at the side of the shrine getting into ritually pure clothes. These clothes are pulled out of red cloth bundles provided by the members of the local committee assigned to assist each of the ritual specialists. These clothes include pure white shirts, *dhotis* tied between the legs, red towels over the loins, and red scarves over the shoulder. The head priest and the *karakum* boys are then garlanded by a representative of the lay committee, and all have red powder marks put on their foreheads and bodies and sandal-paste dots on their foreheads. During these preparations a prominent role is played by the representative of the lay committee (who in the case of the Canefield festival was an Afro-Guyanese), who places the marks on the foreheads of the participants, throws quarters of a lime in the four directions to ward off evil spirits, and joins with the head priest in certain special rituals of preparation before the image of the Tēvi and the *karakums*, into which the presence of the Tēvi is once again to be placed.

When these preparations are completed, the whole company moves out into the compound, where female worshipers appear for the first time, having gathered just inside the gate. Now the interpreter takes the *utaki* drum and talks into it until it again begins to vibrate. As the presence of the Tēvi descends onto the head priest, he begins to tremble, throws cleansing saffron water over himself, takes the fire test, and goes into the bob-and-weave dance. The other ritual specialists follow suit, and the *karakums* with the presence of the Tēvi are brought from the temple and placed on the heads of the two boys who held them the night before.

At this point, the focus shifts to another of the ritual specialists, the sacrificer, who is about to use a 2-foot long sword to cut off the head of a cock. The head priest throws saffron water on the cock to purify it, and the sacrificial priest heats his sword in the fire before the head priest blesses it (fig. 12.4). As both priests dance, the lay donor holds the cock out. As the sword comes down, the head comes off, and the head priest blesses it. The torso of the cock is thrown to the open area near the kitchen where it will hang the next morning.

The procession is now ready to go out the gate to the streets of the settlement. The drums now seem most insistent, and there is great excitement as the presence of the Tēvi enters the street. Just in front of the temple, a crowd waits to line up as individuals bring their petitions. Bowing before the head priest, the petitioner makes offerings for

Figure 12-4. Cock being blessed with holy water and the touch of margosa leaves before being sacrificed in Guyana. *Karakums* on the heads of the boys at the back contain the presence of the goddess.

the deity who is possessing the priest. The drums suddenly stop so the priest/goddess and interpreter can hear the petitioner. Then after an ecstatic comment in Tamil̲, such as "*ramba kaṣṭam*" (which normally means "that is a great difficulty" but in this situation seems to be more theological and mean something like "that is a great evil" or "that is a real demon"), he prescribes a solution by asking the petitioner to do certain forms of worship. The interpreter explains this to the petitioner and actually takes quite a bit of time and whispers carefully in his or her ear. When there is clearly an evil spirit possessing the petitioner, the priest grasps the forelock of the petitioner and "holds" the spirit until it can be convinced to leave. Finally, the priest rubs the *margosa* leaf wand over the body of the petitioner. He then signals for the drums to begin again and dances on to the next petitioner. When the procession finally proceeds down the street, the Afro-Guyanese lay leader performs a purifying ritual at each corner by cutting a lime into quarters and then flinging each quarter in a different direction to ward off evil spirits. He then worships the Tēvi in the priest and *karakums*, and people from that street join in. As the procession goes on, people from each home gather by the side of the street to worship and in some instances to come forward to make petitions. Finally, in the early hours of the morning, the procession makes its way back to the temple compound. After dancing three times around the shrine of the Tēvi, the *karakums* are returned to the shrine, and the head priest holds each of the others until their dance stops. He then dances into the doorway of the shrine of the Tēvi. Then, as the possessing Tēvi leaves him, he suddenly dives full length into the shrine, and members of the lay committee ease his plunge to the ground. After a brief worship, all the ritual clothes are changed, and then each of the participants enters the shrine of the Tēvi in lay clothes for a brief, personal time of thanksgiving.

On the third and last day of the festival, there is a symbolic reversal of the arrangements on the second night when the Tēvi went to each home of the village. At noon on the third day, the people of the settlement and the surrounding region come to the Tēvi with their petitions and their offerings of thanksgiving. Stories abound of healings that have occurred since the last night. As a minimum, everyone partakes of the special *kañci* rice water prepared for the worshipers, but most bring special offerings, each offered as the special deity for whom they are brought is worshiped.

The sequence of worship is the same as always, and the worship of the "North Indian" deities is first. In Canefield, Ganeṣa is in a shrine with Śivan̲, so they are worshiped first, and then the neighboring shrine with Kṛṣṇa and Hanuman. The first of the South Indian group to be worshiped is Caṅkani Kar̲uppu, or the black god in charge of personal quarrels and other problems in one's life. He is reputed to be especially capable of dealing with the curses of enemies. Offerings to him involve large numbers of black male goats, black cocks, and bottles of rum. Many people also ask that he "beat" them with the 12-foot braided whip he carries (fig. 12.5). As the worshiper kneels and holds up an arm, or rolls onto his or her back and holds up a leg, the priests soak the whip in saffron water and then crack the whip loudly around the petitioners's arm or leg.

Worship then moves to the shrine of Munīsvaran̲, the white god just opposite Caṅkani. There a similarly large number of white male goats and white cocks are sacrificed, and copious quantities of rum and especially cigarettes are offered. Worshipers seem to come to this deity with their "psychological" problems, and women especially

Figure 12-5. Worshiper requesting a whipping with a rope in Trinidad.

go into trance, anxiously presenting themselves before this deity. Worship at the Nakura shrine was not elaborate in the Canefield festival, but reportedly at some festivals the Muslim worshipers are almost in the majority and this part of the worship is extensive.

Worship before the Tēvi is, of course, the most extensive of all. Here too animals are sacrificed, but copious amounts of milk and saffron water are also poured out, and fruits and foods of all kinds are brought as offering. In general, the tone promises healing from disease, fertility, and general prosperity or well-being. The worship of the Tēvi includes music and elaborate chanting from the hymnbook or *Māriyammaṉ Talattu*. Worship finally ends with a grand climax at the shrine of Maturai Vīraṉ. There the worshipers' possession states last the longest, and the offerings of animals, rum, and cigarettes are the most abundant. This deity is considered the "master" of all affairs, and whatever the petitions made to others (including the Goddess) need to be repeated here to make them effective. Here also the whole company of worshipers seems to join together, and as they crowd into the shrine in states of ecstasy, the mass of humanity seems to be crying out with one voice.

With the end of the formal worship, quiet descends on the compound, and everyone consumes *kañci* water and generally seems to be busy with personal concerns. But almost no one leaves, and an hour later one of the drums suddenly calls out once again, and the wildest of activity begins as one worshiper called out "the *śaktis* are going to be

Figure 12-6. Worshiper seeking exorcism of a spirit in Trinidad.

raised." Once again, the head priest is quickly possessed, but this time a dozen other ritualists and two dozen worshipers seem to be in similar states. Everyone seems to be asking to be "whipped" with the rope and to be given camphor fires to test the spirit. Finally, something like a queue develops in front of the head priest, and the *jāri* or exorcism of possessing spirits starts to take place (fig. 12.6). As each person presents himself, or, more commonly, herself before the priest, a confrontation ensues. The priest through the interpreter talks directly with the spirit involved and challenges it, bargains with it, and tries to force or seduce it to leave. Using the *margosa* leaf stick to both beat and push the spirit out, the worshiper is finally assured that the spirit is gone, and he or she can keep it away by performing the worship specified.

Although exorcisms are a part of the worship of Māriyammaṉ in India, queues seldom wait for hours while this part of the worship takes place. One of the reasons why the struggle with evil spirits is such a powerful part of the Māriyammaṉ ritual of Guyana is that unresolved social tensions define the life of so many individuals.

The ghosts of the colonial past are by no means gone. In a fascinating article, Brackette Williams (1990) interpreted the "Dutchman ghosts," which so many people bring to the South Indian *pūjaris*, as a form of "history writing" on the part of the people, who feel mysteriously oppressed by the vaguely understood events of two centuries ago that have so dramatically affected their lives. The dramatic ritual of being beaten by a 12-foot-long whip, set in a theological context of serving as a test of the genuineness of one's possessed state, is the most vivid reminder possible of the power relations that existed when white people brought Africans and Indians to Guyana and then "beat" them into a reluctant obedience. By associating these mysterious powers of the past with the "Dutchman," who had disappeared before the Indian immigrants arrived, the whole cluster of events that have led to the present and uncertain future can be mythologized and called up to be reckoned with.

The ghosts of the more recent past are no less troublesome than those of two centuries ago. While the Afro-Guyanese and Indo-Guyanese fought for freedom from colonial authority together, their political leaders dramatically parted company when independence came. In many ways the two communities have similar histories. During the early days of slavery, many Africans went into the nearby Amazonian forests to live, and these people, called "Maroons," still haunt the political leaders of neighboring Surinam. The freed African slaves of British Guiana stayed in the neighborhood of the plantations but demanded the wages and working conditions they felt just and developed an amazingly well-educated and coherent civilization by the time the British colonial leaders were ready to leave. When the Indians started to move into the settlements along with the Africans, they were impressed with the benefits of education, and they too entered the school system with enthusiasm. But when one of the Indo-Guyanese students went off to the United States to study dentistry and returned to take the lead in calling for independence from colonial authority, the Afro-Guyanese community, which was generally better educated and more experienced in government service, was most surprised. It was not long before the Indo-Guyanese leader, Cheddi Jagan, was pushed aside, and the Afro-Guyanese took leadership into their hands. Thirty years later, the political leaders in the two communities have yet to learn how to work together.[15] In the lives of individual people, there is an underlying uncertainty, which says that mysterious "enemies" may at any time make life difficult once again.

Even though the people who come to the Māriyammaṉ temple festivals to exorcize their ghosts are generally not political leaders in society, they still suffer from the social and psychological anxieties that accompany political uncertainty. The Māriyammaṉ worshipers of Guyana from the beginning have been a South Indian minority within the (Indian) community, and they occupied the bottom rung in a many-tiered society defined by power and violence. Like the slaves before them, the Indian laborers did not accept the violence of the system without a fight. And the worshipers who come to this festival clearly think of it as arming them once again for a battle. The male associates of the Tēvi are each thought of as familiar with one or another form of violence, and worshipers expect them to deal with the specific fears petitioners bring to them. But the Tēvi herself graciously empowers each one, by assuring all that it is she who heals and she who provides the fertility necessary to give life its continuity. In discussing similar forms of Māriyammaṉ worship in the Antilles Islands nearby, Benoist (1984) suggested that although Māriyammaṉ had the highest position, Maturai Vīraṉ and other deities had the greater "power." I would say that whereas the other deities confront the specific fears of the worshipers, this festival to Māriyammaṉ is a demonstration of the limitations of violence. The Tēvi empowers each worshiper who attends, precisely because she transcends the conflicts of political and ethnic power brokers. The festival is ultimately an experience of reverence, in which all human offerings and all the concerns of people from many ethnic and religious backgrounds are brought to the feet of the Tēvi. In the end, it is she who possesses or, as the worshipers express it, "plays with" her devotees. In her presence their anxieties are conquered and they are enabled to return to their problematic lives with a new perspective and an odd abandon.

13

Suburban Promises

A *Kavati* Festival in South Africa

There are now about a million Indians among the 20 million citizens of South Africa. The story of how the ancestors of these people came to leave India and settle in South Africa begins around 1860.[1]

Indentured Indian laborers had been taken systematically to a variety of places around the world beginning in the 1830s. By the 1850s, estate owners in Guyana and Trinidad were complaining about how difficult it was to manage the South Indian laborers from the port of Madras, so when British planters in South Africa decided that they too would try planting sugar cane, the colonial authorities decided to send most of the South Indian laborers to South Africa. These laborers landed in the port of Durban and were assigned to sugar estates to the north and south of the city right along the coast. Almost immediately traders from Gujarat arrived, and this largely Muslim community set itself up in the city of Durban, even though it took as its first task the servicing of the Indian laborers' needs.

The later part of the nineteenth century was a turbulent time in South Africa. The British had taken the upper hand in Capetown and Durban, but the Dutch settlers, who had been there earlier, resented that and marched inland looking for political freedom. When prospectors discovered gold and diamonds in the inland Transvaal territory, the scramble for supremacy among the Europeans led to the Boer War between the Dutch settlers and the British colonial authorities. In the midst of this confusion, some of the African tribes, such as the Xhosa and Zulus, learned how to conduct local wars in ways that gained them some measure of respect. However, the two colonial powers continued their struggle for control through most of the twentieth century. In the midst of this colonial struggle in an African land, the misplaced Indian community had little choice but to work out its own destiny.

At the beginning of the twentieth century, the future of the Indian community looked anything but bright. The sugar industry had not been as big a success in South Africa as it had elsewhere, and the British were not sure what role the Indians might play as they sought to cling to colonial power long enough to control the mines and hold off the aspirations of both the Boer settlers and the Africans. Mohandas Gandhi had arrived on the scene just as the uncertainties were reaching their peak and, with single-minded focus on the question of Indian civil rights, was able to convince the British authorities that however precarious their long-term role might be, the Indians had certain rights and should be allowed to pursue their destinies within that framework.

Before long, it was clear that the choice of most of the Indians centered on the city of Durban. South Indian farmers cleared the swamps to the northwest and southwest of the city and set up vegetable gardens that supplied the still-famous Indian market of Durban. The Muslim merchants opened shops all along Grey Street, which the colonial authorities had assigned to them, and developed the most crowded bazaar in the city. Other Indians who arrived in the city found that they usually could get work on the railway, which had a major workers' colony in the northern outskirts of the city.

Even during the early years (1860–1900) on the sugar estates, we know that small Māriyammaṉ temples were everywhere, and it appears that the pattern of worship was quite similar to that developed among the South Indians in Guyana (chapter 12). With the move to the vicinity of Durban at the turn of the century, however, there was an important shift in cultural and religious outlook. One of the factors in the shift in cultural outlook probably resulted indirectly from Gandhi's political initiative, in that the political activity of the Natal Indian Congress unified all the Indian people and gave the South Indian indentured laborers an opportunity to identify with their higher-status Indian associates. Two specific cultural changes within the South Indian community came about at the turn of the century as people sought to leave their low-status background behind. First, as South Indian laborers moved from the sugar estates to the Durban area, many changed their family name and simply adopted one of the five or six landowners' caste names of South India. Today names such as Reddy, Naidu, Moodly, and Pillai have become almost universal, and people still joke about their grandparents' decision to make this change and how complex it has made the still-common practice of arranging a child's marriage with a partner of equal status. Second, many of those with sufficient means to undertake the building of a temple chose to set aside the Māriyammaṉ tradition of the sugar estates and build temples to either Murukaṉ or Śivaṉ. As a result of this development, the South Indian Hindu worship pattern around Durban now has three distinct styles: goddess temples with sacrifices, exorcisms, and local priests in locally designed buildings; Murukaṉ temples designed by architects from India, with goddess temples nearby at which sacrifices and firewalking rituals are held; and more elaborate Śivaṉ temples built by Indian architects, with minimal shrines for the goddess within the temple grounds. The festival here takes place in the most important of the Śivaṉ temples, the Umgemi Road Temple on the northern outskirts of the city.[2]

The Umgemi Road Temple was built in 1910 by Kothenar Ramsamy Pillai (1863–1938), generally considered the greatest of the temple architects who came from India to South Africa around the turn of the century (fig. 13.1). It is a lovely South Indian-style temple with an orthodox *vimāṉa* or dome over the major deity and space for Vināyakaṉ (Gaṇeṣa) to the left and Murukaṉ and his two wives to the right. These three deities face in the orthodox eastern direction, and the popular shrine of the Tēvi is set in a niche in the north wall facing south, again in the orthodox arrangement for a South Indian Brāhmanical temple. The main deity is called Śrī Vaithyanatha Easwar, or Śivaṉ, as the Lord of Healing. To the north of the main temple are more recent Viṣṇu and Māriyammaṉ temples, and in front of all three is a large festival ground with magnificent trees brought from India.

Figure 13-1. Śivaṉ temple in Durban, South Africa.

The place of this temple in the sacred geography of the city of Durban is not easy to describe. As I described earlier, the sugar plantations were spread along the coast to the north and south of the city. In addition to the small Māriyammaṉ temples near the plantations, the railway terminus to the south of the city, Isipango, has a much larger Māriyammaṉ temple (even though locally built, with an inventive reed base holding up the plastered dome *vimāṉa*), which is the site of a major festival in April (in local parlance "the Easter festival") with traditional sacrificial rituals and trance behavior. In the towns leading to the plantations (particularly to the north), Gujarati Hindu merchants built Viṣṇu temples in a North Indian style, and in 1911 a Brāhman priestly family started to serve the Samtseu Road temple of Viṣṇu, which is in the same railway colony as the Umgemi Road temple to the north of the city. The largest blocks of South Indians lived in Cato Manor and Clairwood to the northwest and southwest of the city, respectively, where they were drawn by the opportunities for vegetable gardening in the swamplands adjacent to the Umgemi and Umbilo rivers. Each of these areas has a number of Murukaṉ temples with goddess temples for either Māriyammaṉ or Tiraupati (Draupadī) beside them. Even though in the 1960s the Indian population was forced out of these areas and moved to settlements further from the city under the apartheid policies of the government, the temples were allowed to stay and are still used in worship and indeed still hold celebrations of the *kavati* festival, which I am about to describe in terms of its celebration at the Umgemi Road temple.

As one can see from this description of the sacred geography, Hindu temples surround the city of Durban in a wide band, precisely because Hindu temples (and for that matter Indian homes) were not allowed within the city. The Muslim merchants were able to build beautiful mosques in their bazaar area along Grey Street, but the Umgemi Road temple near the railway colony on the northern edge of the city was as close to a city temple as the Hindus were allowed. As the political struggles of South Africa slowly evolved in the course of this century, the Umgemi Road temple came to serve as an anchor to all Hindus seeking to find a role in the turbulence.

The general outline of South Africa's recent history is well known. Some racist features of the British colonial era were already being challenged by Mahatma Gandhi at the turn of the century. By the 1930s, the British city council in the city of Durban was desperately trying to find new ways of limiting the Indian presence in the city, by insisting that more and more areas close to Indians and that British residents not continue to sell their properties to the Indian moneylenders. In Durban these efforts were a desperate effort of a British clique, and in the 1930s Indians were steadily making major advances in education and business. In the realm of religion, both Indian Christian churches and Hindu reform movements were quite active.

A somewhat different form of turbulence was soon to come, however, as the National Party government led by Boer settlers elaborated its apartheid policy, which divided the population into the four racial groups of "White," "Indian," "Colored," and "Black," each with different political rights, education systems, and residency requirements. The Indians of Durban in the 1960s were uprooted from their homes in places such as Cato Manor and Clairwood and moved to the two new cities of Phoenix, 30 kilometers to the northwest, and Chatsworth, 30 kilometers to the southwest. Even though this dislocation was resented, it did give the Indian community a dramatically more specific identity, and it indirectly provided the festival traditions of the South Indian temples, which stayed open in the old areas, with a new role as a public display of Indian identity.

By the time of the festival celebration I witnessed in 1996, one more wave of turbulence had arrived. In 1994 the apartheid system collapsed, and the African National Congress government of Nelson Mandela took power. Indians had played a prominent role in the struggle against apartheid, and Mandela appointed Indians to prominent positions in his cabinet. Nevertheless, in Durban the economically and educationally better off Indians found themselves racing with the more numerous Coloreds and Blacks for the scarce housing, employment, and educational opportunities suddenly made available in the city. For some Indians, it seemed a good time to enter a more democratic and modern social order; for others, it seemed a time to consolidate ties with one's own community. For everyone, it was a time to feel nervous about one's personal future, to feel concerned about personal safety as crime rates soared; in short, it was a time for prayer.

The Festival

In South Africa, January is a holiday month. In 1996 the priests at the Umgemi Road temple were complaining that they could not keep up with their work as a line of new people drove their new cars into the worship area just in front of the main temple to receive the ritual of blessing before going out into the streets of a city with one of the highest rates of "hijacking" and car theft in the world. Inside at the shrine of the Tēvi, female students and their parents lined up to ask for help with the exam results, which were expected in a few days. Off to the side, their male counterparts were taking a vow to fast and carry a *kavati* or shoulder shrine in the dance procession to be held in a few days.

Tai Pūcam is a festival holiday in early February that is celebrated in all South Indian Śivan temples, but the ritual of carrying *kavati* is not usually a central part of Tai Pūcam celebrations in India. The carrying of *kavati* is a special ritual act found primarily in Murukan̲ festivals, but in South Africa the carrying of *kavati* has become the central festival act of both the Śivan̲ and Murukan̲ traditions. In any case, the carrying of *kavati* is now thought of as the central feature of the Tai Pūcam festival in the Umgemi Road temple of Durban.

The festival begins in the usual way for an orthodox Brāhmanical temple with the raising of the flag and the planting of seeds in a pot of mixed soils 10 days before the climactic dance procession. For the tenth day, the festival images of Murukan and Vināyakan̲ (Ganeṣa) are brought out to a table near the snack bar, where people who have not been able to attend the temple earlier in the festival can ask junior priests to say a "fast-food" ritual prayer for them. For the processional day, the grove-like area in front of the temples is swept clean and roped off so that it can be treated as a sacred area where shoes are not worn.

Early in the morning some of the teenaged boys who have been fasting hesitantly bring the modest *kavati* or shoulder shrine they will carry in the procession, and place it toward the back of the roped off rows where the 2,000 participants will line up. Somewhat later, the more professional *kavati* dancers arrive with a number of assistants and place their elaborate structures closer to the front with their supply of special (yellow or red) clothes, turmeric powder, coconuts, cymbals, *vēls* or spears, dumbbells, and shoes consisting of pointed nails to walk on. Finally, the half dozen places just at the front beside the great rock in the northwest corner of the grove are filled in by local politicians and prominent businessmen (fig. 13.2).

Inside the temple a fire sacrifice or *yakkiyam* (Sanskrit: *yajña*) is led by the head priest for much of the morning, and at the end of it the lay head of the temple board carries an exquisite *kavati* in the old style (a *kavati* originally was a bamboo stick slung across the shoulders with pots of milk on either end, and the idea was to dance wildly before Murukan̲ without spilling the milk) from the *yakkiyam* (Sanskrit: *yajña*) out to the rock where the procession is to start (fig. 13.3). The priest brings the embers of the fire to the rock and lights the fire under the large cauldron of milk there, before returning to the temple for the balance of the celebration. In a pavilion near the fire, thousands of tiny brass pots are set on tables, and lay officials, with their mouths covered so as not to pollute the milk, pour the milk into the pots and carefully cover each one with plastic wrap before they are returned to the dancers.

With the arrival of the fire embers at the starting rock, the rows of waiting dancers begin to go into a frenzy. As the dancing begins, the minority of women among the dancers becomes more prominent, for many are exceptionally good dancers and some go into dangerously severe trances. Some of the women seem to ignore the protocol of the procession altogether. One young woman in a snake outfit begins a dramatic serpentine dance, and a widely respected older woman performs excorcisms in the name

Figure 13-2. Political figures lined up to lead *kavati* procession in Durban.

Figure 13-3. Businessman and chair of the temple board starting the procession in Durban.

of Māriyammaṉ while dancing right in front of the rock. Once the frenzy reaches a certain level, it is considered safe to insert the metal hooks (it is believed that the frenzy takes the blood in from the surface of the skin), and experienced older men begin inserting hooks under the skin of the leading participants. When the dancing begins again, milk pots, coconuts, and anchors lines for the *kavati* all hang from hooks in the skin (with a few even pulling a large *kavati* set on wheels with ropes anchored to their skin). With the hooks inserted, the dancing frenzy again becomes unbearable, until eventually the lay leader of the temple board returns from the temple and leads the procession around the temple grounds. The energy within the procession surges to the front, and the first wave of 30 or so *kavati* dancers (mostly politicians and businessmen) need to be protected from the surging crowd behind by a row of temple staff tied together with *dhotis*. Only a few dozen of the 2,000 marchers know the intricate steps of the *kavati* dance used in India, and their cymbals have to try to hold the beat in the absence of the teams of drummers that would lead a similar procession in India.

After circling the congested temple grounds three times, the procession pours into the temple, and the *kavatis* are quickly handed out the side window, while those in the procession make their milk offerings to the deities. By late afternoon the clutter of cars blocking a couple of lanes of the highway outside the temple begins to move along, and the Black African temple servants begin to sweep up the piles of leftover sandals and plastic bags that litter the temple grounds.

Conclusion

South African Hindus take great pride in describing themselves as the largest Hindu community outside of India. They are less quick to point out that the Indian community's most prominent political and intellectual leaders are Muslim and that the number of Indian Christians is growing dramatically. Perhaps even more unnerving to traditional Hindu leaders is the fact that in the newly integrated society of South Africa, the shopping malls seem to be everyone's favorite destination, and the ultra-modern Hare Kṛṣṇa temple beside the Chatsworth mall is by far the busiest temple in the country.

At first glance, the *kavati* festival, with its severe ascetic practices and its concern with pollution and ancient forms of music and dance, seems a strange contrast to this urban sophistication and modern taste (in much the same way as it is in Malaysia and Singapore). But one is even more puzzled after meeting the individual vowkeepers and processionists, when one realizes that the most modern among the students, businessmen, and politicians are the active participants in the festival. Clearly, participation in the *kavati* festival has become an antidote to the great uncertainties that surround life in modern South Africa. Will the politically aggressive Zulus, who make up the large majority of the population in the state of Natal, stand aside as the Whites hand over the business and professional leadership of Durban to the highly educated Indians? Will families be broken up as Indian professionals find that they must go abroad in the future to find work? Are the new opportunities to return to India going to be attractive when visitors to India are finding that they have drifted further away from the homeland than they thought they had during the years in South Africa? Dancing at the *kavati* festival does not change the uncertainty of the surrounding environment, but it does anchor one in one's own community, while at the same time affirming the community's right to its share of the public domain.

Festivals are always about social status and social solidarity in some measure, but for a suburban teenager I met in Durban, it was a tortuous route in parental logic that finally convinced him to take his vow and make his bid to be part of the high-status Hindu community of Durban. His grandfather openly talked of the way their low-caste name had been changed and still preferred worship at the Māriyamma<u>n</u> temple and working with his hands. He even called himself "Bob" so the Black Africans who came to his repair shop would not feel uncomfortable. His wife, however, moved strictly within Indian circles and kept all the vows of fasting she heard about from the higher-status Indian women. The parents had made it into low-level clerical jobs, and the family's hope was that the grandson would now make it into medical school. The family's closest Indian friends were the Moodlys ("true Moodlys" they clarified). Mr. Moodly was on the board of Umgemi Road temple, and his son was a medical doctor trained abroad. The grandson destined for medical school explained that the real problem was his marks and he would have to do something about that, but this vow his grandmother wanted him to do "couldn't hurt," and even if it didn't get him into medical school, "it might help in some other way." In the end, he marched quietly near the back of the procession and joked with his school chums that he had to do it for his grandmother.

Each individual faced the choice of identifying with the local Indian community and joining the procession or siding with the newly integrated social order of South Africa and the wider secular world. The Indian community's leaders faced a similar dilemma as they tried to decide how to describe their community's celebrations in the newly "open" public arena. The fight to save the temples of Cato Manor and Clairewood had been successful in the 1960s partly because the National Party wanted to give the Indians favors denied to the Colored and Black communities. At that time, some Indians decided to refuse such favoritism within the evil apartheid system and insisted on defining themselves as part of the unjustly treated "Black" community. Most, however, went along with the opportunities offered for more public forms of worship, a better education, and better housing in the new Indian-only colonies, and they contributed generously to a gaudy temple on the grounds of the university assigned to Indians. Now, in 1996, the dilemma was presented in a new form. Many Indians were thankful for the opportunity to participate in an open and integrated society and for the African National Congress government's willingness to include Indians in positions of power. But the Zulu leader Buthelezi had a different vision, one of separate communities, with political alliances developed on the basis of certain constitutionally defined privileges. Most of the conservative Hindu leaders at this festival acknowledged that they liked his idea because they saw the vision of separate communities as the only way to protect a position of privilege for a minority that constituted hardly 5% of the national population. These leaders thought the police should allow them to march with the *kavati* on the main roads, and the newspapers should report on their community activities. Other people in the crowd thought that the integrated society pushed by the ANC was a good thing and that the police should not allow the procession onto the public roads. Some even said that the temple at the university is now an embarrassment, because the apartheid era's designation of an institution as open to only one community is now gone, and the majority of the students are no longer Hindu.

The celebration of the Tai Pūcam festival and the use of *kavati* dance in a festival take place in many parts of the world without raising the intense social and political questions associated with the celebration in South Africa. One can assume that the social and political atmosphere will soon change in one direction or the other and that the celebration of the festival in a few years will have quite a different meaning for the participants. The history of the South Indian community settled in South Africa has seen more social and political turmoil than most Hindu communities around the world. The participants in this festival probably imagine that another major social or political crisis is only a few years down the road. They hope that the solidarity they have learned to express in this celebration will keep them united and perhaps prepare them for the next crisis.

14

A Bath for Dancing Śivan̲ in the Cold of Canada

Adapting a Festival to a New Environment

During the past half century, many South Indians and Śrī Lankans have emigrated to other lands. With its cold climate and open spaces, Canada offered a dramatic physical contrast to the regions from which these immigrants came, and the social and emotional contrasts could hardly have seemed less drastic. At first, like most immigrants in Canada, those from South India and Śrī Lanka worshiped as best they could with other people from their homelands,[1] but they longed to have a temple of their own.

The temple for Tamil̲-speaking people on Bayview Avenue north of Toronto is an orthodox South Indian–style temple. Six to 10 traditional priests from South India are on duty at all times, and the temple has a busy and vibrant worship atmosphere every day of the year.

The design of the temple was set down by the great ascetic sage Śaṅkarācārya of Kāñcīpuram and is meant to include all the deities that would be worshiped in Brāhmanical temples in South India. Dozens of separate shrines for these deities are maintained by the priests, and the vast concourse in which they are set reminds a worshiper of the great corridors (*pirakārams*) of a South Indian temple. The arrangement of the deities involves two main groupings, with one group on the worshiper's left as one enters for the family of Śivan̲, and one on the worshiper's right for the family of Viṣṇu.[2] Each of these groups has one towering *vimān̲a*, which will eventually extend well above the roof. The towering *vimān̲a* of the Śivan̲ family houses the second son Murukan̲ (Kārttikēyan̲), and the other houses Perumāḷ (Viṣṇu) himself. These two family groups are united both visually and religiously by a smaller *vimān̲a* in the center for Vināyakan̲ (Ganeṣa). Because the image of Vināyakan̲ and the Tēvi (Durgā) were the only ones on the site for some time, and because Vināyakan̲ is directly in front of the main doorway, the temple is often popularly called the Ganeṣa Temple. Clustered near Murukan̲ are major shrines of Śivan̲, Parvati, and Śivan̲ Naṭarājan̲ or Dancing Śivan̲, and facing the images of all the gods are shrines of each of the goddesses.[3]

Much of the initial energy involved in developing a great temple such as this had to be spent on obtaining images and having them properly empowered. Priests with experience in the worship of the different deities had to be found. The worshiping community was initially small, but it suddenly enlarged dramatically when the war situation in

Śrī Lanka led to a large immigration of Śrī Lankan Tamiḻs. The Śrī Lankan group now makes up the majority among both the worshipers and the organizers of the temple, even though the original planners were South Indian professionals who are still active.

The decision to include festival activity in the life of the temple was risky. Because people have rich memories of childhood celebrations that were deeply moving to them, they want to see them reenacted exactly as they are remembered. Unfortunately, however, popular festival activities are not often carried out the same way in two different places, so where there are people of differing backgrounds, there is likely to be disagreement about what is important in the celebration.

The festival people chose to celebrate in Toronto is popularly called *Ārttirā Taricaṉam* (Sanskrit: *Ārdrā Darśana*), or the Vision of Grace, and centers on the bathing of Dancing Śivaṉ. Most people have seen a short version in their local temple, but these are really imitations of the great 10-day festival of Dancing Śivan in his home temple of Citamparam, the only place where Dancing Śivaṉ is the central object of worship.

The Festival as Practiced in India and Śrī Lanka

In the home temple of Dancing Śivaṉ in Citamparam, the Dīṭcitar priests carry on a unique ritual tradition (Younger 1995). In Citamparam the two major festivals are at the two solstices, with the more important one in the month of Mārkaḻi (December/January) on the day or "star" (*nakṣatra*) of Tiruvāturai, and the other in the month of Āni (June/July) on the day of Uttiram. In both cases, the 10-day festivals climax with the 4 AM Bath or *Apiṭēkam* (Sanskrit: *Abhiṣeka*) of the images of Dancing Śivaṉ and the Goddess, in which pots of water, milk, curd, honey, sugarcane juice, a mixture of five fruits, lemon water, coconut water, apple juice, grape juice, rose water, water from the Ganges River, and finally sandal-paste water are poured over the images.

The Mārkaḻi festival has an added feature: it involves an honoring of the great hymnwriter Māṇikkavācakar in a number of its rituals. The famous *Tiruvempāvai* hymn he wrote is sung in the presence of his image just beside the inner sanctum of Dancing Śivaṉ in the late afternoon of days 2 through 8 (not as in other places where it is part of the bath ceremony on day 10). The hymn is sung by the *ōtuvar* or traditional hymnsinger employed by the temple, but women performing Mārkaḻi vows, which involve taking early morning baths in the cold winter streams and reciting this hymn as they do, often bring their hymn booklets and hum along with the *ōtuvar*. In preparation for this hymnsinging, the *ōtuvar* undergoes elaborate rituals making him a personification of Māṇikkavācakar, and at the end he and the image of Māṇikkavācakar are taken to the inner sanctum of Dancing Śivaṉ, where they are honored and thanked by the deity. In addition to being present for the singing of his famous hymn, the image of Māṇikkavācakar is also honored by being carried backward (in a posture of devotion) before the festival images of the deities during the regular morning processions on days 2 through 8. Māṇikkavācakar's image is not carried in this manner in the evening processions or in the movements of the main image from the inner sanctum during the last 2 days of the festival.

In most Śivaṉ temples of South India and Śrī Lanka, this famous festival of Citamparam is copied in festivals that center on the *apitēkam* (Sanskrit: *abhiśeka*), or bathing of the subsidiary images of Dancing Śivaṉ found in those temples. In the great

Maturai temple, for instance (from which most of the priests in Toronto have come), there is an especially elaborate celebration of this festival because Māṇikkavācakar was raised near Maturai and served as minister in the court of Maturai before retiring to Citamparam and a life of meditation.

The main Śaiva temples of Śrī Lanka date from the time of the great Cōḻa Empire, which included both South India and Śrī Lanka. In the nineteenth century a reformer named Aramukan Navalar attained great prominence in Śrī Lanka with a simplified or "Protestant" version of Śaiva Siddhānta theology and temple practice that he taught. As a result of his influence, and other factors that distinguish temple practice in South India and Śrī Lanka, the Śrī Lankan Tamiḻ Śaivas place a much greater emphasis on laypersons singing the Tamiḻ hymns than do the Śaivas of South India. In addition, because of a shortage of Brāhman priests and professional *ōtuvar* hymnsingers in the temples of Śrī Lanka, many temples manage without these professionals. These differences in the religious histories of South India and Śrī Lanka have had an interesting impact on how the two communities understood the tradition of worship they were trying to reestablish when they joined together in the temple in Toronto. The differences would be especially noticeable when the two communities tried to join to celebrate this festival.

Modifications in the Canadian Environment

Driving through the lonely streets of Toronto on December 21 at 3:30 in the morning, I wondered what leaps of imagination would be necessary to make it possible to celebrate the Bath of Dancing Śivan̲ and the beginning of a new "day of the gods" in Canada. Arriving in the icy parking lot to find only one other vehicle, a van stuck in the ridges of ice as its driver struggled to back up to the door and unload sound equipment, I knew the leaps were going to be great.

Inside the temple, the most subtle differences were immediately obvious. It was warm inside, and everything came under the glare of electric light. The mystery of the creeping dawn of the winter solstice at 4 AM in Citamparam was over in Toronto the minute I entered the door. There, in the glare of many lights, were the priests and their helpers bustling about. The mysterious and semi-divine Dīṭcitar priests of Citamparam seem to move dreamily in the mythic distance, but here the priests were talking excitedly about where exactly they should place the table that was to hold the images to be bathed. The images themselves sat unattended and unadorned on the table as I walked around it, and I recalled the day in Citamparam when 200 husky farmers tried to help the priests lift the image of Dancing Śivan̲ as it left the inner sanctum and were barely able to control the great weight it had magically accumulated over the months inside the sanctum (Younger 1995, pp. 60–61). As the tables for images and offerings slowly took shape and sound equipment was set up, the crowd gathered, and the stage created in our full view began to take on some of the mystery that would allow us to see in the dance of Śivan̲ the promise that we would witness the beginning of another "day of the gods."

The crowd was a bit late for the 4 AM start in 1994 because the printed notice of the festival said that the climax of the festival or the bath would take place at 4 PM. Later notices crossed off the PM and wrote in AM, but worshipers who arrived were buzzing with the question that occurred to all of us: were we celebrating the solstice as it began the "day of the gods" in India—in which case we should have been celebrating at 4 PM the evening before so as to be synchronized with worshipers in India—or were we going to celebrate a Canadian beginning of the cosmic year at the familiar 4 AM time? One of the prominent Brāhman organizers cut the debate short by asserting that the notice error had been that of the printer and "of course, we are celebrating the beginning of the day of the gods, so it would have to be in the morning." Doubtful eyes indicated that he had not really heeded the argument many forwarded that "things had to be done exactly as they were at home."

As the worship began, the most difficult adjustments needed for this festival ritual were soon evident. As the worshipers gathered on the carpets rolled out before the tables of images, a Śrī Lankan man handed out hymnbooks he had arranged to print especially for the festival. Soon the crowd began following along in the hymbooks and singing after him antiphonally, as he sat erect in the middle of the crowd and sang out one verse after another. The tone of his singing was classical and strong, and the audience of worshipers improved dramatically as they imitated the tunes he sang, many of which they had heard before on recordings but had apparently never sung themselves. The priests hinted a few times that they were ready to begin the bath, but the hymnbook was not finished, and the singer had no intention of leaving it incomplete. The priests began the ritual anyway, and the audience had to divide its attention for a time, until the ritual details of the bath became totally absorbing and the singing faded away.

Just to the side of the priests pouring the many pots full of juice, milk, and other substances onto the images, a microphone was set up so that one of the Brāhman lay organizers of the temple, assisted by one of the priests who was a Smārta Brāhman and also knew a bit of Sanskrit, could recite the Sanskrit verses that traditionally accompany the bath. In India, this recitation is done by the priests performing the bath or by priests off to the side and is inaudible, but in this case it was given much more prominence in that it was sung with the text in hand, and it determined the pace at which the priests who were performing the bath could proceed.

Mediating between the lay Śrī Lankans, who wanted more ways to participate in the worship, and the Brāhmans and priests, who wanted to be free to perform the ritual as correctly as they could, was a Śrī Lankan woman who appeared to be in charge of everyone. She stood on the side opposite the Sanskrit recitation and told worshipers who arrived where to put their offerings on the tables, told a few male assistants when to take those offerings and refill the huge tubs of juice, milk, and so on from where the bathing substances were taken, and when to empty the tubs collecting the materials draining from the bath. She also handed the various bathing substances to the assistant priest, who then handed them on to the priest performing the bath. In many ways, this woman regulated the most ritually correct parts of the ceremony, but she was also able to play the role of the leading devotee and seemed deeply moved by the appearance of the images as they were bathed. In both these roles, she was the model through whom the Tamil̲ Canadians from both Śrī Lanka and South India came to understand the inner meaning of this dearly recalled but vaguely understood form of worship.

Even if the Śrī Lankan woman was able to satisfy both those who wanted ritual correctness and those who wanted lay participation in the bath, she could not suppress the latent disagreement when the ceremony moved on to the singing of Māṇikkavācakar's hymn. As this part of the ceremony began, the priests called an older Śrī Lankan gentleman up to the side of the altar. In his youth he had been a professional *ōtuvar* temple singer, and he occasionally still performed that role when the Toronto temple had a ritual role for an *ōtuvar*. In an elaborate ceremony the priests turned him into Māṇikkavācakar, by tying a special orange cloth around his head, performing a number of other ceremonies invoking the presence of Māṇikkavācakar, and finally bringing him food offerings from the deity. During the later part of this ceremony, a Śrī Lankan woman of about his age stood beside him, and he seemed to try to get the priest to share some of the blessings with her. Those of us in the audience were puzzled, and wondered if this was his wife, but the priests pointedly refused to offer any of the blessings to her and presumably knew what was about to happen. The *ōtuvar* sang the introduction to the hymn uncertainly and then handed the book to the lady. She then sang the first verse in a classically trained voice with a deeply devotional tone. The priests were a bit stunned, but, after hesitating for an awkward 5 minutes, they eventually presented her with some of the offerings sent to Māṇikkavācakar by the deity at the end of each verse. As the ritual continued through the 20-verse hymn, the audience generally appreciated the singing, but the buzz through the crowd began the debate as to whether the priests should have refused her the offerings from the deity. When the singing finished, the *ōtuvar* was sought out once again by the priests so that he could receive the final thanks from the deity. During the pause the priests again lost control of the crowd, and a young Śrī Lankan woman took the microphone and sang a popular devotional song. The exasperated priests finally found the *ōtuvar* and finished that part of the ceremony. In the end, the grand final procession of the images wound its way around the concourse, and all participated with great joy.

Conclusion

In general, the Hindu temples in Canada are daring and innovative about the ritual forms they are using. Most services are congregational, involve long sermons, and are held at 10 AM on Sunday morning. The temple described here is a notable exception, in that it has tried to construct an orthodox South Indian temple building and bring priests from South India to perform both the daily and festival rituals in a traditional way. However, modifications are inevitable in such a radically new environment, and it is not yet clear what impact they will have on the overall meaning of the worship experience of the participants in this festival.

Although it was not easy to reproduce the many natural associations worshipers make with the season of Mārkaḻi in South India and Śrī Lanka, the overall impact of the faithfully reproduced ceremonial of this festival is exceedingly beautiful. Under the glare of electric lights and in the magnified sounds of the microphones, the priests and musicians seemed to perform their roles with an overall precision and punctuality that indicated much more central direction than would be the case in India. One of the priests even arranged to have a friend film the final procession for him. To the extent that worship is enhanced by beautiful ritual, this ceremony has taken on more polish than those it seeks to emulate ever had. Central direction was what festivals in South

India and Śrī Lanka seemed not to have, and it was their ability to reflect the diverse feelings of the community which made them so vibrant. In this setting, it is hard to see how the festival can avoid being "pulled inside" the temple precincts and become part of the ritual arranged by the officers and priests of the temple. Aesthetically, that seems to work well, but will its social function remain the same if it does?

One of the important differences between the temples of South India/Śrī Lanka and those of Canada is that whereas the temples in South India and Śrī Lanka had management committees of laymen, they generally served a local ruler or a group of land owners or businessmen, whereas in Canada the entire membership has a role in management. The important impact of this participation is that it is not necessary for the popular forms of worship to be in the festival activities outside of the control of the temple authorities. In this temple, for instance, the Śrī Lankan majority has been able to elect one of its own as president of the temple board, so that the wishes of the Brāhman founders of the temple and the priests they have brought from South India do not always prevail. It is not clear what resolution will end the disagreement as to whether a woman can sing the hymn of Māṇikkavācakar (which is apparently now common in Śrī Lanka), but the democratic procedures used in the temples of Canada provide for debate when ritual reformers can set forth their views. At the moment, Brāhmanical reformers want the Sanskrit recitation to be even more prominent than it is in Citamparam, and some Śrī Lankan reformers will not be satisfied until women are able to sing the hymn Māṇikkavācakar, although male himself, put so beautifully in the voice of a female crying out to God. Whether debates such as this get resolved within the temple management procedures themselves, or become part of other, more far-reaching disagreements about cultural adjustment, only time will tell.

The wider cultural debates that lie on the periphery of this beautiful festival celebration were not really completely absent from the celebration. Late in the ceremony, I was approached by a member of the audience dressed in a western style, and smelling a bit of alcohol from the night before. He had asked who I was and announced quickly that he supported the guerilla movement called the Tigers, who are trying to win a separate state for the Tamiḻs of Śrī Lanka. He said he found this ritual and talk about a "day of the gods" to be "total nonsense." In interviews with both the Brāhman founders of the temple and the prominent Śrī Lankan leaders, I also discovered that none of their children was at the festival, even though a slightly older generation of young parents was there with many small children. It bothered the leaders that the "lost generation" of those born just after the first of the immigrants arrived in Canada has chosen, for the time being at least, not to follow the traditions their parents are so keen to establish in Canada. They wanted to know my views on why this was so and were surprised to hear that some of their children were in my classes on Hindu ritual at the university. The wider cultural debates the worshipers at this festival are involved with involve politics, ethnicity or minority group status, and aesthetics, as well as theology and purity of tradition. Whether the festival will serve to contribute to those debates or act as a forum in which a few hundred people can postpone hearing those debates is a question only time will answer. If it does not contribute to those debates, it will not be a true "festival" as South India and Śrī Lanka have known that phenomenon over the centuries.

Conclusion to Part III

The six festivals included in part III do not form a single "type" like those included in parts I and II do. The Vēḷaṅkaṇṇi festival described in chapter 9 has become so successful that it alone might constitute the "modern" type of South Indian festival. It now has its own offshoots. Scholars describe the Madras procession of the Vēḷaṅkaṇṇi church as the "most modern" of South Indian festivals (Waghorne 1997) or the village healing cult of Santi as the most complete intermingling of Hindu and Christian symbols (MacPhail 1993). Both Hindu and Christian leaders frown on this development, but their hesitation about making a clear statement of approval or disapproval indicates their respect for the rich tradition of popular religion associated with festivals in South India.

The two Kerala festivals described in chapters 10 and 11 allow us to turn away from the questions of mass culture circling around Vēḷaṅkaṇṇi and look at the detailed moves religious leaders sometimes make to maintain the loyalty of their fellow worshipers on the local level. Nowhere is religious leadership more experienced at maintaining the loyalty of its following than in Kerala, where for centuries the Hindu, Muslim, and Christian communities have had roughly equal numbers, and each of those communities has had sharp divisions. In Mannarkat, the Jacobite Syrian Church uses its festival to enhance its position against the larger Christian denominations of the Kottayam region and at the same time to demonstrate its ties with the Hindu majority environment of Central Kerala. In Murukapuḻa, in an oddly similar strategy, an Iḻava leader strengthens his temple's position against the Reform Iḻavas when he designs a festival that appeals to Untouchable and high-caste Hindus, as well as the Iḻavas.

In the contexts of "diaspora" life, religious leaders have both more freedom and less freedom in celebrating festivals within their communities. On one hand, they usually do not have to celebrate the festival at all, and people will understand that organizational problems or logistics problems in the alien environment simply made it impossible. On the other hand, once they undertake the festival, the zeal for a faithful performance of the festival as remembered by the participants becomes a much more central factor than it would be in South India or Śrī Lanka, and innovation for its own sake is clearly discouraged. The 3-day festivals of Guyana and Trinidad are somewhat difficult to organize, for poverty, political instability, and emigration affect local communities dramatically. Yet the effort to have a ritually perfect festival that ignores, or triumphs over, the problems of the environment has become a major concern. In South Africa, the same set of issues are turned around, and the festival celebration is used to remind the Indian community, and the wider public, that Hindus are a well-organized community and intend to have a say in the defining of the new social and political environment.

The celebration of the festival in the temple in Toronto, Canada, is valuable for this study because it provides an opportunity to see the process of developing a festival at first hand. Probably all festivals began with somebody bringing a memory of a previous religious encounter to a new situation, but in the context of Toronto, a number of able leaders are trying to propose that the Toronto festival reproduce the different memories they have brought from Śrī Lanka and South India. Reconciling these differing memories will be a challenge in itself, but even when that reconciliation has occurred, there will be a further challenge as an effort is made to make the symbols of the cosmic dance of Śivaṉ meaningful to a generation born and raised in Canada. Those who recall the bathing of the deity in the misty dawn of Citamparam will still shiver when coconut water is poured over the body, but those seeing it for the first time in the glare of electric lights might find it harder to assume the proper feeling. Processions through the streets around the temple are so central to South Indian festivals that the Toronto temple was purposely built with large open areas where indoor processions could be held, but will the complex social implications of the processional retain the same meaning when held indoors? If one attends the Toronto festival regularly for 10 years, one will know how modifications are made in the process of developing a ritual of popular religion.

Conclusion

Festival religion in the South Indian tradition is a distinctive and impressive form of religious life. The studies presented here show that this phenomenon has a long history and that it still enjoys a popular following far beyond the geographical bounds of South India. Do these festivals share general characteristics?

The three special features of this festival tradition, which seem to be present in all its many local manifestations, are ecstatic religious behavior, the ritual enactment of story fragments, and a dynamic sense of community formation. The interaction of these three features seems to define any given festival and lends it the psychological, theological, or political dimension for which it is known.

The most visually dramatic part of a festival is often the ecstatic behavior of the worshipers. In some ways this ecstatic behavior reminds one of "pentecostal" behavior in a large number of different traditions, but some intense features associated with the ecstatic states in the South Indian tradition seem a bit different.

Much of the intensity comes from the role of the *viratam* (Sanskrit: *vrata*) or vow the worshiper takes some time before the festival. In almost every festival, I was told about vows that people took when their child was sick or they felt disturbed in some way. Then often after a period of doubt and difficulty preparing for the festival, the vowkeeper was greatly relieved to be able to perform the preparatory penance and go into a trance. A central figure, such as the man in Murukapuḻa who danced in a cauldron of oil, went over the story of his vow again and again, empahsizing that it had been years since the Tēvi had possessed him and insisting that he had been deeply frightened for months that even though he had taken the vow, she would again not possess him.

In addition to the vow itself, intensity is added to the ecstatic behavior because of the extremes of mortification often associated with the vow. Hooks inserted into the flesh and objects penetrating the tongue or cheek are some of the painful forms of mortification that impress bystanders. But rolling, walking, or dancing great distances in the blazing sun is also carried to the extreme, and even the average participant in the festival consumes little food, abstains from all sexual activity, and engages in many severe forms of physical exertion.

The intesity associated with the vow and the physical exertion raise the individual's experience to an even higher level of religious consciousness as the ecstatic individuals merge with the mythic narrative associated with the festival. In the goddess festivals, the worshipers tend to speak of the Tēvi "possessing" the ecstatics, or "playing" with the crowd through them. In other contexts, the Ayyappaṉ worshipers are said to "become" Ayyappaṉ, and the worshipers of Śivaṉ or Viṣṇu are said to become one of the saints who had direct experience of deity. In each case, the ecstatic becomes part of the sacred presence that gives the festival its wonder.

A second feature of South Indian festivals that links the ecstatic behavior of individuals with the divine realm is the set of story fragments associated with each festival. Some of these story fragments link with myths also found in more elaborate literary form, but most involve ritual enactments that ecstatic worshipers are seeking to identify with or miraculous experiences of saints associated with the place where the festival is held. The "theology" manifest in these story fragments expresses in one narrative form the nature of the divine presence and the great variety of human concerns associated with the festival. In the context of the festival, the deities' romance, marriage, family argument, and fight with demonic forces are enacted in such a way that those events become associated with the ritual energy of the festival itself and with the specific aspirations of ecstatic experience.

When the crowds in Kataragama "identify" with the romance and joy of the deity's marriage to the tribal girl/goddess Valli, they are not forgetting the reverence due to divinity so much as they are expressing the transforming experience any worshiper undergoes in union with the divine. In Koṭuṅkaḻūr the energy seems to come from the other side, as the transforming wonder associated with the union is not so much the emphasis, but the story fragments point to a wild erotic power that leaves the worshipers with the satisfying feeling that they have been swept away.

In many of the stories, the nature of deity is not really the point of departure at all, and the deity stands to the side as the worshipers seek to emulate the saint who could so beautifully describe the soul's transformation in its longing for the divine. When the political ideals found their way into the story, as they did so clearly in Kandy, or more indirectly in the balanced cosmological patterns of the Tiruvāṉaikkā festival, one must look for the divine story or myth that grounds the cosmic patterns in their origin. Human and divine links characterize the story fragments partly because they describe the experience of the ecstatics, who are humans reaching into the divine, but also because the festival as a whole is understood as a scene where a human community has succeeded in bringing the divine into its midst. Written forms of myth or theology are really works of imagination expressing a human understanding of the divine, whereas these story fragments are direct manifestations of ritual action involving religious engagement of the divine. Even though these story fragments are frustratingly incomplete in narrative form, they compensate us with rich psychological understanding and social insight. They lead us back to the third feature of the festival tradition, the dynamically defined community.

The third feature of the South Indian festival tradition is its power to renew the community of worshipers and their society. This dimension of the tradition is hard to see at first, precisely because it is so transparent and obvious. The vast crowds are not only an objective fact about the festival but also a part of the meaning of the festival that leads the worshipers to discussion, reflection, and even reverence.

Part of the relevance of the great crowds is that the festival helps overcome the sharp social divisions in South Indian society. Ecstatic behavior and story fragments often provide opportunities to highlight those divisions and bring them to the festival for recognition. Women make no effort to hide the fact that their vows and subsequent ecstatic trance provide them with new status in their husband's home. Worshipers of the Tēvi of Koṭuṅkaḷûr delight in her anger with her quasi-demon husband and her wealthy in-laws, and domestic tension underlies the story fragments of Tiruvāṉaikkā and Śrīraṅkam as well. Having the "Untouchable" ecstatic smear his burning oil on the Iḻava owner of the Murukapuḻa temple is an explicit modern allusion to caste status problems, but similar status issues surround the marriage of Lord Kataragama to a tribal girl/goddess, or the exorcising of the colonial demons who set the communities of Guyana at odds with one another. Only slightly more disguised are the social divisions defined by religion, so that the efforts of festival rituals to establish Hindu/Christian, Hindu/Buddhist, and Hindu/Muslim links are fascinating unconscious efforts to turn a division into a blessing.

In the long run, the story of a festival is an inclusive story, and the community defined by the festival is a wondrous story of social divisions and hidden tensions overwhelmed by a self-transcending experience that touched the divine and now promises to make everyone's life bearable. In the more "orthodox" worship within the temple, caste groups worshiped separately so that ritual restrictions could remain. The festival form was the "subaltern" form in which the community's all-inclusive boundaries were redefined, and the sacredness of the whole recognized.

In a less structured society, this annual redefinition of "who we are" might not be necessary, but South Indians have an intensity about the definition of identity that seems to travel with them wherever they go. If their rigidly defined marriage regulations and temple rituals provide the superstructure for many of their achievements, the inclusiveness and warmth of their festival celebrations enables them to redefine the boundaries of their identity in a rich variety of local forms.

Notes

Introduction

1. In *The Home of Dancing Śivaṉ: the Traditions of the Hindu Temple in Citamparam* (1995) I tried to discover "what went on" in one of the most famous temples of South India by examining the inscriptions, archaeology, and evolving legend tradition of that temple. The hymns associated with the temple and the legend books written for visitors to the temple were useful but only when they became datable pegs in a much larger stream of nonliterate tradition.

2. The most prominent among the anthropologists to take the South Indian tradition of festival religion seriously was Obeyesekere (1966, 1977, 1978, 1981, 1984, 1988), but Beck (1972, 1981) also put festivals at the heart of her social analysis. The autobiographical account by Daniel (1984) of his trip to Sabarimalai in the middle of an important book on theory is also testimony to the important place festivals have in anthropologists' efforts to understand South Indian society and culture. McKim Marriot's early (1955) study of festivals in North India and Ann Gold's (1988) much quoted study of Rajasthani pilgrims were important contributions to the wider study of popular religion in India.

3. Among students of religion the pioneering effort to study South Indian festivals was made by Dennis Hudson in two excellent essays entitled, respectively, "Two Citrā festivals in Madurai" (1971) and "Śiva, Mīnākṣi, Viṣṇu—Reflections on a Popular Myth in Madurai" (1977). A group effort to find a proper theoretical framework soon followed in *Religious Festivals in South India and Sri Lanka*, edited by Guy R. Welbon and Glenn E. Yocum (1982), and some of my early articles (Younger 1980, 1982a, 1982b, 1982c, 1982d, 1983) provided data on a number of important festivals. Clothey (1983) included festivals in his theoretical study of South Indian ritual, and Hiltebeitel (1988) and Harman (1989) used detailed analyses of festival celebrations in examining religious phenomena of particular goddesses.

4. The literature on North Indian pilgrimages is extensive. Deleury (1960) and Bhardwaj (1978) provided a solid base of evidence some time back, and Stanley (1977), Morinis (1984), van der Veer (1984), Aziz (1987), and Gold (1988) have all provided studies of different locations.

5. Lévi-Strauss (1969) and Dumont (1953, 1957) have been important figures in explaining how this system functions.

6. Discussions of ritual theory (see especially Bell 1992) have tried to figure out where interpretive activity fits. Frits Staal (1975) has even argued that ritual should be acknowledged to be "meaningless"—that is, it does not need a "meaning" other than itself.

7. "Bakhtin studies" has become a major academic field in itself, with new translations, analyses, and criticisms coming out all the time. His major study of Dostoevsky was first published in 1929, but only after many years of exile in Kazakhtstan and other difficulties with Soviet authorities was it republished in 1963. The study of Rabelais was rejected for publication in the 1940s and published in Russia only in 1965. Many of his essays, while written earlier, have only been published recently.

A very creative use of his ideas in the study of Asian religion was Stan Mumford's (1989) *Himalayan Dialogue*. Some indication of the current controversies surrounding his scholarship can be found in a collection of essays edited by Peter Hitchcock (1999).

8. One of the most difficult parts of Bakhtin's argument is his division of world history into three "chronotopes": the medieval carnival being the "ancient matrix" wherein the individual is part of the cycle of nature; then the "individual life sequence" of modern Europe when the individual was "sealed off" from the world to develop one's own economic and religious destiny; and a new era when the "ancient matrix" returns in a "reflexive" manner to allow the personal sense of time to reenter a larger "historical consciousness."

He tries to make this "return" of the "ancient matrix" appear to be a new utopia, but one might also wonder if his glorification of the earlier era does not in itself reduce its multivocal qualities.

Because South Indian festivals continue to be celebrated with great zeal, the problem of how their meaning for ancient or medieval participants is passed on to a modern era is an internal one, and not one a scholarly observer has any special responsibility for. In the next section of this Introduction, I reflect on the problem of how to deal with the claims to antiquity that are part of the festival celebrations, but I will present them as one example of the great variety of religious experiences and not make them, as Bakhtin does the "carnival," into the voice of an earlier era that has an especially urgent message for our day.

9. The most frightening example of this transfer that I have witnessed is not described in this study but was described in detail in Younger (1995) on pp. 60–61. An interesting variation on this transference is the "appearance" of Mary in the window opening described in chapter 10.

1. Return to the Mountains

1. The name "Ayyappaṉ" is now universally used by the worshipers, but it seems a bit like a nickname or a name of address. Most people think it is a combination of "Ayyaṉ" or "respected" with "Appaṉ" or colloquial for "father." Some scholars see a connection with a village deity called Aiyanār in Tamiḻnāṭu (Adiceam 1967), but few worshipers see a similarity, and now, the myth and ritual of the two deities are quite different.

The deity is equated by the worshipers with Dharma Śāstā, whose images are found throughout Kerala (Sarkar 1978), and is also commonly called HariHara, or the child of Viṣṇu (in female form as Mōhinī) and Śivaṉ, in accord with one of the myths about the deity that I explain later.

2. E. Valentine Daniel in the fascinating book called *Fluid Signs* (1984) describes in detail the physical and psychological challenges involved when he made a trip to the shrine with some fellow pilgrims.

3. Eapen's *A Study of Kerala History* (1983) is a reliable guide to the general history of the region.

4. One result of the great crowds is that the pilgrimage experience is dispersed and fragmented, so that each group traveling together has only passing contact with other worshipers. In an effort to keep some central elements of the myth and ritual in place, dozens of booklets about

the festival have been published in Malaiyāḷam, Tamiḻ, and English and are available all over South India. I examined about a dozen of these and found that the familiar stories were told in a number of different ways. Even the books of Pyyappan (1962) and P. T. Thomas (1973) are really elaborate versions of the pamphlet myths.

2. *On the Edge of the Forest*

1. The thorough work of C. G. Seligmann and Brenda Z. Seligmann (1911) is helpful both because it is from an earlier era and because they studied the Veddas who knew the Kataragama area.

2. The Seligmanns argued that the Vedda worshiped a deity named Kande Deviyo or Mountain God from whom their many *yaku* or spirits of the dead derived their authority. Worshipers to the festival all know this tradition, and most honor it by including a visit to the mountain in their worship. Recent court disputes about who controls the holy sites on the mountain will not be dealt with in this study, but they do indicate that this spot is gaining, not receding, in religious importance (Gombrich and Obeyesekere 1988; Wijayaratna 1987).

3. Wirz in 1954 described the temple as for Viṣṇu.

4. There were two important setbacks to the Hinduization of the sacred place when the Buddhist government authorities renovated the site. One was that the popular Ramakrishna Mission guest house right in front of the Tevayanai temple was closed and turned into a government museum. The second was that the small shrine of Bairava, a wild form of Śivaṉ to whom priests and others go for their final act of worship, and where mind-altering drugs and noisy crowds are sometimes found, was moved outside the wall of Lord Kataragama's compound to a garden beside the river.

5. The ritual of "water cutting," which now closes all major festivals of Śrī Lanka, has been variously interpreted. In the context of this festival, it is not a simple final priestly act but the dramatic climax of the whole festival, and the water sports that follow reflect the erotic excitement at the heart of the festival.

6. When I attended the full festival, in 1990, the part of the ritual performed by a Vedda chief was reinstated after 40 years. Boranda, the previous chief, had refused to come to the festival after Śrī Lankan independence because the democratic government refused to give him the gold coins that the traditional rulers had always given on behalf of the deity. His son, Kaaira, returned to perform this ritual duty in 1990.

7. Gananath Obeyesekere, who has written extensively about this festival (1977, 1978, 1981, 1988) emphasizes the fact that the relationship portrayed in this festival ritual is an "illicit affair" with a "secret woman" (*hora gani*) or mistress. I see no evidence that the main ritual officiants agree. I agree with Wijayaratna (1987, p. 382) that the excitement of the proper Vedda marriage bond is being portrayed. True, the ceremonial aspects of a Brāhmanical Hindu wedding that one finds in some South Indian festivals are not present here. The excitement and community involvement are consistent with Vedda custom, and the Seligmanns (1911) describe the Vedda defense of the monogamous marriage relationship as intense (including sometimes putting offenders to death), even though the Vedda marriage ceremony itself is minimal.

8. The account of Duttagamini's emergence from Rohaṇa and fight with Elara are in the *Mahāvamsa* (Geiger 1912) of the sixth century, but the claim that he worshiped at Kataragama and indeed built the temple are found only in later legend books from about the fourteenth century (Gombrich and Obeyesekere 1988, p. 425).

9. Devout Hindus, who believe the whole worship center to have been a Hindu shrine slowly being taken over by others, argue that Kalyanagiri came there in the sixth century BCE. More reasonable claims are the seventh or the fourteenth centuries of the Common Era. See

especially Kalyanasundaram (1980) and Arunachalam (1964), which are cited in Wijayaratna (1987, p. 211).

10. Normal Hindu practice is to cremate the dead, but monks go through a death ceremony when they are initiated, and when they later on release their spirit, the body is placed in a vault in a seated position and becomes a place for reverent ceremony.

11. Gombrich and Obeyesekere (1988, p. 164) say that Palkutibawa was a Muslim *pir*, but I think they were confused in this because the title "*bawa*" is used for both Muslim and Hindu holy men. Muslim worshipers certainly do revere Palkutibawa as the one who brought their own saint, Kamrai Nabi, to Kataragama.

12. Obeyesekere (1978) goes into this aspect of the festival in great detail.

13. In 1990 one of the tea plantation laborers agreed to do the hook swinging from the scaffold in midafternoon for the sake of the television crew and found that he could not do it. He felt that he had angered Lord Kataragama by not keeping this practice a purely devotional one and even wondered if he would be able to do it again for the night procession.

14. Gombrich and Obeyesekere (1988) provide figures for different periods in the past century and suggest that about 550,000 is the present attendance.

15. The articles on Kataragama by Pfaffenberger (1979) and Swearer (1982) focus almost completely on this issue of political integration.

16. In 1990 when I attended the festival, Premadasa, as the new president of the country, flew to the festival. He went to pray first of all at the Buddhist *stūpa* or Kiri Vehera and then at the temple of Lord Kataragama, where he seemed to find it difficult to understand the ritual.

17. In 1989 a member of the JVP, or radical Sinhala youth movement, threw a hand grenade at the government minister in the procession wounding him and killing a number of the *ālatti ammas*.

3. *The Goddess of Koṭuṅkaḷūr*

1. Obeyesekere's (1984) *The Cult of the Goddess Pattini* discusses the stories of Pattini found in Śrī Lankan villages and concludes with a historical chapter tracing the cult to the Koṭuṅkaḷūr temple.

2. Bhagavatī of Cheṅkanur, for instance, is reputed to have monthly menstruations that are ritually recognized by worshipers, and Bhagavatī of Chottanikara is reputed to do miraculous healings.

Many of the smaller goddess temples seem to be ritually linked to Koṭuṅkaḷūr. Some throw an ember from their worship fire toward Koṭuṅkaḷūr, and others have a secret door pointing toward Koṭuṇkaḷūr (chapters 10 and 11).

3. The ancient synagogue in Cochin is a major tourist attraction, but ancient synogogues in places such as Parur are nearer Koṭuṅkaḷūr.

4. Thozhiyur, Kunankalam, and Parur still have the "old style" Christian houses crowded together in the middle of the town. Somewhat later in history, the Christian trade center shifted to Kottayam further south, where it could control the trade as it came out of the mountains, and that city is the major Syrian Christian center today.

5. Sarkar (1978, p. 57) describes these two temples as among the "earliest stone temples of Kerala." The Śivaṉ temple is usually called Tiruvañcikulam, and the Viṣṇu temple is usually called the Kṛṣṇa temple at Tirukkulacekarapuram.

6. Obeyesekere (1984, p. 535) seems to transpose the numbers when he gives the date as 1431.

7. Because these stories exist primarily in the oral forms used in such settings, there are many different versions, and there is no easy way of determining which versions are earlier.

Obeyesekere (1984), who started his study of this story tradition by looking at the Pattini stories of Śrī Lanka, believes that the Śrī Lanka stories were taken to Śrī Lanka from Kerala when the stories were part of a Jaina/Buddhist tradition and that the stories then emphasized the righteousness of the heroine. He believes that later on the influence of the Kāli tradition modified the stories so that they came to emphasize a wilder and more vengeful heroine (p. 541). This argument assumes that the central feature of the story is the psychological makeup of the main character. It also assumes that the diffusion of cultural traits between South India and Śrī Lanka took place in a sufficiently clear pattern so that one can reconstruct the cultural history of the region in terms of a few major migrations of people and ideas (p. 523).

I have tried to view the existing local tradition as it might have evolved over the centuries, in the light of what is known about the local social and political history. In this context, it is certainly probable that stories about the goddess Kāli and the demon Dāruka, found all over India, did influence the local stories to some extent at some point in that history. What is not so clear, however, is that the pre-Kāli stories about goddesses called Kaṇṇaki, Śrī Kurumba, or Cīrma involved a less impassioned heroine. The pre-Kāli stories seem to involve male figures who are more closely tied to the goddess (more like men are in the matrilineal settings of Kerala society) than the clearly demonic Dāruka of stories from elsewhere in India, but the passion is all the more palpable when it works its way through those domestic entanglements.

8. Some studies of the *marumakkattāyam* system imply that it is followed by the Nair caste only, but that is not the case. The Nairs are certainly the most notable, primarily because as landlords their *taravāds* often represent a significant concentration of power, but in parts of Kerala all communities seem to have practiced *marumakkattāyam* at one time. Some still do, including some of the Christians and Muslims.

The *marumakkattāyam* system of inheritance should not be confused with the other notable aspect of the Nair marriage system. Nair women often arrange *campantams* or "common law" relations with Namboodri Brāhman men. Although this arrangement is, of course, made possible because of the woman's freedom within the *marumakkattāyam* system, it is more directly the result of the Namboodri inheritance system, which allows only the eldest male a proper marriage in order that all property rights in the family can be kept intact as they are passed on to the next generation. The Namboodris themselves, of course, are migrants from North India and follow one of the patrilineal systems of inheritance prevalent there.

Because of the influence of patrilineal Hindu customs in other parts of India, most *taravāds* now arrange for their daughters to undergo an orthodox Hindu marriage ceremony as a child, but the inheritance is still matrilineal, and the grown women are still free to arrange *campantams* as they see fit.

9. The famous military schools of the region were called *kalaris*, and the mercenaries the *caver*.

10. The best known of the many translations of this story is Dikshitar (1939).

11. Sarkar (1978, p. 106) says of this image: "A subsidiary shrine in the Bhagavatī temple-complex at Kodungalur contains a much defaced image of a Mātṛikā, known popularly as Vasūrimālā (garland of small-pox). Originally the image belonged to a Sapta-mātṛikā panel and most likely it is a figure of Chāmuṇḍā datable stylistically to the eighth century."

12. The title of Induchudan's (1969) controversial book, *The Secret Chamber*, indicates his deep interest in this chamber. He argues that the chamber actually holds the remains of a historical heroine named Kaṇṇiki, and this contention offends the ritual regulation that human remains would not be found in a temple. He is right to argue that saints and ascetics are often interned in sepulchers and in monastic settings and other places. In India these sepulchers become the focus of much popular worship for Jains, Buddhists, Hindus, Christians, and Muslims alike, but proper Hindu temples are not normally associated with such places of worship. Modern

worshipers are not sure what to make of the closed chamber on the west side of the temple and tend to ignore it.

13. Rows of seven female images, or sometimes just seven plain stones, are found somewhere in the courtyard of most Kerala temples. When the cult of seven mothers became popular and who the people of Kerala understand the seven to be are not clear. Students of iconography, such as Banerjea (1974), provide a standard list of Brahmāṇī, Māheśvarī, Kaumarī, Vaiṣṇavī, Vārāhī, Indrāṇī, and Cāmuṇḍī.

14. The image does not seem to follow any standard iconographic model. Eight armed figures of Durgā are, of course, common. Induchudan (1969, p. 5) describes a severed male head in the lower right arm, a palm leaf manuscript, trident, and sword in the other right hands. In the lower left he describes a bell, and in the other hands an anklet, snake, and pot.

15. Many festivals are associated with the "star," or day of the lunar month on which they climax. The Bharaṇi asterism in the month of Mīnam (March–April) is even more prominent than usual in the popular labeling of this festival.

16. The Toṟṟam Pāṭṭu that they sing constitute a rich oral tradition. A few of these songs have been committed to writing on palm leaf manuscripts, but the worshipers seemingly delight in the great variety of narrative versions found in the oral recitations at the festival. See Chandera (1973), Choondal (1978), Menon (1959), and Obeyesekere (1984) for summary accounts.

17. Not all *veḷicapāṭu* who arrive are part of the traditionally authorized number, and probably somewhat over half perform a less ritualized version of the skull slicing in front of other gentlemen further back from the temple entrance. I could not learn where their swords were taken and suspect that it involved a less formalized ritual than for the main group.

18. This is the most striking example I know of in the South Indian festival tradition of the festival activity taking an explicitly anticlerical character, much as the "carnival" tradition of Europe did. This festival is also close to the "carnival" tradition described by Bakhtin (1984) in the explicit use it makes of body imagery and sexuality.

19. This "polluting" of the temple takes place exactly one month before the climax of the festival, or on Bharaṇi day in the month of Kumbham (February–March). This ritual feature, as well as others connected with the different offerings disallowed during the festival, and the sequence in which certain groups are supposed to arrive at the festival, are all described in Induchudan (1969) but are not widely known among contemporary worshipers.

20. In 1900 a colorful account of the festival was written by T. K. Gopal Panikkar in *Malabar and Its Folk*. He describes copious amounts of blood from the cock sacrifices and the drinking of great quantities of toddy (which I did not see in 1985), and he also refers to the "priestesses" distributing consecrated turmeric in the inner sanctum.

21. During the last few days of the festival, the persons who go into trance during their dances are most often women. These women believe they are possessed by the Tēvi and paint their tongues red so that as they sink into the trance their tongue lolls far out of the mouth, just as the tongue of Kāli does in the iconography.

4. *Wandering and Romance with Lord Raṅkanātaṉ*

An earlier version of this study (Younger 1982d) appeared in *Modern Asian Studies*, and had a different focus.

1. Auboyer (1969); Hari Rao (1967, 1976); and Younger (1993) all provide overviews of the temple architecture and religious life.

2. *Aham* 137 is a love poem in which the poet looks into the sad face of his lover and says:

Your face has lost its lustre and resembles the sandy and thickly wooded river bank in Araṅkam [ancient name of Śrīraṅkam] with the hearths quenched and things strewn hither and thither after the celebration of the Paṅkuṇi festival.

3. This festival is referred to in an inscription (*Annual Reports on Epigraphy 1936–7*, no.75) of 1073 CE during the reign of the the Cōḻa emperor Kulōttuṅka I and during the lifetime of Rāmānuja. A later inscription (*Annual Reports on Epigraphy 1936–7*, no.57) dated 1565 CE gives a detailed account of the provisions a *jīyar* (ascetic) made for bathing the deity in the river on the ninth day (just as it is done today). A half dozen other inscriptions refer to donations for the festival.

4. In an earlier version of this chapter (Younger 1982a), I developed the whole account of the festival around the problem of interpretation. The problem of interpretation is not so prominent in this version, but I will still try to use some of the general themes in the temple tradition to interpret the festival activity.

5. This is the Caṇṭēśvara temple built in 903 CE at the time of the marriage of Pūti-Āticca-Pitariyar, the daughter of the Katumbalam chieftain Tennavan Iḷnṅkōvēlār, and the grandson of the Cōḻa emperor Ātitya I (880–907) (*South Indian Inscriptions III*, nos. 96 and 126). In the inscriptions connected with the building of the temple, the village is called Isānamaṅkalam and is described as a *brahmatēya*, or a village given by the king to a group of Śaiva Brāhmans.

5. The Family of Śivaṉ in the Kāvēri River Valley

An earlier version of this study appeared in *Studies of Religion* (Younger 1982b).

1. Ray (1959) and de Silva (1983) both provide good histories of this development.

2. A thorough analysis of the many relevant inscriptions is in Younger (1983).

3. See, for instance, *Annual Reports on Epigraphy 1891*, no. 31; with the full text in *South Indian Inscriptions III*, no. 76.

4. *Annual Reports on Epigraphy* (hereafter *ARE*) *1891*, no. 18 (full text in *South Indian Inscriptions IV*, no. 419); *ARE 1908*, no. 486; *ARE 1936*, nos. 119, 120, 121, 122, 124, 125; *ARE 1937*, no. 5.

5. His account of the Tiruvāṉaikkā temple is found in Pillai (1975).

6. Monks and Kings Intervene

1. Ray and Paranavitana (1973, p. 766) have suggested that "the metamorphosis of Upulvan (Varuṇa) to Viṣṇu took place some time after the reign of Parākramabāhu VI (1410–1468)." We know, however, from Knox's account (1958, see also the next section in this chapter) that the deity was still called by the earlier names in the late seventeenth century. The change was almost certainly something ordered after the eighteenth century by the Buddhist reformers, who had long understood "Viṣṇu" to be the protector deity of the Buddha.

2. Utpalvan is often compared with the Vedic god Varuṇa, who appears to be a sky-god in the *Ṛg Veda* but is referred to as the "god of the waters" in later references. In the classifications of different terrains in the Tamiḻ grammar, *Tolkappiyam*, for instance, the coast or *neytal*, is said to be governed by Varuṇa. It is certainly interesting to think of Śrī Lanka as protected by a Varuṇa-like deity, in that so much of it is coast.

3. *Ayūdhas* are used as *utsava* or symbols of deity that can be carried about in festivals. They are found in South India as well as Śrī Lanka, but small images, or *utsava mūrtis*, are more common in India. *Ayūdhas* were apparently earlier forms in which deities were symbolically represented.

4. The ceremony connected with the *kāpa* includes the priest carrying miniature bows and arrows into the forest. These bows and arrows are then left on the pot holding the *kāpa* throughout the festival. They probably serve just as a reminder of the hunting and gathering economy that long prevailed in these mountains, although Paranavitana has raised the possibility that they could link the festival with the god Rāma, whose symbol is the bow and who is sometimes worshiped along with Alutnūwara in Śrī Lanka (Ray and Paranavitana 1973, p. 763).

5. It is interesting that the seventeenth-century version of the festival involved the three deities associated with the first three regions or *tiṇais* mentioned by the Tamil̲ grammarian, Tolkāppiyan̲: the *kuṟiñci* or mountainous regions of Kataragama/Murukan̲, the *neytal* or coast of Upulvan/Varuṇa, and the *pālai* or dry lands of the goddesses.

6. One of the obscure ritual features of the festival is that during the second half, or the last five days of the processional part of the festival, palanquins, cloth-covered boxes called *randōlis*, are carried at the end of the long procession associated with each deity (except for the procession of the tooth relic of the Buddha). The popular explanation of the crowd is that these *randōlis* contain the consorts of the deities involved. Quite a bit of worship is directed toward these *randōlis* (they are more accessible than the symbols of deity on the back of the elephant), and this part of the festival is actually called the Randōli Perahara. The priests do not open the cloth coverings, but did say that the boxes contain very old weapons (*ayūdhas*) and caskets that hold the power of the deity.

7. In 1998 the political symbolism of the temple was reawakened when the government was preparing to celebrate 50 years of independence at this spot, and just days before the celebration suicide bombers of the Tamil̲ Tigers entered the Temple of the Tooth, blew themselves up, and damaged the temple severely.

7. *Singing the Tamil̲ Hymnbook*

An earlier version of this study appeared in *History of Religions* (Younger 1982c), and was reproduced in Spencer 1987. Vasudha Narayanan's (1994) major study of this recitation ceremony was not available when this chapter was written.

1. There was a dispute a generation back about which branch of the family of *araiyars* should have the privilege of carrying on this service before the deity. While the case dragged on in court, the temple authorities decided that the two branches of the family should serve on alternate nights, an arrangement that remains.

2. A number of worshipers explicitly explained their roles to me, and a number used the analogy of the present cabinet government in India, with Nammāl̲vār as prime minister, Tirumaṅkai as defense minister, and Uṭaiyavar as home minister.

3. Asceticism plays a relatively minor role in Śrīraṅkam religious life today. The *Kōyil Ol̲uku* or temple chronicle tells us that this was not always the case, for a great *jīyar* or ascetic named Kūranārāyaṇa once performed many miracles, arranged for the digging of new irrigation channels after a flood, and revamped the priestly offices. Because of his following, the *Chronicle* tells us, the priests were forced to give him an official role in the temple. The memory of this great man and that of Rāmānuja, who gave up married life to become an ascetic, are blended in the explanation offered by the *Chronicle* as to why the holder of the offices of the Śrīraṅkanāta Jīyar now receives one of the three highest honors.

4. In chapter 4, which deals with the *ati* or "original" festival of this temple, I analyzed what might be the primordial patterns in the worship of this place.

5. Āṇṭāḷ, the female hymnsinger, is not included in the seminar of recitation. One of her hymns, called the *Tiruppāvai*, recited at another point in the festival, is especially associated with the month of Mārkal̲i. I was never given a satisfactory explanation as to why her image is not included in the seminar, but one must assume that in part of the tradition, at least, she is not considered an *āl̲vār*.

6. In other versions of the story he was trying to take the gold ring from the toe of the deity when he accidentally touched the deity's foot, a gesture implying worship.

7. In the chronology of the *Chronicle*, this story is set in the year corresponding to 2656 BCE.

8. The date of CE 823, which is given for this event, is relatively accurate. The overall impression of the date is, of course, quite distorted by the fact that the Muslim invasions and many of the later kings' donations are described as having already taken place.

9. There are three problems with the traditional dating of Rāmānuja. The first is that, whereas Rāmānuja is said to have been persecuted and chased out of Śrīraṅkam by the Cōḻa king, Kulōttuṅka I, who reigned from 1070 to 1120, that king left 70 inscriptions on the temple's walls and gave generous gifts to the temple.

The second is that, whereas Rāmānuja is said to have fled west to the Hoysala country and converted its Jaina ruler to Vaiṣṇavism about 1070, no Hoysala inscriptions support this tradition, Viṣṇuvardhana did not come to power until 1120, and the other name he used, Biṭṭigadēva, was not confined to his early career and is probably a Vaiṣṇava (and not a Jaina) name in any case.

And the third problem is that, whereas Rāmānuja is said to have taken the Viṣṇu image that had been thrown out of the temple at Citamparam and installed it in Tirupati, inscriptional evidence seems to indicate that the image was thrown out by Kulōttuṅka II and installed in Tirupati by King Ghaṭṭidēvaṉ about 1140, or sometime after the traditional date for the death of Rāmānuja.

In the light of these problems, T. N. Subramanian (1957) has suggested that the traditional assumption that Rāmānuja enjoyed an ideal lifetime of 120 years from 1017 to 1137 might be abandoned. A more reliable picture emerges if he is presumed to have died about 1155–6 and other events are fit in accordingly.

My concern here is not with the actual biography of Rāmānuja, but with the fact that the *Chronicle's* account of his activity in the temple is a reconstruction written 300 years later and is not supported by inscriptional evidence.

10. In the *Chronicle*, with its distorted chronology, the great Cōḻa king Rājendra I, who reigned 400 years earlier, supervises this test.

11. This account in the *Chronicle* is, of course, the basis for the arrangement I called the "one-day footnote" to the festival, and it is a group of priests claiming to be descendants of the Amudaṉār who do the singing on that day.

8. Dance and Trance in the Presence of Māriyammaṉ

A rather different version of this research appeared in *Journal of American Academy of Religion* (Younger 1980).

1. I think most South Indians would consider the two severe forms of mortification of the body in worship to be "hook swinging" and "walking on burning coals" and would think of them most naturally in connection with the worship of Māriyammaṉ. I suspect that there were some people "walking on burning coals" at Samayapuram the year I was there, but I concentrated on the crowd along the roadway and did not see them. I did see them in the festival for Māriyammaṉ of Samayapuram, which takes place later in the year when she goes to the riverbed in Śrīraṅkam. The coals there were extremely hot, and the two trained practitioners moved slowly, while the crowd watched this miraculous feat with amazement (Younger 1982a).

I take the imitation of these forms of mortification, which we have already examined in chapter 2 and will see again in chapter 11, as borrowings based on the reputation these forms of worship have achieved in Māriyammaṉ worship.

2. According to early missionary accounts (Whitehead 1921), the sacrifice of chickens or goats was one of the main forms of offering to Māriyammaṉ. In villages of South India this practice is still carried on a bit secretly, but in Guyana and Trinidad (chapter 12) it is a central part of the temple ritual. In Samayapuram the temple managers and priests have been adopting Brāhmanical styles of worship, and animal sacrifice would have to be carried out in a hidden way, if at all.

3. The possession states, which many people think of first when they think of Māriyammaṉ, are still a central part of village worship in South India; in Guyana and Trinidad the priests are

the first to go into trance and make possession a major part of the worship (chapter 12). In the large-scale and somewhat Brāhmanical atmosphere of Samayapuram, the possession states are not as prominent.

9. *Healing Mother Vēḷaṅkaṇṇi*

A rather different version of this study appeared in *Sacred Journeys*, edited by Alan Morinis (Younger 1992).

1. These questions could, of course, be asked about new dimensions of the the Ayyappaṉ festival as well. It also no longer draws its participants from the local society, and broadly defined ideological issues swirl around the reports about the celebration and drag it into modern religious debates.

By placing it in part I, I am, of course, indicating that I think that the ritual action of the Ayyappaṉ festival still reflects a local social setting and that the voices of the celebration are still consistent with the multivocal exuberance of the ancient festival style. Forces that would bring this celebration into modern debates may at some time prevail, but I do not think the ancient character of the festival has been lost, in spite of the huge numbers attending today.

10. *The Window Opens in Mannarkat*

1. The best discussion of the larger question of Christian/Hindu interaction in the religious world of Kerala is Corinne Dempsey's (2000) new book, *Kerala Christian Sainthood: Collisions of Culture and Worldview in South India.*

2. The atmosphere around the festival site is surprisingly like those one sees in Māriyammaṉ festivals in Tamiḻnāṭu. The more traditional comparison would certainly have been with the Kerala temples of Bhagavatī, especially with the one nearby. On the other hand, the reputation of Vēḷaṅkaṇṇi has been spreading far and wide, and her healing rituals are somewhat similar to those of Māriyammaṉ, so it is not impossible that Mannarkat worshipers might have been influenced by those out-of-state developments in festival style.

11. *Can Śivaṉ Be "Re-formed"?*

1. I am indebted for many of these insights to George Jacob (more recently a bishop of the Mar Thoma Church), who was living in the village to conduct his doctoral research at the time I visited there.

12. *Dance and Trance in a New World*

1. This account, of course, simplifies a rather complex colonial history. The Dutch settled the area in the seventeenth century, and after a series of slave revolts and other difficulties, the British and French took over parts of the area in the late eighteenth century. In the western or British section, the sugar estates occupied most of the coastal land, which was drained with a network of canals and locks. Those estates were run with African slaves until the British parliament freed the slaves in the 1830s. The estates in British Guiana then tried to procure laborers from a number of places. Portuguese, who were working on sugar plantations on the island of Madeira, were the first to come in 1835, but the authorities in Madeira objected to losing their labor force, and by 1881, when this source dried up, only 32,216 had come. The Portuguese quickly moved from the sugar estates to become the petty merchants of the towns, and they are still prominent in business in Guyana (Menzez 1995). Chinese laborers were brought in between 1852 and 1884, but there were only 13,533 of them. Many were soon in the restaurant

business and are still a clearly visible minority in Guyanese society. By comparison, there were 238,909 Indian laborers brought in. Guyana became an independent nation in 1966.

2. Dwarka Nath (1970) provides details on each ship in the early decades. He also points out that the chief interpreter of the Immigration Department (the most prominent Indian in the colony at the time) was Veeraswamy Mudalier, who was a Tamiḻ. He was first appointed in 1845, and continued to be a highly respected civil servant late into the century. There was another large influx of South Indian immigrants after the turn of the century.

3. Many scholarly accounts take for granted that there was a "homogenization" of the Indian population in the barracks, or as some put it, "even before they left the port in India." It is obvious that the strictest of caste rules could not be kept in these circumstances, but talk of full homogenization does not seem to be supported by the evidence. The two dozen temple *pūjaris* I interviewed, and the two dozen temple presidents as well, all testify that they remember their parents and grandparents speaking Tamiḻ. They also insist that they are of pure South Indian stock; that during the time they lived on the estates, South Indians usually married South Indians; and that the South Indian naming ritual, marriage ritual, and death ritual were always distinct.

In support of their contention that the South Indian family system may have remained reasonably intact is the evidence I stumbled across while examining the "ship register" of a ship called the *Roman Emperor* which arrived in Trinidad from Madras, December 3, 1858. There were 143 women among the 378 persons aboard. Seventy-one of these were women accompanying their husbands, 41 were young girls with their parents, 18 were with other relatives, and only 13 were "single women" (ship records, Trinidad and Tobago Government Library). In any case, throughout South India marriage with near relatives on the mother's side is encouraged, and it is conceivable that the South Indian immigrants were able to keep their marriage system in place.

4. In Rose Hall, Corentyne, for instance, it was pointed out to me that the Afro-Guyanese and South Indians ("Madrasis" in the local vocabulary) shared a common cemetery on one side of the road, whereas the North Indians ("Hindus" in the local vocabulary) shared the other cemetery across the road with the Muslims.

5. In the French colonies of Reunion, Martinique, and Guadalupe, where South Indian laborers were in the majority, Māriyammaṉ worship is also found (Benoist 1984; Horowitz 1963; Horowitz and Klass 1961; Nagapin and Sulty 1989; Singaravelou 1975).

6. It is, however, prominent in a temple in St. Augustine, Trinidad, which was built in the 1970s.

Some of the literature on this form of worship just uses the popular designation and refers to "Kālī Mai Pūja," and some even fail to make the important clarification that the priests always speak of the deity as "Māriyammaṉ" (Bassier 1987; Khan 1977).

7. Maturai Vīraṉ is a deity similar to the deity usually called Aiyanār in South India (Adiceam 1967). For the sake of North Indians, he is also called Bairava or "Khal Bheyro," a fierce form of Śivaṉ associated with a dog.

8. This is probably the black deity described by Louis Dumont in his famous article (1959) on the "structural analysis" of the three deities of Māriyammaṉ, Aiyanār, and Kaṟuppanār and their correspondences with social groups in a Tamiḻ village.

For the sake of North Indians, this deity is equated with "Dee Bābā," or the proprietor or protector of the land.

As we will see later, the worshipers often describe him in the context of Guyana as the "Dutchman," who settled the territory and whose spirit is still thought of as fiercely guarding it.

9. The President of the Canefield temple pointed out to me the green marbles used for the eyes of this image, and said "he is the white man . . . to whom God gave the distant vision or foresight to be able to cross the oceans and find this country." It is puzzling to have both the "black" power, Caṅkani, and the "white" power, Munīsvaraṉ, associated with colonial masters, but that is the way the worshipers speak of them.

10. Bassier (1987) argues that, like the Rastafarians, this ritual tradition enjoyed a "revitalization" during the years of political repression in Guyana in the 1970s. There is probably some truth in this argument, but it tends to discount the long years of tradition that precede the 1970s and are best seen through the eyes of the more conservative temples. Jayawardena (1967) and Vertovec (1992), on the other hand, are dismissive of the "Madrasi" temples and even suggest that they might disappear, but this view also discounts their impressive history.

11. Those at Stewartville or Leonara, Herstelling, Ganga Ram, and Ngg.

12. Notably, the temple at Black Bush Polder and those in Trinidad where he had considerable influence.

13. The fact that there is such a rigid tradition of a 3-day festival is puzzling because the festival of Māriyamman̲ described earlier from India took 10 days. One might explain the shorter duration as the longest time available, given the constraints of the sugar estates' work schedule. The other possibility, however, might be that an old tradition of 3-day festivals in the nineteenth century was subsequently modified in India to bring the Māriyamman̲ festivals into line with the festivals of the more Brāhmanical temples.

In a report on the festival as celebrated in 1923, Leslie Phillips describes it as a 3-day festival but says that it is celebrated only once in 5 years. Oral tradition in a number of temples seems to recall this arrangement in their temple as well.

In his study of the South Indian traditions of Guyana, Singh (1975) argues that the festivals are to be held in January or August. Some of the earliest known ones use those dates, but Phillips reports on a March one in 1923. I heard of some scheduled for February, March, and May as well. The Canefield one is ordinarily held in August, but because of personal difficulties on the arrangement committee, it was postponed to October.

The most common date for Māriyamman̲ festivals in India today seems to be May.

14. I will use the English "possessed" as the most natural word that comes to mind to describe this state. The local vocabulary is "to play with" the Tēvi, but this is used as a technical phrase and probably translates the Sanskrit "*līlā*" or the active side of the Tēvi's manifestation.

15. One of the more thorough of the many studies of this period is Sallahuddin (1994).

13. *Suburban Promises*

1. Thorough studies of the records of the ships that carried indentured workers to South Africa have been carried out. The records themselves are available in a special library in Durban Westville University. The work of Bhana and Pachai (1984) and Bhana and Bain (1990) are the most reliable.

2. The excellent study of these temples by Mikula, Kearney, and Harper (1982) makes it easy to locate the temples.

14. *A Bath for Dancing Śivan̲ in the Cold of Canada*

1. Although not relevant to the present story of a particular festival celebration, the history of the Hindu community's adjustment to life in Canada is interesting and involves the use of every conceivable style of Hindu practice. Briefly stated, the historical stages are as follows.

Stage 1 involved the professionals who arrived in the '50s and '60s trying to take an intellectual approach. They tended to look to "Vedanta" to provide a way of uniting all religions and all forms of thought. When they could, they would band together and invite Vedanta Society *swāmis* to give lectures to the public on Vedanta or science.

Stage 2 in the late '60s and '70s involved a huge influx of Sikh and Hindu laborers from Punjab. In trying to establish a single Indian community, people gathered together to sing informal *bhajans* and give reverence to poster pictures of deities and *gurus*.

Stage 3 in the late '70s and '80s saw each language group and each religious group by itself raise huge amounts of money to build as orthodox a temple as was feasible. During this time the temple north of Toronto was built.

A new stage, which I call stage 4, now seems well under way as the newest immigrants and the second generation of Hindus born in Canada seem to be attracted to small shrines of individuals who do healings and exorcisms for a mixed clientele.

2. When the temple was built, it was decided that the entrance should face the road, but that meant that the deities face west, when the ritually proper direction is east. Some worshipers now express regret about that decision.

3. The north-facing Turka (Durgā) shrine (the ritually correct position) is in the area of the Śivaṉ family. It is more substantial than those of the other goddesses.

References

Adiceam, Marguerite E. 1967. *Contribution à l'étude d'Aiyanār-Śāstā*. Pondicherry: Institut François d'Indologie.

Ames, Michael. 1964. "The Structural Relation of Magical Animism and Buddhism in Śrī Lanka." *Journal of Asian Studies*. 23:21–52.

Annual Report on Epigraphy (*ARE*) *1887–*. Madras: Archaeological Society of India.

Arunacalam, P. 1964. "The Worship of Muruka." *Journal of the Royal Asiatic Society* (*C.B.*) 29(77):249ff.

Auboyer, J. 1969. *Sri Ranganathaswami: le temple de Vishnu à Srirangam*. Paris: UNESCO.

Aziz, Barbara. 1987. "A Pilgrimage to Amarnath: The Hindu's Search for Immortality." *Kailash: Journal of Himalayan Studies* 9:2–3.

Bakhtin, M. M. [1919] 1993. *Toward a Philosophy of the Act*. Austin: University of Texas Press.

——. [1929, 1963] 1984. *Problems of Dostoevsky's Poetics*. Minneapolis: University of Minnesota Press.

——. [1965, 1968] 1984. *Rabelais and His World*. Bloomington: Indiana University Press.

——. 1981. *The Dialogic Imagination*. Austin: University of Texas Press.

Banerjea, J. N. 1974. *The Development of Hindu Iconography*. New Delhi: Munshiram Manoharlal.

Bassier, W. M. Z. 1987. "Kāli-Mai Worship in Guyana: A Quest for a New Identity." In Singh, I. J. Bahadur, ed. *Indians in the Caribbean*. London: Oriental University.

Beck, Brenda E. F. 1972. *Peasant Society in Koṅku: A Study of Right and Left Subcastes in South India*. Vancouver: University of British Columbia Press.

——. 1981. "The Goddess and the Demon: A Local South Indian Festival and its Wider Context." In *Puruṣārtha*. Paris: Editions de L'école des hautes etudes en sciences sociales.

Bell, Catherine. 1992. *Ritual Theory, Ritual Practice*. New York: Oxford University Press.

Benoist, Jean. 1984. "Entre l'Inde et le monde créole." In *Indian Labour Immigration*. Mauritius: Gandhi Institute.

Bhardwaj, Surinder. 1973. *Hindu Places of Pilgrimage*. Berkeley: University of California Press.

Bhana, Surendra, and Joy Bain. 1990. *Setting Down Roots: Indian Migrants in South Africa 1860–1911*. Johannesburg: University of Witswatersburg Press.

Bhana, Surendra, and B. Pachai. 1984. *A Document History of Indians in South Africa*. Johannesburg: David Philips.

Breckenridge, Carol Appadurai. 1978. "From Protector to Litigant–Changing Relations between Hindu Temples and the Rājā of Ramnad." In *South Indian Temples*, edited by Burton Stein. New Delhi: Vikas.

Brown, Leslie. 1956. *The Indian Christians of St. Thomas*. Cambridge: Cambridge University Press.

Carman, John. 1974. *The Theology of Rāmānuja*. New Haven: Yale.

Chandera, C. M. S. 1973. *Kannikiyum Cheermakkavum*. Kottayam: College Book House.

Choondal, Chummar. 1978. *Studies in Folklore of Kerala*. Trivandrum: College Book House.

Clifford, James, and George Marcus. 1986. *Writing Culture: The Poetics and Politics of Ethnography*. Berkeley: University of California Press.

Clothey, Fred. 1983. *Rhythm and Intent: Ritual Studies from South India*. Madras: Blackie and Son.

Daniel, E. Valentine. 1984. *Fluid Signs*. Berkeley: University of California Press.

Deleury, G. A. 1960. *The Cult of Vithoba*. Poona: Deccan College Press.

Dempsey, Corinne. 2000. *Kerala Christian Sainthood: Collisions of Culture and Worldview*. New York: Oxford University Press.

Derrett, Duncan M. 1971. "An Inscription Dated 1584 Concerning Reform of a Matha." In *Studies in Indian History and Culture*. volume presented to P. B. Desai. Dharwar: Karnatak University Press.

de Silva, K. M. 1983. *A History of Śrī Lanka*. Berkeley: University of California Press.

Diehl, Carl Gustav. 1956. *Instrument and Purpose: Studies on Rites and Rituals in South India*. Lund: C. W. K. Gleerup.

Dikshitar, V. R. Ramachandra. 1939. *The Silappadikaram*. Oxford: Oxford University Press.

Douglas, Mary. 1973. *Natural Symbols*. London: Pelican.

Dumont, Louis. 1953. "The Dravidian Kinship Terminology as an Expression of Marriage." *Man* 53:34–39.

——. 1957. *Une Sous-Caste de l'Inde du Sud: Organisation Sociale et Religion des Pramalai Kallar*. Paris: Mouton.

——.1959. "A Structural Definition of a Folk Deity of Tamilnad: Aiyanār the Lord." *Contributions to Indian Sociology* 3:75–87.

Durkheim, Emile, and Marcel Mauss. [1903] 1963. *Primitive Classification*. Translated by Rodney Needham. Chicago: Chicago University Press.

Eapen, K. V. 1983. *A Study of Kerala History*. Kottayam: Kollett Publication.

Geertz, Clifford. 1973. *The Interpretation of Cultures*. New York: Basic Books.

Geiger, Wilhelm, trans., assisted by Mabel H. Bode. 1912. *Mahāvamsa: The Great Chronicle of Ceylon*. London: Pāli Text Society.

——, trans., assisted by Mabel Rickmers. 1953a. *Cūḻavamsa, Part I*. London: Pāli Text Society.

——, trans. 1953b. *Cūḻavamsa, Part II*. London: Pāli Text Society.

Gold, Ann Grodzins. 1988. *Fruitful Journeys: The Ways of Rajasthani Pilgrims*. Berkeley: University of California Press.

Gombrich R., and G. Obeyesekere. 1988. *Buddhism Transformed: Religious Change in Sri Lanka*. Princeton: Princeton University Press.

Habermas, Jurgen. 1976. *Communication and the Evolution of Society*. Boston: Beacon Press.

Hardy, F. 1978. "Ideology and Cultural Contexts of the Śrīvaiṣṇava Temple." In *South Indian Temples*, edited by Burton Stein. New Delhi: Vikas.

——. 1983. *Viraha-Bhakti: The Early History of Kṛṣṇa Devotion in South India*. Delhi: Oxford University Press.

Hari Rao, V. N., trans. 1961. *Kōil Oḻugu*. Madras: Rockhouse and Sons.

——. 1967. *The Srirangam Temple: Art and Architecture*. Tirupati.

——. 1976. *History of the Srirangam Temple*. Tirupati.

Harman, William P. 1989. *The Sacred Marriage of a Hindu Goddess*. Bloomington: Indiana University Press.

Hiltebeitel, A. 1988. *The Cult of Draupadi*. Chicago: University of Chicago Press.

Hitchcock, P. ed. 1999. *Bakhtin/"Bakhtin" Studies in the Archive and Beyond.* Special edition of *South Atlantic Quarterly*, 97:3–4.

Horowitz, M. M. 1963. "The Worship of South Indian Deities in Martinique." *Ethnology* 11.3:339–346.

Horowitz, M. M. and M. Klass. 1961. "The Martiniquan East Indian Cult of Maldevidan." In *Social and Economic Studies* 10:93–100.

Hudson, Dennis. 1971. "Two Citrā Festivals in Madurai." In *Asian Religions*, edited by Bardwell Smith, 191–222. Chambersburg, PA: The American Academy of Religion. Republished in 1982. In *Religious Festivals in South India and Sri Lanka*, edited by Guy R. Welbon and Glenn E. Yocum, 101–156. New Delhi: Manohar.

——. 1977. "Śiva, Mīnākṣi, Viṣṇu—Reflections on a Popular Myth in Madurai." *The Indian Economic and Social History Review* 14.1:107–119. Republished in 1978. In *South Indian Temples*, edited by Burton Stein. New Delhi: Vikas.

Induchudan, V. T. 1969. *The Secret Chamber: A Historical, Anthropological and Philosophical Study of the Kodungallur Temple.* Trichur: Cochin Devaswom Board.

Jayawardena, Chandra. 1963. *Conflict and Solidarity in a Gianese Plantation.* London: Athlone.

——. 1967. "Religious Belief and Social Change." *Comparative Studies in Society and History.* 8:211–240.

Kalyanasundaram, S. 1980. *A Short History of Kataragama.* Colombo.

Khan, Abriham. 1977. "Kali-Mai Puja in Guyana." *Religion* 7:35–45.

Knox, Robert. 1958. *An Historical Relation of Ceylon.* Dehiwala, Śrī Lanka: Tisara Prakasakayo.

Kumar, K. Indra. 1971. *Fire Walking–The Burning Facts.* Colombo.

Lévi-Strauss, Claude. 1958. *Anthropologie structurale.* Paris: Librairie Plon.

——. 1962. *La Pensée sauvage.* Paris: Librairie Plon.

——. 1969. *The Elementary Structures of Kinship.* Boston: Beacon Press.

——. 1970. *The Raw and the Cooked.* London: Harper and Row.

MacPhail, Richard. 1993. *Santi's Lila.* PhD dissertation. Hamilton, Ontario: McMaster University.

Mahalingam, T. V. 1957. *Journal of Oriental Research* (Madras), 25:78–79.

Marriot, McKim. 1955. "Little Communities in an Indigenous Civilization." In *Village India*, edited by McKim Marriot. Chicago: University of Chicago Press.

Menon, Chelanattu Achutha. 1959. *Kali Worship in Kerala: Part I and Part II.* Madras: Madras University Press.

Menzez, Mary Noel RSM. 1995. *The Portuguese of Guyana.* Georgetown.

Mikula, Paul, Brian Kearney, and Rodney Harper. 1982. *Traditional Hindu Temples of South Africa.* Durban: H. Temp.

Morinis, Alan. 1984. *Pilgrimage in the Hindu Tradition.* Oxford: Oxford University Press.

——. 1992. *Sacred Journeys: The Anthropology of Pilgrimage.* Hartford, CT: Greenwood Press.

Mumford, Stan Royal. 1989. *Himalayan Dialogue.* Madison: University of Wisconsin.

Nagapin, Jocelyn, and Max Sulty. 1989. *La Migration de l'Hindouisme vers Les Antilles.* Paris.

Narayanan, Vasudha. 1994. *The Vernacular Veda: Revelation, Recitation and Ritual.* Columbia, SC: University of South Carolina.

Nath, Dwarka. 1970. *A History of Indians in Guyana.* London.

Obeyesekere, G. 1966. "The Buddhist Pantheon in Ceylon and Its Extensions." In *Anthropological Studies in Theravada Buddhism*, edited by Manning Nash. New Haven: Yale University Press.

——. 1977. "Social change and the Deities: The Rise of the Kataragama Cult in Modern Sri Lanka." *Man* 12:377–396.

——. 1978. "The Firewalkers of Kataragama: The Rise of Bhakti Religiosity in Buddhist Sri Lanka." *Journal of Asian Studies* 37.3:457–476.

——. 1981. *Medusa's Hair: An Essay on Personal Symbols and Religious Experience*. Chicago: University of Chicago Press.

——. 1984. *The Cult of the Goddess Pattini*. Chicago: University of Chicago Press.

Obeyesekere, G., and Richard Gombrich. 1988. *Buddhism Transformed: Religious Change in Sri Lanka*. Princeton: Princeton University Press.

Panikkar, T. K. Gopal. 1900. *Malabar and Its Folk*. Republished 1983. New Delhi: Asian Educational Services.

Payne, B. 1999. "Bakhtin and Cassirer: The Philosophical Origins of Bakhtin's Messianism." In *Bakhtin/"Bhaktin": Studies in the Archive and Beyond*, edited by Peter Hitchcock. *South Atlantic Quarterly*, special issue, 97.

Pfaffenberger, Bryan. 1979. "The Kataragama Pilgrimage: Hindu-Buddhist Interaction and its Significance in Sri Lanka's Polyethnic Social System. *Journal of Asian Studies* 38.2:253–270.

Phillips, Leslie. 1923. A Kali-Mai festival in Guyana. Pamphlet.

Pillai, T. M. Narayanaswamy. 1975. *Tiruvānnaikākkōvil*. Madras: University of Madras.

Pyyappan. 1962. *Lord Ayyappan the Dharma Sasta*. Bombay: Bharatiya Vidya Bhavan.

Ray, H. C., and S. Paranavitana. 1959, 1960, and 1973. *History of Ceylon*. Vol. I, Part I; Vol. I, Part II; and Vol. II. Colombo: University of Ceylon.

Renou, Louis. 1965. *The Destiny of the Veda in India*. Banaras: Motilal Banarsidass.

Sallahuddin. 1994. *Guyana: the Struggle for Liberation 1945–92*. Georgetown, Guyana.

Sarkar, H., ed. 1978. *An Architectural Survey of Temples of Kerala*. New Delhi: Archaeological Survey of India.

Seligmann, C. G., and Brenda Z. Seligmann. 1911. *The Veddas*. Cambridge: Cambridge University Press.

Seneviraratne, H. L. 1978. *Rituals of the Kandyan State*. Cambridge: Cambridge University Press.

Singaravelou. 1975. *Les Indienes de la Guadeloupe*. Bordeaux: Imprimière Deniaud.

Singh, I. J. Bahadur. 1975. *South Indian Traditions*. Georgetown: University of Guyana.

Smith, Raymond T. 1959. "Some Social Characteristics of Indian Immigration into British Guinea." *Population Studies* 13:34–39.

Smith, Wilfred Cantwell. 1963. *The Meaning and End of Religion*. New York: Macmillan.

South Indian Inscriptions. Vols. 1,2,3,4. New Delhi: Archaeological Society of India.

Srinivasachari, P. N. 1970. *The Philosophy of Viṣiṣṭādvaita*. Madras: Adyar Library.

Staal, Fritz. 1975. The meaninglessness of ritual. *Numen* 26.1:2–22.

Stanley, J. M. 1977. "Special Time, Special Power: The Fluidity of Power in a Popular Hindu Festival. *Journal of Asian Studies* 37.1:27–43.

Subramaniam, T. N. 1957. *South Indian Temple Inscriptions*. Vol. 3, Pt. 2. Madras: Government Oriental Manuscripts Library.

Swearer, Donald K. 1982. "The Kataragama and Kandy Asala Peraharas: Juxtaposing Religious Elements in Sri Lanka." In *Religious Festivals in South India and Sri Lanka*, edited by Guy R. Welbon and Glenn E. Yocum, 295–312. New Delhi: Manohar.

Tamiḻ Lexicon. 1936. Madras: Madras University Press.

Thomas, P. T. 1973. *Sabarimalai and Its Sastha*. Madras: Christian Literature Society.

Tiruvāṉaikhā Stalapurāṇa. 1968. Ten Intiyā Kṣētrakal. Śrīraṅkam: Sri Vāni Vilas Press.

Tolkāppiyam. 1916. Madras: Minerva Press.

Turner, Edith, and Victor Turner. 1978. *Image and Pilgrimage in Christian Culture: Anthropological Perspectives*. New York: Columbia University Press.

Turner, Victor W. 1969. *The Ritual Process*. Chicago: University of Chicago.

——. 1974. *Dramas, Fields, and Metaphors*. Ithaca: Cornell University Press.

van der Veer, P. 1984. "Structure and Anti-structure in Hindu Pilgrimage to Ayodhya." In *Changing South Asia: Religion and Society*. Edited by K. Ballhatchet and D. Taylor. Hong Kong: Asian

Research Service, for the Centre of South Asian Studies, School of Oriental and African Studies, University of London.

van Gennep, Arnold. 1960. *The Rites of Passage*, translated by Monika Vizedom and Gabriella Caffee. Chicago: University of Chicago Press.

Vertovec, Steven. 1992. *Hindu Trinidad*. London: Macmillan.

Wach, Joachim. 1951. *Sociology of Religion*. Chicago: University of Chicago Press.

Wadley, Susan, ed. 1980. *The Powers of Tamil Women*. Syracuse: *Foreign and Comparative Studies, South Asian Series*, no. 6, Maxwell School of Citizenship and Public Affairs, Syracuse University.

Waghorne, Joanne. 1997. *Vēḷaṅkaṇṇi Festival of Madras*. Paper at the American Academy of Religion, San Francisco.

Welbon, Guy R., and Glenn E. Yocum, eds. 1982. *Religious Festivals in South India and Sri Lanka*. New Delhi: Manohar.

Whitehead, Henry. 1921. *The Village Gods of South India*. Madras: Oxford University Press.

Wijayaratna, Mohan. 1987. *Le culte des dieux chez les bouddhistes singhalais*. Paris: Cerf.

Williams, Brackette. 1990. "Ritual, Colonial and Colonized Interpretations of the 1763 Berbice Slave Rebellion. *Journal of Historical Sociology* 3.2:133–64.

Wirz, Paul. [1954] 1972. *Kataragama: The Holiest Place in Ceylon*, translated by Davis Berta Pralle. Colombo: Lake House.

Younger, Paul. 1980. "A Temple festival of Māriyammaṉ." *Journal of the American Academy of Religion* 48.4: 495–517.

——. 1982a. "DMK politics and a Māriyammaṉ festival." *Religion and Society* 19.4:18–27.

——. 1982b. "The Family of Śiva in an Irrigated Coconut Grove: The Traditions of the Tiruvāṉaikkā Temple." *Studies in Religion* 2:145–63.

——. 1982c. "Singing the Tamiḻ Hymnbook in the Tradition of Rāmānuja: The Adyayanōtsava Festival in Śrīraṅkam." *History of Religions*. 21.3:271–293. Reproduced in 1987 in George W. Spencer, ed., *Temples, Kings and Peasants*. Madras: New Era.

——. 1982d. "Ten Days of Wandering and Romance with Lord Raṅkanātaṉ": The Paṅkuṇi Festival in Śrīraṅkam temple." *Modern Asian Studies* 16.2:325–358.

——. 1983. "The Role of Landlords, Kings and Priests in the Operation of a South Indian Temple." In *Śrīnidhih: Perspectives in Indian Archaeology, Art and Culture*, Shri K. R. Srinivasan Festschrift, edited by K. V. Raman, 243–256. Madras: New Era.

_____. 1992. "Velankanni Calling: Hindu Patterns of Pilgrimage at a Christian Shrine." In *Sacred Journeys*, edited by Alan Morinis. Hartford, CT: Greenwood Press.

——. 1993. "Srirangam." In *Temple Towns of Tamilnadu*, edited by George Michell, 79–93. Bombay: Marg.

——. 1995. *The Home of Dancing Śivaṉ: The Traditions of the Hindu Temple in Citamparam*. New York: Oxford University Press.

Index